LIMERICK

D1609806

Do Mhairéad, Seán Óg agus Donncha.
Grá mo chroí sibh.

Limerick

The Irish Revolution, 1912–23

John O'Callaghan

FOUR COURTS PRESS

Set in 10.5 on 12.5 point Ehrhardt for
FOUR COURTS PRESS LTD
7 Malpas Street, Dublin 8, Ireland
www.fourcourtspress.ie
and in North America for
FOUR COURTS PRESS
c/o IPG, 814 N. Franklin St, Chicago, IL 60622.

A catalogue record for this title
is available from the British Library.

ISBN 978-1-84682-742-6

Printed in England
by TJ International, Padstow, Cornwall.

Contents

Illustrations

Credits

1, 2, 4: Ludlow Collection; 3, 11, 13, 18, 19, 23, 25, 30, 31, 32, 35: Limerick Museum; 5: Liam Irwin; 6: Limerick City Library; 7: Brian Murphy; 8, 9: Des Long; 10: John Colivet; 12; University of Limerick Glucksman Library Special Collections; 14: Helen Litton; 15, 16: Imperial War Museum; 17: Tom Donovan; 20: The Haselbeck Collection, copyright Patricia Haselbeck-Flynn; 21: The National Archives, London; 22, 33, 34: Hogan Collection, National Library of Ireland; 24: Mercier Press; 26: Dan Neville; 27: Kerry O'Brien; 28: Tom Toomey; 29: Hogan-Wilson Collection, National Library of Ireland.

MAPS

Abbreviations

AOH	Ancient Order of Hibernians
ASU	Active Service Unit
ATIRA	Anti-Treaty IRA
BMH	Bureau of Military History
CBS	Crime Branch Special
Cd.	Command Paper (British parliamentary papers)
CD	Contemporary Document, Bureau of Military History
CE	*Cork Examiner*
CI	County Inspector, RIC
CO	Colonial Office, TNA
CSO	Chief Secretary's Office
DÉ	Dáil Éireann Secretariat files, 1919–22
DÉCC	Dáil Éireann Courts (Winding Up) Commission papers
DED	District Electoral Division
DÉLG	Dáil Éireann Local Government Department
DF	Department of Finance
DI	District Inspector, RIC
DLPC	Des Long private collection
DORA	Defence of the Realm Act
EH	*Evening Herald*
FJ	*Freeman's Journal*
GAA	Gaelic Athletic Association
GHQ	General Headquarters
Hansard	House of Commons debates
HO	Home Office
HQ	Headquarters
IE	*Irish Examiner*
IFS	Irish Free State
IG	Inspector General, RIC
IGC	Irish Grants Committee
II	*Irish Independent*
IMA	Irish Military Archives
IPP	Irish Parliamentary Party
IRA	Irish Republican Army
IRB	Irish Republican Brotherhood
IT	*Irish Times*
ITGWU	Irish Transport and General Workers' Union
IWFL	Irish Women's Franchise League

IWM	Imperial War Museum
IWSLA	Irish Women's Suffrage and Local Government Association
LA	Limerick Archives
LC	*Limerick Chronicle*
LCC	Limerick County Council
LGB	Local Government Board
LL	*Limerick Leader*
LM	Limerick Museum
MS	Manuscript
MP	Member of Parliament
MSPC	Military Service Pensions Collection
MWFL	Munster Women's Franchise League
NA	National army
NAI	National Archives of Ireland
NLI	National Library of Ireland
NMI	National Museum of Ireland
RIC	Royal Irish Constabulary
ROIA	Restoration of Order in Ireland Act
SF	Sinn Féin
TNA	The National Archives, London
UCDA	University College Dublin Archives
UDC	Urban District Council
UIL	United Ireland League
ULGLSC	University of Limerick Glucksman Library Special Collections
WO	War Office, TNA
WS	Witness statement to Bureau of Military History

Acknowledgments

Many people have been extremely generous to me during my time research-
ing revolutionary Limerick. In particular, I wish to thank John Logan, for his
friendship; Shane Walsh, Tom Toomey and Pádraig Ó Ruairc, for sharing
their expert knowledge; Bernadette Whelan, for her support; Patricia
Haselbeck-Flynn, Helen Litton, John Colivet, Dan Neville, Tomás
MacConmara, Sinead McCoole, Tom Donovan, Des Long, Brian Murphy,
Marianne Gallagher, Ruán O'Donnell, Cormac O'Malley, Charlie Quaid,
Johnny Conn, Liam Irwin, William O'Neill, Matthew Potter, Brian
Hodkinson, Martina Evans, Máirín Uí Chonghaile, John Cleary, Nóirín Uí
Fhlatharta, Colm Ó Flatharta, Sharon Slater, Liam Hogan, Mike Maguire,
Ken Bergin, Jean Turner, my colleagues in St Angela's College, Sligo, and all
of the others who helped in a myriad of ways. Editors Mary Ann Lyons and
Daithí Ó Corráin invested much time in the text of this book and Mike
Brennan created its maps, for which I am grateful. I am indebted also to the
staff of a variety of archival institutions and libraries: the National Archives
of Ireland; the National Library of Ireland; Military Archives; University
College Dublin Archives; the National Archives, London; the Imperial War
Museum, London; Special Collections, Glucksman Library, University of
Limerick; Limerick Archives; Limerick City and County Library; and
Limerick City and County Museum. Most importantly, I wish to acknowl-
edge my parents, my mother Ann and my late father John, along with my sis-
ters and brother and their families. This work is dedicated to my wife
Mairéad and our sons Seán Óg and Donncha.

The Irish Revolution, 1912–23 series

Since the turn of the century, a growing number of scholars have been actively researching this seminal period in modern Irish history. More recently, propelled by the increasing availability of new archival material, this endeavour has intensified. This series brings together for the first time the various strands of this exciting and fresh scholarship within a nuanced interpretative framework, making available concise, accessible, scholarly studies of the Irish Revolution experience at a local level to a wide audience.

The approach adopted is both thematic and chronological, addressing the key developments and major issues that occurred at a county level during the tumultuous 1912–23 period. Beginning with an overview of the social, economic and political milieu in the county in 1912, each volume assesses the strength of the home rule movement and unionism, as well as levels of labour and feminist activism. The genesis and organization of paramilitarism from 1913 are traced; responses to the outbreak of the First World War and its impact on politics at a county level are explored; and the significance of the 1916 Rising is assessed. The varying fortunes of constitutional and separatist nationalism are examined. The local experience of the War of Independence, reaction to the truce and the Anglo-Irish Treaty and the course and consequences of the Civil War are subject to detailed examination and analysis. The result is a compelling account of life in Ireland in this formative era.

Mary Ann Lyons
Department of History
Maynooth University

Daithí Ó Corráin
School of History & Geography
Dublin City University

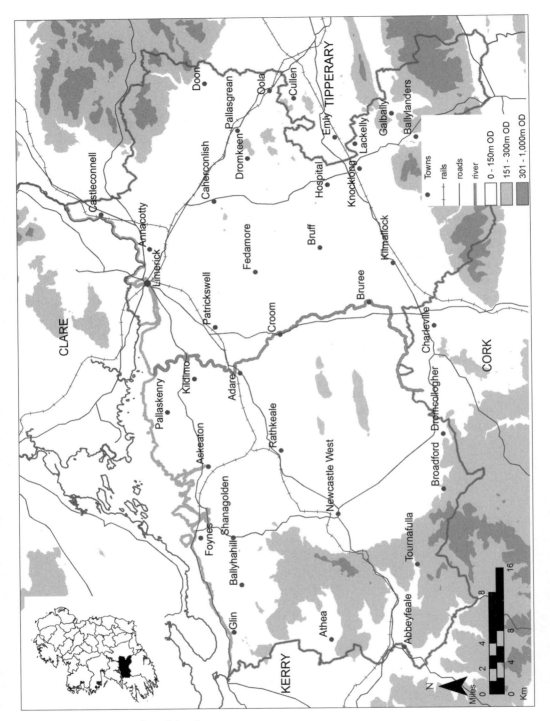

1 Places mentioned in the text

1 Limerick in 1912

Remarkably, on 27 May 1923, just weeks after the Civil War ceasefire, a commemorative monument to Irish Republican Army (IRA) Volunteers who had died in the War of Independence was unveiled in Murroe, a village about ten miles east of Limerick city. This twenty-foot-high limestone carving must have been commissioned before the end of the Civil War and was probably the first such memorial raised in the country; more significantly, it signalled that Civil War differences had been set aside locally, at least, if not further afield. Dr John Harty, archbishop of Cashel and a Murroe native, addressed the thousands of people attending the ceremony and set them a difficult task. It was their communal duty to remember the sacrifices of the previous decade while looking to the future. But to strike the right balance, they would have to 'forget the immediate past'.[1] Simply wishing it away, however, would not be enough to mitigate or undo any element of the revolutionary tumult of the 1912–23 period, during which Limerick, city and county, was a key political, social and military battleground. Much of the change that occurred was welcomed in Limerick but the revolution produced both winners and losers, and no group was entirely satisfied with its outcome.

County Limerick is roughly rectangular in shape, with the Shannon estuary forming fifty miles of the longer, northern boundary (see map 1). This is the only county boundary that is clearly defined by a topographic feature, although the Ballyhoura mountains straddle a section of the southern border while the Slieve Felim range sits in the north-east corner, the Galtees in the south-east corner and the Mullaghareirks in the south-west corner. In very broad terms, the county can be divided into two distinct physical regions. To the west of a line through Kildimo–Adare–Ballingarry, a series of hills run from Loghill on the Shannon, between Foynes and Glin, to Dromcollogher on the southern boundary, extending beyond Abbeyfeale. This uplands territory included large expanses of bog in the early twentieth century. Poorer soil and smaller farms meant subsistence farming was more prevalent here than elsewhere. From mid-Limerick to the Slieve Felims and Galtees lies the flat land of the Limerick plain, part of the region known as the Golden Vale. This lush farmland provided for a strong commercial agriculture economy in 1912. The River Shannon, along with the River Maigue and the River Deel, navigable as far as Adare and Askeaton respectively, had been replaced as significant communication channels by the development of a modern rail and road network from the mid-nineteenth century. Limerick's central location in the mid-west of the country meant that important national primary rail and road routes converged on the city. The Great Southern & Western Railway linked Limerick to other major cities including Dublin, Waterford, Cork and Galway, as well as Athlone in the midlands and Sligo in the north-west. Many of County Limerick's smaller population centres also had access to the railway. Limerick harbour, with its floating and dry docks, was the site of the premier commercial port on the western side of the island. There were five large mills operating on the Dock Road in 1912, for instance, all of which had to be supplied through the port (see map 2). Grain was a major import, along with coal and timber. But the lack of direct rail and canal connections to the docks was a major deficiency, both systems terminating a mile away.

Limerick's 1911 population of 143,069 had decreased steadily from 330,029 in 1841.[2] The city's 38,518 residents made it a metropolis by Irish standards, exceeded only by Belfast, Dublin and Cork.[3] The county had few large population centres and its inhabitants were widely dispersed.[4] Excluding the city, Limerick had only two urban districts: in 1911, 2,585 people lived in Newcastle West and 1,705 in Rathkeale.[5] Almost 65 per cent of Limerick's population lived outside towns of 500 inhabitants or more. The comparative figure for the province of Munster was 69 per cent, and nationally, 66.6 per cent.[6] While cohort decline was endemic in many counties ravaged by emigration and late marriage age, the population of Limerick city and county dropped by less than 6,000 people between 1901 and 1926. Clare and Tipperary, by contrast, both lost about 30,000 people in the same period.[7] This surface stability in Limerick camouflaged catastrophic demographic fluctuations among its Protestant community, however. The vast majority of Limerick's population was Roman Catholic: 101,502 people (97 per cent) in the county and 34,865 people (90.5 per cent) in the city. Traditionally, most Protestants were urban dwellers and in 1911 there was a more substantial Protestant minority in Limerick city than in the county. There were 2,316 Episcopalians (almost exclusively members of the Church of Ireland) in the city, 847 Presbyterians and 213 Methodists. There were 2,550 Episcopalians in the county, 136 Presbyterians and 273 Methodists.[8] The death rate exceeded the birth rate among Limerick's small Quaker cohort in every decade since the 1830s. Quaker 'energy and dynamism' had been central to the development of business life in the city in previous centuries but the community had entered 'near fatal decline' by the turn of the century.[9] During the fifteen tumultuous years between the 1911 census and the 1926 census, there was a dramatic decline in the Protestant population. While the balance of Limerick's population contributed to diffusing religious tensions and meant that there were no battles for communal or economic dominance of the kind that provoked large-scale conflict elsewhere in the country, there were isolated instances of sectarianism in Limerick city and county.[10]

One charge justifiably levelled against Catholic Limerick was that it was 'notorious for the intimidation of Jews and Protestant evangelists'.[11] Dr J.J.

Long was sent to Limerick by the Irish Church Missions in 1899, tasked with opening a dispensary for the city's poor. A robust proselytizer, he saw off physical assaults, legal challenges and boycott, led by the Redemptorists' Confraternity of the Holy Family, for more than twenty years.[12] The Limerick pogrom of 1904, a unique event in an Irish context, was incited by demagogic Redemptorist preaching to the 6,000 strong confraternity. The small Jewish community was scapegoated for the poverty that gripped much of the city. Subsequently, the pogrom was largely erased from social memory. An interesting development in 1904 was the closure of Christian ranks against the Jews. The *Limerick Leader* published several letters from Catholics and Protestants heartily supporting the crusade. When the persecution of Limerick's Jews was debated in the House of Commons, Michael Joyce, MP for the Limerick city constituency, asked: 'Is there any intention to introduce legislation to safeguard the people against extortionate usurers who charge 200 or 300 per cent profit on shoddy articles?'[13] The specifically anti-Semitic boycott of 1904 was similar to those that had gone before in Limerick and indeed a precursor to more that would follow in 1917–23 in that it illustrated how suggestion could lead to intimidation and mark one section of a community out as an internal enemy. But Limerick was by no means exceptional by international standards. Similar dynamics were at play in former imperial territories in Central and Eastern Europe as nationalist forces mobilized in the wake of the 1914–18 war, although the scale of the displacement of people and the ferocity of the violence employed there was vastly greater than anything that occurred in Ireland.

Limerick's economy was predominantly agricultural. In 1911, when 17.8 per cent of Ireland's population worked on the land, the proportion in Limerick was slightly lower at 17.2 per cent. An average sized county, comprising 680,898 acres (more than 1,000 square miles), Limerick accounted for 3.3 per cent of the total area of the island.[14] A natural advantage enjoyed by Limerick was its location at the heart of the country's premier dairying terrain. Because the rich pastureland of the Golden Vale ran through the county, the vast majority of Limerick farmers – 88 per cent – were involved in dairy production.[15] The general milk yield per Limerick cow was higher than the national average and more of the milk supply went to the creamery than in any other county.[16] Some 58.5 per cent of Limerick's population lived on agricultural holdings. Seventy-five per cent of Limerick farms were less than 50 acres in size.[17] If the proportion of agricultural holdings in a county valued at £15 or less is taken as a rough index of the prevalence of poverty, rural Limerick was relatively prosperous. Just over 48.5 per cent of residents on agricultural holdings in Limerick lived on land valued at £15 or less, while the corresponding figures for Munster and Ireland were 53.1 per cent and 58.9 per cent respectively.[18] Small farms dominated, but with its significant

number of large farms and creameries, County Limerick was strong economically. Despite the occasional case of animal smuggling during the foot and
mouth outbreaks of 1912–14, Limerick escaped its depredations, unlike
Waterford where a two-month ban on all livestock movements led to factory
closures and lay-offs among railway and dock workers.[19]

The bacon industry united city and county and was perhaps Limerick's
greatest asset. A semi-industrial, provincial city, Limerick was celebrated as a
bacon-making capital, its products selling at a premium internationally. Pigs
delivered from farm to city centre were driven through the streets to be slaugh-
tered. The presence of four large factories, namely Matterson's and O'Mara's
on Roche's Street, Shaw's on Mulgrave Street and Denny's, which had sites on
both William Street and Mulgrave Street, drew the moniker 'Pigtown'. As well
as being the city's largest employers, they provided an extensive range of cheap
foodstuffs, including pigs' heads, crubeens and entrails. These Limerick firms
were among the first to use ice, which made curing possible all year round
from the late nineteenth century. By the 1890s, Shaw's ran its cooling rooms
on electricity and had its own lifts and telephones. This heavy investment in
technology helped to make it one of the largest curers in the world.[20] Pigs made
Limerick famous but the Limerick Clothing Factory was the busiest in the
country and was working at full capacity from 1914 to 1918, making uniforms
for the British, Australian and American armies. Goodbody's, Russell's and
Bannatyne's led the flourishing flour milling industry. Large department stores
such as Todd's, McBirney's and Cannock's employed hundreds. Cleeve's
Condensed Milk Company employed 3,000 people in nineteen factories, creameries and bakeries around Munster, the majority of them in Limerick. The revolution would take a heavy toll on Cleeve's, in particular.

The prosperity that was evident among the business classes did not reach
all quarters of the city, however. Among working-class people, poverty
remained rampant. They continued to experience low wages, job insecurity,
ill-health, high food prices, poor housing and high rents. Councillor Michael
O'Callaghan, the owner of a tannery on Gerald Griffin Street that benefitted
from government contracts, spoke against the mooted introduction of restrictions on food prices in early 1915.[21] There were over 1,000 tenements in the
city, accounting for 20 per cent of the housing stock. One-room flats made
up another 15 per cent.[22] Much of this accommodation was sited in Georgian
buildings vacated by the middle and upper classes in their rush to the afflu-
ent surroundings of the suburbs. Limerick Corporation had done little to
relieve the situation, building only 133 dwellings under the artisan housing
and sanitary acts between 1887 and 1914.[23] In 1915 Michael McGrath, superintendent medical officer for public health, adjudged that Limerick city was
'very much behind the times as regards the provision of sanitary accommodation'. A third of city dwellers lived in dirty and overcrowded conditions –

mainly in the Englishtown, Irishtown and Carey's Road areas – without running water or sewerage systems. Dr McGrath warned that depositing human waste on the streets caused disease. Until the practice was eradicated, 'it will be utterly impossible to have a healthy city.' Scarlet fever, typhoid and diphtheria all killed people in Limerick city in 1915. Tuberculosis was a major culprit, responsible for 119 fatalities. There was a high rate of infant mortality: 100 children under the age of one died in 1915.[24]

Living conditions in County Limerick were also often poor. In 1910 the *Limerick Leader* pinpointed a house in Rathkeale as being 'a specimen of the wretched hovels that are to be found in some of the congested areas.' It was fifteen or sixteen feet long and ten feet high, with a door that 'the average sized person would find difficult to enter without stooping.' The thatched roof was decaying.[25] But the provision of housing was slowly improving in rural Limerick (and at a much faster rate than in the city). From the 1880s, hundreds of good quality labourers' cottages had been built by the Boards of Guardians under the Labourers' Acts and let at low rents. The creamery system was established and road work was organized by direct labour. The combined effect of such developments was the retention of a steady population during the early years of the twentieth century. In 1913 the *Leader* reported on 'deserving poor people' in rural areas living in 'hovels that ... a respectable pig would not live in.'[26] At the same time, however, it praised recent developments in agriculture in the county and credited land purchase as being the key feature in the improvements.[27]

In 1876 just eighteen landlords owned 167,000 acres or 25 per cent of the entire county between them. The absentee earl of Devon owned 33,000 acres around Newcastle West with a valuation of £14,525. The largest resident landlord was the earl of Dunraven, Windham Thomas Wyndham-Quin. His 14,298 acres were valued at £10,814. His Adare Manor home was the most valuable in Limerick. The majority of Limerick's estates were sold not under the land acts of the 1880s and 1890s but under Chief Secretary George Wyndham's 1903 Land Purchase Act. Dunraven was instrumental in establishing the Irish Land Conference of 1902–3, which eventually found a middle ground between landlords' demands and tenants' means. Dunraven represented landlord interests but was viewed as an honest broker in the settlement. Tenants could now afford to buy and landlords benefitted from a 12 per cent state-sponsored bonus on top of the agreed purchase price. Dunraven was one of the first Limerick landlords to sell. From 1906 to 1909, he recouped £133,031 for 10,505 acres. Charles Barrington received £52,518 for 4,797 acres in 1913 and £374 for another 36 acres in 1914.[28] More than half of Limerick tenants (about 10,000 farmers) had purchased their land and were secure in their holdings by 1913–14.[29] A decade later, 76 per cent of the total acreage of Limerick had been purchased by tenants.[30]

On 31 March/1 April 1911, census day, there were 294 Royal Irish Constabulary (RIC) men in fifty-seven posts around Limerick (see map 5). This was less than half the number of policemen that there had been twenty or even forty years earlier when there was a high prevalence of agrarian agitation and seditious organization in Limerick.[31] Of the 294, 89 per cent were Catholic and 67 per cent came from a farming background. There were thirty-five men in William Street barracks in the city but numbers did not reach double figures in any other station, some of which were just huts.[32] Henry Yates took up the role of County Inspector (CI) of the RIC in Limerick in 1912. An Englishman who had entered the force as an officer cadet nearly thirty years earlier, he occupied this crucial position until the summer of 1920, by which time he was in his sixties. Yates's *modus operandi* during the delicate intervening years was often cumbersome and heavy-handed. The British army was also visible in Limerick and its largest bases were at the New Barracks, Ordnance Barracks and Strand Barracks in the city (see map 2).

The IPP, champions of home rule, were the exclusive representatives of Limerick at the imperial parliament in Westminster from 1874 until eclipsed by Sinn Féin (SF) at the 1918 general election. In place of direct government from London, home rule proposed a limited measure of control over domestic affairs for a Dublin parliament. In a revision of constituencies in the mid-1880s, Limerick City lost one of its two seats and County Limerick was divided into East Limerick and West Limerick, both of which returned one MP. There was no further change to the constituencies until 1922 (see map 3). John Redmond led the IPP from 1900. Michael Joyce, a Shannon river pilot, and thus a key figure in ensuring the success of Limerick port, represented the Limerick City constituency from 1900 until 1918. P.J. O'Shaughnessy, from a business and farming background in Rathkeale, did likewise for West Limerick. William Lundon was MP for East Limerick from 1900 until his death in 1909. William's son, Thomas, succeeded him and occupied the seat until 1918. The Lundons were farmers from Kilteely. MPs were not paid until 1911 and Joyce, Lundon and O'Shaughnessy all spent considerable periods of time away from home. Limerick's abject parliamentary fund subscriptions did little to ease their personal expenses. Like most provincial representatives in parliament, they generally left the national question to the party leadership and concentrated on local Limerick issues (although Joyce, as president of the United Kingdom Pilots' Association, was central to the Pilotage Act of 1913).

From the end of the nineteenth century the IPP was represented at grass-roots level by the United Irish League (UIL). The UIL was a powerful force in Limerick politics but it was primarily rural and agrarian in its orientation and its failure to appeal to the urban working class was a permanent weak-

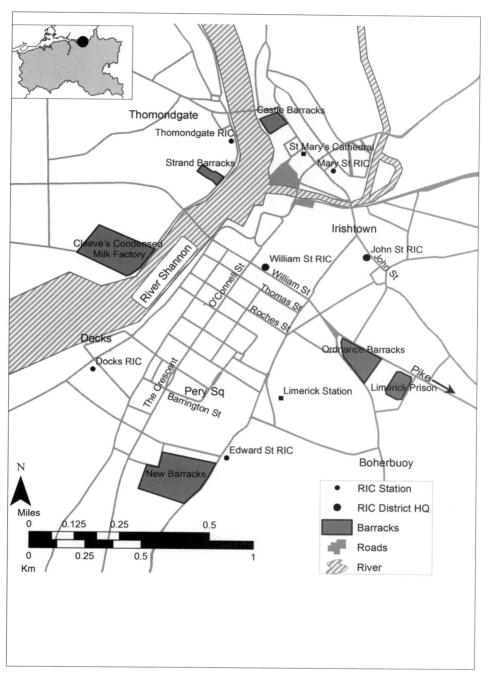

2 Limerick city

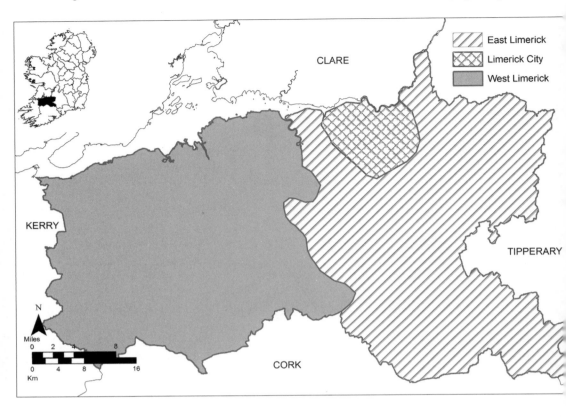

3 Parliamentary constituencies in 1910

ness. The League peaked early in the new century and continually high branch and membership statistics were in fact misleading. In reality, it eventually became little more than an electioneering unit. The Ancient Order of Hibernians (AOH) came to rival the UIL as the primary route into political office in the home rule movement and supplanted the UIL as the most dynamic organ of the IPP in Limerick city in the early 1910s, stepping into the breach as the land question was sidelined. The AOH was primarily urbanbased and the change in the pattern of popular political participation in Limerick reflected the detachment of many farmers from politics, satiated as they were by land reform.

The UIL reached its numerical peak in Limerick between March 1902 and March 1903 with over eighty branches and up to 5,500 members.[33] It was at its busiest in 1907, holding over 100 meetings. This surging activity was largely in response to the 'Ranch War' of 1904–8, which aimed to force landlords to sell estates at prices set by tenants and to redistribute grazing land. However, statistics on cattle-driving, boycotting and the letting of farms demonstrate that compared to the midlands, Connacht and Clare, the Ranch War was not fought with much enthusiasm in Limerick. While agrarian agitation smouldered in a number of private quarrels, the county was, for the most part, undisturbed. The absence of large-scale unrest can be attributed to the fact that the inequitable division of land between a minority of graziers who farmed livestock on extensive grassland farms and the mass of uneconomic smallholders was not as pronounced in rural Limerick as it was in the midlands and west.[34] The *Limerick Leader*, the self-proclaimed 'faithful organ of the National Party',[35] was not taken in by UIL figures purporting to demonstrate its rude good health and instead pointed to 'a strange want of activity' and signs of the generational divide that was to prove so important:

> The complaint is universally made that the League does not succeed in winning to its ranks the young men of the country, and those who make this complaint usually lay the blame on the young men. As far as we can see, however, the blame is to be laid on the older Leaguers themselves.

One branch did nothing at three successive meetings except pass votes of sympathy with the relatives of deceased parishioners and on one occasion actually held a meeting specifically for that purpose.[36] The *Leader* consistently charted the slow demise of the UIL over the following years. Towards the end of 1909 there was a spate of allegations and counter-allegations made by the League and the Hibernians, which patently contained some truth, that each body was forming bogus branches in an attempt to rig the forthcoming nationalist conventions for the selection of parliamentary candidates ahead of the January 1910 general election.[37] For instance, between 1906 and 1917 the only press accounts of UIL activity in Kilmallock, where there had not been an active branch since at least 1905, appeared in December 1909. The local branch was supposedly revived and managed to appoint delegates to the impending nationalist convention. Yet no meeting was advertised, the leaders of the old branch were not consulted, and there was no further activity in the town. Moreover, while UIL branches in Limerick were numerous, members and money were not. In March 1914 there were seventeen members of the UIL per thousand of population in Limerick. The comparative figure for Clare was twenty-five.[38] Indeed, counties with only a fraction of the number of branches had more members and regularly contributed more to the parliamentary fund than Limerick. This gives rise to the suspicion that many of the branches in Limerick may have become nominal or 'purely electoral' in their purpose, existing only on paper, and that party politics may have been irrelevant to many members outside of election time. If this was the case on a broad scale (and it was in Waterford at least[39]), then the dominant position of the IPP in the nationalist movement before the 1916 Rising was even more precarious than has been traditionally portrayed by historians.

By the start of 1910, the numerical and financial strength of the AOH ensured that it received the full backing of the IPP leadership. In February the west Limerick executive of the UIL formally accused the AOH of 'packing' the nationalist conventions to select candidates for the recent election with their own delegates in order to out-vote League members. P.J. O'Shaughnessy claimed that branches of the AOH had been founded for the specific purpose of out-voting his supporters and defeating his nomination. The UIL wanted the AOH barred from future conventions.[40] There were conspicuous irregularities in the City constituency in January when impersonation to the extent of 600 votes took place on behalf of Michael Joyce (a prominent member of the Limerick city division of the AOH, as well as a dedicated Leaguer), and again before the December 1910 general election when 900 potential Redmondite voters were struck off the registry at the electoral revision court on the intervention of William O'Brien's All for Ireland League, which ran a candidate against Joyce in both January and December.[41] The Catholic bishop of Limerick, Edward O'Dwyer, was a virulent critic of the Hibernians, whom he suspected of fostering anti-clericalism; he accused Joe Devlin, who was both president of the AOH and secretary of the National Directory of the UIL, of attempting to build a dictatorship.[42] O'Dwyer would not sanction his clergy to provide chaplaincy services to the Hibernians and, in May 1912 a priest in Limerick would not permit AOH members to receive communion or attend funerals as representatives of the organization.[43] The animosity between the UIL and the AOH was not the only symptom of dissension in nationalist ranks. There was much rancour between what the police referred to as the UIL and AOH's 'Official Nationalists', and the All for Ireland League, founded by O'Brien in 1909, though little of the violence that marked their rivalry in Cork. O'Brien's League had twenty-five branches in Limerick by the end of 1910.[44] The 1911 corporation consisted of twenty-seven nationalists, ten members of the All for Ireland League and three 'Sinn Féiners'.[45] In the June elections to local authorities, O'Brienites also made considerable gains but their progress ceased by the end of 1911, partly due to their *détente* with local unionists.[46]

As towns replaced farmland at the epicentre of politics (see map 4, p. 66, for local government divisions), the urban-based AOH outstripped the UIL in Limerick during the years before 1914. The acrimony between them should not obscure the fact that the UIL and AOH were very similar organizations. Their most frequent items of business involved expressions of condolence to the families of deceased colleagues, and making formulaic resolutions in favour of IPP tactics and John Redmond's leadership. Joint meetings were not unknown and League branches occasionally met in Hibernian halls. The growth of the AOH in the south was closely linked to its brokerage of a social insurance scheme which ran efficiently in Limerick, despite being less popular than elsewhere.[47] At the end of 1912 there were 80,000 AOH members nationally and 189,927 associates of the insurance section, while the UIL boasted 1,234 branches with 130,007 members. The following summer, there were 3,158 Hibernians in Limerick and 3,982 subscribers to the insurance scheme, along with fifty-six branches and 2,539 members of the League. Only Cork, Galway, Mayo and occasionally Roscommon had more UIL branches.[48] In contrast, only a few SF branches were active in the country at the time. As will be shown in chapter 4, for all their impressive numbers, however, these nationalist bodies proved to be little more than paper tigers in 1917–18.

In the shadows of the home rule movement, four women's suffrage associations had branches in Limerick, namely the Irish Women's Suffrage and Local Government Association (IWSLA), the Irish Women's Franchise League (IWFL), the Munster Women's Franchise League (MWFL) and the Irish Women's Franchise Federation. Their members were usually well-educated, middle-class women. In December 1910 the IWSLA had managed to convince Limerick Corporation to adopt a resolution supporting women's suffrage. They gained attention and support by moving from drawing-room meetings to hiring the Athenaeum Hall in the city at Easter 1911, when Hanna Sheehy Skeffington addressed the group. Both the IWSLA and the IWFL had representatives elected as Poor Law Guardians in 1911. Limerick County Council subsequently passed a resolution favouring the vote for women.[49] Michael Joyce was a rare supporter in the IPP but Bishop O'Dwyer wished to protect women from the 'squalid strife of political parties'.[50] At an MWFL meeting in Limerick in January 1913 Michael Colivet of the AOH, and a future SF and Volunteer leader, displayed pretty typical anti-suffragette hostility. His tone was echoed in the *Leader*, which dismissed the event as a '"screech"' and the broader suffragette movement as a Tory scheme to undermine home rule.[51] Another MWFL occasion in the county courthouse on 29 April 1913 had to be held behind closed doors, with admission by ticket only and a police presence on the door. Shots had been fired as a similar gathering in Cork broke up in disorder the night before.[52] In October Sheehy Skeffington was forcibly ejected from a home rule rally that Redmond was addressing in the city.[53] After 1916 the feminist movement became increasingly peripheral as the revolution accentuated the martial characteristics of republicanism, but it still managed to make progress. In 1918 the government introduced legislation to give the vote to men over twenty-one years and to women over thirty who were householders or married to householders. In 1922 the constitution of the Irish Free State (IFS) acknowledged the right to vote of all citizens over twenty-one, but only after the general election of that year.

SF had no national electoral success before 1917. A 'Sinn Féin' hurling club was formed in Limerick city in December 1905 but it never entered competition. A 'Sinn Féin' swimming club met regularly during the summer months for several years. These sports clubs were social rather than political outlets for Irish-Irelanders. The first branch of the SF political party in Limerick was established in the city in August 1907. In November 1908 the secretary revealed that 'the season just closed had been an uneventful one, as the summer is our fallow season, and the work accomplished practically nil'. Sinn Féiners took a handful of seats on Limerick Corporation in 1908 and 1911 but they were probably elected as representatives of other bodies. In September 1909, when there were four nominal branches of SF in Limerick but no registered members, the secretary of the city branch wrote to *Sinn Féin*, the party newspaper, to invite the 'large number of Sinn Féiners in Limerick (men and women) who are not members of our branch, and probably not aware of its existence' to become members.[54] There was no rush to join. Party work mostly involved promoting Irish manufactured goods and Irish language and culture in tandem with the Gaelic League. As with the suffrage associations in their early days, meetings were held in private residences.

The most significant pre-Rising disrupter of the IPP stranglehold on Limerick was the Fenian John Daly. The Local Government (Ireland) Act of 1898 facilitated challenges to the landlord and merchant classes that had previously monopolized Limerick city and county politics. Labour won a majority on Limerick Corporation in January 1899 but the local constitutional status quo was not upset by any hint of social radicalism. The only political philosophy shared by the Labour contingent, John Daly among them, was some form of nationalism. During three consecutive terms as mayor, from 1899 to 1901, Daly specialized in separatist gestures. In April 1900, for instance, Sir Andrew Reed, RIC Inspector General (IG), reported that the whole of Ireland, with one exception, was looking forward to the visit of Queen Victoria:

> In Limerick the scandalous action of John Daly ... has stirred up and keeps inflamed the worst possible spirit of disloyalty and sedition amongst the low class of extremists who are unfortunately numerous in Limerick, and entirely under Daly's influence.[55]

Daly's dictatorial tendencies eventually undermined his standing within his own clique and the balance of political power in Limerick city swung back in favour of the IPP. Daly's preferred form of nationalism and that of some constitutionalists had much in common, however. Limerick East MP William

Lundon was an ex-Fenian and his understanding of home rule, as he publicly explained it in 1903, did not mean

> a little parliament in Dublin that would pay homage to the big one, but a sovereign and independent one and if he had his own way he would break the remaining links that bound the two countries ... he was trained in another school in '67 ... and he was not a parliamentarian when he walked with his rifle on his shoulder.[56]

Lundon's oratory exemplified the 'Faith and Fatherland' character of IPP rhetoric. The claim for home rule reflected pragmatism regarding the balance of power in Anglo-Irish relations, more than it did pro-imperial sentiment for an Anglicized Ireland. The abstract quality of home rule effortlessly complemented evocations such as Lundon's. Coupled with the credit it claimed for ameliorative British social and democratic legislation, the populist patriotism of the IPP secured its grip on the 'hearts and minds' of a majority of nationalists.

A key personality in southern unionism, Lord Dunraven practiced conciliation politics by building trust between moderate home rulers and unionists as a foundation for a mutually agreeable measure of devolved self-government. Lord lieutenant of County Limerick from 1894 to 1926, Dunraven won a place on the first Limerick County Council in 1899. While campaigning, he made no secret of his support for the outgoing grand juries, comprised of leading ratepayers, whose administrative duties would now be assumed by the new entities. Because he did not back the demand for a Catholic university, Dunraven also had to contend with Bishop O'Dwyer's opposition. Though defeated for the chair of the county council, he was appointed head of the finance committee. He was elected to the council again in 1902 but excluded from membership of the finance committee. Dunraven's committee record had been patchy but this was a remarkable snub from a popular body to the Anglo-Irish aristocracy.[57] The 1898 Local Government Act provided for grand jurors to be co-opted on to the first councils. Nationalists tolerated this as the symbolic baton of power passed from the old to the new. The second council was less welcoming. The nationalist minority was routinely denied full participation in local government in the north of Ireland and County Limerick's councillors were perhaps exacting a comparable measure of control over Dunraven. It was a missed opportunity to keep Limerick unionists inside the tent. The conciliationist approach depended on the type of cooperation and good faith that had made the 1902–3 Land Conference such a success but it buckled irreparably when Dunraven's Irish Reform Association released its devolution manifesto in 1904. Nationalists were unenthused and unionists were appalled. Chief Secretary Wyndham resigned along with the rest of the Conservative/Unionist government in 1905, just two years after introducing his great land reform. Irish nationalists and unionists became increasingly intransigent thereafter.

The nationalist–unionist political divide in Limerick was also evident in the existence of rival youth organizations in the city. Originating in London in 1891 as a follow on to Sunday School, the Church Lads Brigade catered for teenagers and sought 'the improvement of boys spiritually, morally, mentally and physically and the means employed were Bible classes, gymnastic training, athletic competitions, and drill on the pattern of the military organisation.'[58] Limerick city's first Church Lads companies were formed in the mid-1890s, including at St Mary's Cathedral, St Michael's, St Munchin's, St John's and Trinity. A battalion was formed in 1896 with its headquarters in the diocesan hall in Pery Square. Strongly supported by notables such as Lord Clarina, the Church Lads regularly paraded the streets of the city accompanied by their own fife and drum band and sometimes with the Union Jack. Their annual sports day was a significant event in the life of Limerick's Protestant community. Annual all-Ireland Church Lads camps involved daily tent, kit and uniform inspection. Some of the lads were armed. They retained close links to the military from their formation and several former members were killed during the First World War. Church halls were used as recreation centres for soldiers during the war. All parochial units of the Church Lads amalgamated into the St Mary's Cathedral company in 1919. This single company, the only one south of the border, survived until the 1940s. Edward Pearson, a military cadet, led the company during the 1920s. During the War of Independence, he organized soccer games between the Church Lads and the band boys of the Oxford and Buckinghamshire Light Infantry and the Royal Welsh Fusiliers. They continued to socialize in the diocesan hall but did not drill or parade.[59]

Na Fianna Éireann was inaugurated by Bulmer Hobson and Countess Markievicz in Dublin in 1909. Inspired by the legendary warrior band of Gaelic Ireland, the purpose of Na Fianna was 'to re-establish the independence of Ireland'. It would achieve this by 'the training of the youth of Ireland, mentally and physically ... by teaching scouting and military exercises, Irish history, and the Irish language'. Members had to promise to 'work for the Independence of Ireland, never to join England's armed forces, and to obey my superior officers'.[60] A branch was formed in Limerick in 1911 and developed close links with the city's Irish Republican Brotherhood (IRB), which had been reorganized under the guise of the Wolfe Tone Club debating society. John Daly sponsored the group and they met on his property. Tom Clarke, who was married to Kathleen Daly, John's niece, wrote to him: ''tis grand to find that you have made the Fianna such a success in Limerick – you are away ahead of anything else in the country.'[61] In May 1912 no fewer than 210 Fianna boys paraded in the city.[62] Seán Heuston, a clerk with the

Great Southern & Western Railway, was closely identified with Na Fianna in Limerick until he returned to his native Dublin in 1913. Heuston was executed for his role in the 1916 Rising. Con Colbert, a native of west Limerick, was also executed after the Rising. It was by assuming overlapping roles in the revivalist and republican networks of the capital that Colbert contributed most to revolution. As a member of the Gaelic League, the IRB, Na Fianna Éireann and the Irish Volunteers, he performed a vital function in navigating the transition between cultural renewal, separatist conspiracy and public declaration of force. Colbert regularly visited John Daly when passing through Limerick city on his way home to Athea. Madge Daly described the 'deep friendship' that developed between them: 'Con's visits were a source of great pleasure to my uncle as he brought him the latest news of the Fianna, the Wolfe Tone clubs and the other national groups in Dublin.'[63]

Na Fianna members were encouraged to display aggression to the RIC and physically to confront their unionist equivalent in Limerick, the Church Lads Brigade. Boyishness and practical training aside, Na Fianna preached Anglophobia and the Church Lads were rampantly imperialist. The most striking difference (one of the few) between Na Fianna and the Church Lads, an explicitly Protestant organization, was in their respective attitudes to religion. Separatist republicanism defined itself in ethical as well as in ideological terms, and Na Fianna emphasized the importance of morality, but, unlike other youth groups of the period, including the Church Lads, rarely made any reference to religion. This was probably because Hobson and Markievicz, both from Protestant backgrounds, as well as recognizing how politically divisive religion was in Ireland, did not want Catholic parents to suspect proselytism where none existed.[64] While Na Fianna was a fixture in Limerick throughout the revolution, the Church Lads' public profile became increasingly subdued.

The upheaval in land ownership was just about to eclipse Limerick's old landlord class in 1912 but Limerick society, in city and county, remained firmly stratified. Economic circumstances and social status were still intimately linked. The landlords can be seen as the greatest social, economic and political losers of the revolution, or as a pragmatic group who took full advantage of the favourable financial terms of a land act designed to loosen their grip on the land of Ireland, from which Ascendancy wealth and power had been derived. The political trappings of the old order were largely ornamental by this point, decades of democratic reform having diluted their privileges. The Church of Ireland had been disestablished. Control of local government had been taken out of minority hands. Extension of the suffrage had benefitted the Catholic majority. Dunraven's Adare Manor was 'the last word in comfort and elegance' but he was not a representative example.[65] The landed gentry had always been a minority of the minority. Most Protestants were not separated from their Catholic neighbours by estate walls. Rather, they lived and worked beside them in towns and cities, and while Protestants were over-represented in the professions and white-collar positions, the rising Catholic middle class was making rapid strides in these areas.

Relations between Catholics and Protestants in Limerick often featured choreographed displays of mutual public respect, but also careful avoidance along parallel paths. Catholic and Protestant farmers might help each other out at threshing time, for instance, but observant Protestants would exclude themselves from Sunday sports, a big part of community life. This self-exclusion could also have been an exercise in self-preservation, a response to the *Ne Temere* decree that demanded that the children of an inter-church marriage be raised as Catholics. This naturally made Protestants anxious about the prospect of their children marrying Catholics. Curiosity, incomprehension or underlying tensions revolved around religious differences and sometimes class distinctions, pockmarked by occasional, often petty, outbursts of bigotry and contempt. But this relatively steady ground shifted dramatically when unionism became suspect, even treasonous. The revolution was deeply unsettling for many Protestants, particularly those who shared some degree of emotional attachment to the British Empire. Military connections or judicial appointments, for instance, rather than being sources of strength, became points of vulnerability. In Limerick, these fault lines were sorely tested during the home rule crisis and further exposed during the War of Independence and Civil War.

After the revolution, many thousands of people, including several hundred from Limerick, retrospectively claimed compensation from the IFS, under the Damage to Property (Compensation) (Amendment) Act (1933), for losses suffered in the course of service to the republican movement.[66] The British Government's Compensation (Ireland) Commission reimbursed loyalists for injuries that they suffered owing to their politics between 1 January 1919 and the truce of 11 July 1921: regrettably, the records relating to Limerick have not survived. The claims of southern loyalists, including Limerick loyalists, to the British government for losses suffered after the truce because of their politics are available in the records of the Irish Distress Committee and Irish Grants Committee (IGC) in the National Archives, London.[67] Like Bureau of Military History (BMH) witness statements – veterans' accounts of their political and military activities during the Irish Revolution – and the Military Service Pensions Collection (MSPC), which relates to the Irish state's payment (or denial) of allowances, gratuities and pensions to veterans of 1916–23 or their dependents, these sources establish some facts and obscure others. Their greatest value is in revealing attitudes and feelings.[68]

This study begins by charting the decline of the home rule movement from its hegemonic position in the early years of the century to its defeat by

SF in the general election of 1918. It then reflects on the process by which the republican movement established a revolutionary counter-state which neutralized British administration in much of the country. While the significance of the political dimension should not be underestimated, the successes of passive resistance must be considered in conjunction with the military campaign of the IRA. A central and recurring theme is how effective a small core of the most committed revolutionaries was in the pursuit of its mission. These activists managed to bring with them a substantial proportion of Limerick people. Conceptualizing or measuring support for a cause during time of war is challenging, however, because political preference was no longer an automatic choice. There was a shifting middle-ground where self-preservation and self-interest dominated in the face of complicated dilemmas and unstable circumstances. The impact of the cumulative 'centrality of minor acts of threat or harm' in dictating people's behaviour should not be overlooked.[69] The violence of 1919–21 centred on confrontation between rebel freedom fighters and an oppressive imperial regime, but it also involved more complex processes. Political and social divisions gripped Limerick from the summer of 1921 until the summer of 1923, when city and county were convulsed by civil war and agrarian and labour disputes were ongoing. It is important to identify those who inflicted and suffered violence, consider what motivated perpetrators, and explore how victims and survivors suffered. Looking at the entire period, the relationship between the revolution and what were essentially local and perhaps even petty personal matters is a key intricacy to negotiate. Most Limerick people were not revolutionaries or counter-revolutionaries and, as far as they could, avoided the extremes of the revolution. And while many succeeded in living lives untouched by antagonism or violence, not everyone was so fortunate.

2 'The unionists went back into their shell': the home rule crisis, 1912–14

Lord Dunraven's experience on the county council in the early part of the century demonstrated how polarized local Limerick politics could be between nationalists and unionists. During the home rule crisis of 1912–14 that division widened. When two general elections in 1910 left Redmond holding the balance of power in Westminster, he traded votes to H.H. Asquith's Liberal Party in return for the promise of a home rule bill. The 1911 Parliament Act reduced the permanent stumbling block of the House of Lords' veto to a temporary delaying power so that the home rule bill introduced in April 1912 seemed set to become law in 1914. The bill proposed nothing so extreme as a republic and it provided for London to retain control over basic elements of sovereignty such as defence and foreign policy, trade and even policing, but Ulster unionists reacted with fury. Adopting an increasingly hard-line position, they resolutely engaged in extra-parliamentary tactics. Limerick unionists, with Charles Barrington to the forefront, took a more measured approach but it was not until 1920 that they retreated from their opposition to self-government for Ireland.

In Limerick the first local battle of the home rule crisis was fought over the relationship between politics and the city and county's ecumenical credentials and reputation. This was an ongoing conflict and although Limerick's Catholic hierarchy was nationalist and its Church of Ireland hierarchy unionist, there was little open dissonance on matters of public policy between the churches. The Right Reverend Dr Raymond d'Audemar Orpen was the Church of Ireland bishop of the United Diocese of Limerick, Ardfert and Aghadoe from 1907 until January 1921.[1] Unlike the Catholic bishop, Edward O'Dwyer, Orpen maintained a low-key public profile. Any Catholic–Protestant tension that may have arisen over the potentially contentious 'Good Literature Crusade' was kept in check. Aimed mainly against English newspapers, the crusade was in full swing during the home rule crisis. Limerick was its epicentre. A Vigilance Association formed in Limerick, as in most large towns, had strong support from the Catholic clergy. Fr Thomas Murphy, the head of the Limerick branch, wrote *The literature crusade in Ireland* in 1912 and published it locally. This booklet was the crusaders' policy document. The movement advocated that Ireland should be cleansed of English contamination and that all ideas incompatible with Catholic orthodoxy be suppressed. On 22 December 1912 the Good Literature Crusade's book-barrow appeared on the streets of Limerick for the first time, its con-

tents priced 'to suit all classes'.[2] On 30 November 1913 a crowd of 4,000
people attended a demonstration against 'unwholesome' literature. It was
backed by both Fr Aidan Mangan, director of the Redemptorist
Confraternity, and Reverend Hackett, Church of Ireland dean of Limerick.[3]
Limerick's religious leaders, certainly those on the Protestant side, seemed to
place a premium on harmony. Limerick's civic leaders, most of them Catholic
nationalists, were also interested in presenting a united front, but only on
their terms. They were more likely to demand confirmation of their generos-
ity to the minority than to relax their political posturing.

In March 1910 W.L. Stokes, the Protestant councillor and high sheriff of
Limerick, had repudiated charges of intolerance in Limerick made by the
family of a Presbyterian clergyman. Two months later, Stokes's fellow
Protestant and successor as high sheriff, William Halliday, paid tribute to the
spirit of religious and political tolerance in Limerick.[4] In early 1912, as a
crude part of the nationalist campaign to assuage 'baseless apprehensions' concerning the likelihood of oppression of the minority in a home rule Ireland,
Stokes's and Halliday's comments were among a host of similar offerings put
forward in the press.[5] In response to allegations of sectarianism, a list of
Protestants employed in positions of significance by Limerick Corporation was
published and it was emphasized that many of these officers had been elected
over Catholics.[6] At a meeting of the west Limerick executive of the UIL in
May 1912, Fr John Fitzgerald called for contributions to finance speakers to
contradict allegations made against nationalist Catholics of being intolerant
towards Protestants and unionists.[7] On 11 July Limerick Corporation recorded
its regret and disappointment that the Protestant minority in Limerick, 'which
had always been shown kindliness and respect', had not spoken out against
the 'bigoted action of their co-religionists in Belfast', where there had been
regular and prolonged outbreaks of anti-Catholic discrimination and violence.[8]
The west Limerick executive of the UIL issued a similar call on 2 August.[9]
Samuel Harris, president of the east Limerick UIL executive, declared that
he and his fellow Protestants in the south of the country were 'treated like
princes' by the Catholic majority.[10]

Matters reached a significant escalation point in Limerick on 10 October
1912, less than two weeks after hundreds of thousands of Ulster unionists
signed their Solemn League and Covenant against home rule. Tory MP and
former Chief Secretary George Wyndham addressed 2,000 Munster members
of the Unionist Alliance protesting the bill at the Theatre Royal on Henry
Street in the city. The *Limerick Leader* editorial of 9 October referred to allegations that Protestant shop owners in the south of Ireland had been 'starved
out' by their Catholic neighbours. The *Leader* challenged Lord Massy, who
chaired the unionist meeting, to rebut the claims. The paper also condemned
the economic and social persecution of many Catholics in Belfast at the hands

of the unionist majority while highlighting the custom and tolerance that Protestant shopkeepers in Limerick enjoyed from the city's Catholics. Whereas Ulster's Covenant had committed to using 'all means' necessary to defeat home rule, Barrington's resolution was that Limerick unionists would apply 'every legitimate means'. It was passed with acclaim. All unionist opposition to home rule placed heavy emphasis on commerce. Barrington opined that while 'the green flag' was 'in our hearts', 'sentiment will not pay the butcher's bill, or put money in our pockets, or buy boots and shoes for our children'. The Union guaranteed 'prosperity and contentment which is everything'. In addition, the unionists of Munster made it clear on this occasion that they saw the continuation of land purchase as central to a peaceful civil society.[11]

Having concluded with a rendition of the national anthem, attendees were met with a barrage of stones as they departed. The *Leader* and the pro-Union *Limerick Chronicle* agreed that the disturbances were further provoked by a new mounted police unit, which had no experience of crowd control, employed 'roughrider' tactics in its attempt to disperse the waiting nationalist crowd. Two nights of rioting followed. Protestant clergymen were assaulted. Business premises, mainly Protestant-owned but some Catholic-owned, were attacked. Windows were smashed in eighty-five properties according to Chief Secretary Augustine Birrell. CI Henry Yates referred to attacks on Protestant churches and halls and the targeting of private Catholic homes in reprisal. Every window in the Protestant Young Men's Association was broken. Quiet was restored when Catholic clergy intervened and the police were confined to barracks. After Fr Mangan addressed a crowd, reported to be in the region of 5,000, on the night of 12 October the demonstration ended. The loss of face suffered by the recently appointed CI was accentuated when the *Chronicle* praised the role of the Catholic clergy and alluded to the RIC's withdrawal from the streets after Yates had drafted 300 extra policemen into the city. The paper also suggested that 'here, all classes and creeds live on terms of the utmost amity and good will. We have long enjoyed a reputation for peace and good order which any city in the world might envy.'[12] In the House of Commons, Unionist leader Edward Carson condemned the 'unprovoked attacks' and 'intolerance'.[13] Michael Joyce's only parliamentary contributions on home rule occurred in the week after the riot, and amounted to defences of Limerick against what he considered as slurs on its good name.[14] The *Leader*, in IPP watchdog mode, closely monitored the records of the three Limerick MPs in Westminster. By the end of January 1913, 233 votes had been taken on the bill. Lundon and O'Shaughnessy were present for all; Joyce missed only one.[15] Their attendance rates remained consistently high during the crisis.

When the Theatre Royal reopened on 21 October 1912, it was boycotted by nationalists, and patrons were assaulted and intimidated. Reinforcements were needed to support the police and military and Catholic clergy once again played a role in quieting unrest.[16] Charles Johnston, a member of Limerick Corporation, was prosecuted for assaulting Canon Robertson of St Munchin's Church of Ireland church, but the case against him was dismissed.[17] Another councillor interpreted the riots as 'the boys of Limerick adopt[ing] the mild protest of breaking windows' to express their resentment at Unionist advocacy of minority Protestant rule.[18] The press blamed 'a crowd of youngsters' and 'a crowd of boys' for the violence.[19] Specifically, the culprits of the 'orgy of glass-breaking' were 'lads' aged from thirteen to fifteen, 'gangs of whom have gone round each night smashing in a spirit of sheer mischief, the windows of Catholics and Protestants, Nationalists and Unionists, with absolute impartiality'.[20] When Na Fianna and the AOH fell out over their respective roles in the riots amid mutual accusations of window-breaking, CI Yates concentrated on this spat rather than his failure to deal efficiently with the disorder in the first place.[21] The majority of recipients of court-ordered compensation for damage inflicted during the riots were Protestants, including Archdeacon Hackett (soon-to-be Dean) and St Michael's Church, as well as the Young Men's Association. The whole episode had played into the hands of the advanced nationalist element in Limerick. After this the unionists of Limerick, in the words of Volunteer Jeremiah Cronin, 'went back into their shell and did not attempt anymore public demonstrations'.[22] The Church Lads Brigade, for instance, no longer paraded the streets of Limerick after October 1912.

In early 1914 W.R. Gubbins, Limerick County Council chairman, described it as extraordinary that Protestants, 'who received every kindness at the hands of Catholics, should not have the courage, the pluck or the common decency to contradict those base and groundless rumours' of Catholic intolerance that were in circulation.[23] Councillors' condemnations of Munster Protestants for not contradicting accusations of Catholic intolerance were menacing in tone: 'the worm may turn … and those people who remain silent now may have reason to regret it'.[24] Samuel Harris lamented that the Protestant merchants of Limerick and elsewhere had not come forward in the press and at public meetings to show that they had no fear of home rule. Similar comments were made by many of his Catholic nationalist colleagues.[25] At the start of March the *Chronicle* reported the claims of a Conservative delegation which had visited the city that Limerick Protestants were living in a 'state of terror'.[26] The mayor, Philip O'Donovan, hoped that unionists, 'who drew very large incomes from the Catholic population, would have come forward and stated that home rule had no terrors for them, and that there was no fear the Catholics would prosecute them'.[27] William Halliday, lauding the harmony that he felt would continue to prevail in Limerick whether or not home rule came to pass, condemned the influence of 'political tricksters'.[28] A number of prominent local Protestants issued a carefully worded statement denying the existence of religious discrimination in Limerick: 'religious and political opinions being almost identical, political intolerance is often mistaken for an attack on religion'.[29] The timing of public displays of this nature was also revealing, displaying as it did a definite orchestration of sentiment in response to pressure from civic officials. At a meeting of Limerick Corporation on 5 March, convened especially to address this controversy, Councillor Michael O'Callaghan strongly encouraged a public unionist dis-avowal of the 'Tory slanders'.[30] When another English political deputation visited on St Patrick's Day, they were hosted by the Protestant Young Men's Association. The message sent and received was that there was no intolerance in Limerick.[31] Around this time Limerick County Council made much of having appointed a northern Protestant, Robert Davidson, as the divisional surveyor for east Limerick, at £300 a year. Headlines trumpeted tolerance over accounts of how he had defeated fully qualified Catholics.[32] Five years later, they were playing the same tune. When Samuel Ruttle, who came from a 'respected' Protestant family, was appointed as a rate collector, it was all the more broad-minded because he had defeated a strong Catholic candidate and, following Davidson, was the second non-Catholic appointed by the council.[33]

All sides promoted the fanciful notion that Limerick was free of bigotry. Even when there was an apparently clear case of 'blind, stark, mad bigotry', the courts did not see it as such. Canon Robertson objected to the inscription on a Catholic tombstone in the graveyard St Munchin's because it called for prayer for the souls of the deceased. This was contrary to Protestant practice and carried a 'whiff of Purgatory'. Mary McNamara of nearby Thomondgate was obstructed in visiting her parents' grave and Roberts wanted the newly erected tombstone removed. Captain James Delmege of the Church Vestry Committee sided with McNamara. James Stewart, the warden of St Munchin's, seemed embarrassed but still followed Robertson's orders. Judge Smith, presiding at Limerick Sessions, was horrified: 'It is the most terrible case of sectarian bigotry I have ever witnessed and coming from the North I know what that is'. He awarded McNamara a decree against the Vestry Committee (minus Delmege). Robertson and Stewart appealed at Limerick assizes before Justice Gordon, who did not see the incident as sectarian and reversed Smith's decision.[34] So, officially at least, there were no bigots in Limerick. Loud pronouncements of tolerance continued throughout the rev-olution. Discordant notes were struck more regularly by representatives of the majority, usually when they felt that Protestants were not strenuous enough in their denunciation of bigotry on the part of their co-religionists elsewhere on the island.

Often away from the political spotlight, employers and workers around Limerick city and county engaged in a slow wrestling match over terms and conditions. Employees rarely enjoyed spectacular successes but they made gradual, intermittent progress during the revolution. An early step in the process occurred between 24 January and 11 February 1913, when the Limerick Dock Labourers' Society engaged the Limerick Steamship Company in industrial action. The union objected to the subcontracting of non-union-ized labour, which had the potential to undercut its members' already low wages and further jeopardize their tenuous job security. When the employers imported workers from Liverpool, substantial additional RIC resources had to be deployed. Whereas a striking labourer died in clashes at Sligo harbour, stone-throwing was the extent of the violence in Limerick.[35] The sympathy of Limerick Corporation, mindful of security costs, was with the dockers. Arbitration resulted in the strike-breakers' departure and the police returned to normal duties. Strikes in Galway and Sligo between March and May 1913 were part of the same social movement that affected urban Ireland and cul-minated in the Dublin lockout of late 1913 and early 1914.

Even during this surge of industrial unrest, however, the politics of home rule remained centre-stage. From 1911 the Orange Order took the lead in drilling and arming men until the Ulster Volunteer Force came into being in early 1913. In reaction, the Irish Volunteers were founded on 25 November 1913 in Dublin. Con Colbert and Ned Daly (nephew of John Daly and another of those executed in 1916), were among the Limerick men present at the inaugural meeting in the Rotunda. Bulmer Hobson, on behalf of the IRB, was heavily involved in its establishment, but the immediate catalyst was Eoin MacNeill's article in *An Claidheamh Soluis*, 'The North began', which called on nationalists to arm themselves in support of home rule as unionists had done in opposition. Just prior to the public inauguration of the Irish Volunteers, Fr John Fitzgerald of the west Limerick UIL, in the presence of P.J. O'Shaughnessy MP, had urged the creation of a force to resist Ulster unionism and 'weak-kneed Liberals'. He threatened bloodshed if home rule was not enacted. In December, however, Thomas Lundon MP told the east Limerick UIL that a militia was unnecessary and urged restraint in commit-ting to the movement until the party leaders gave direction.[36] His comments reflected nationalist reservations about the possible significance of the Volunteers and their potential to undermine Redmond. A signal of the strength of the home rule movement at this point, however, was the fact that 12,000 people turned out to hear Redmond speak in Limerick city on 12 December 1913.[37]

The local IRB made arrangements to establish the first corps of Volunteers in Limerick. At a public meeting in the city's Athenaeum Hall on 25 January 1914, Mayor Philip O'Donovan stated that should the movement 'be in any way hostile to the cause so ably advocated by Mr Redmond and the Irish Parliamentary Party he would not officially support it'. However, the

IRB, in the guise of the Wolfe Tone Club, and acting as representatives of trade unions, were able to dominate the original provisional committee of the City Volunteers. Patrick Pearse and Roger Casement addressed the Athenaeum meeting, and later reported favourably to Tom Clarke on the response of those present, with practically every man there joining up.[38] Perceiving the Volunteers as a vehicle for radicalization, Pearse told John Daly that he had pitched his speech

> in a key intended to find a response in the Home Rule heart as well as in the Nationalist heart, more properly so called. I believe that the rank and file of the Home Rulers are ready, if properly handled, to go as far as you have gone and I hope to go. Here again the Volunteer movement seems to be the one thing that will bring them into line with us.[39]

CI Yates reported that Daly 'and his followers are the principals in this [Volunteer] movement as a large section of the Nationalists believe there is no necessity for it at the moment'.[40]

As elsewhere, however, the organization grew rapidly around the city and county and Redmond could not afford to dismiss it. Volunteer coordinator Ernest Blythe 'visited almost every small town and village' in Limerick in March 1914.[41] British double standards acted as catalysts for expansion. The 'Curragh incident' in March illustrated that the army's officer class would not support any government moves to quash unionist resistance to home rule. The Ulster Volunteers again led the way in illegal gun-running. Under the eyes of the state apparatus, they imported 25,000 German rifles and three million rounds of ammunition in April 1914. The Irish Volunteers' response was relatively underwhelming. They smuggled 1,500 bargain-basement single-shot, 1871 German Mausers and 50,000 rounds of ammunition. This necessitated an astounding seaborne adventure in capricious conditions that had a strong Limerick dimension. Mary Spring Rice of Mount Trenchard, Foynes, and her cousins, Conor and Kitty O'Brien were instrumental in the financial and logistical elements of the gun-running. The episode enhanced the prestige of the Irish Volunteers and altered external perceptions of the organization. It was also a reminder that not all Protestants were unionists. One of the Mausers, which armed the 1916 rebels, was symbolically reserved for John Daly and delivered to him by Tom Clarke.[42] In mid-May Limerick County Council resolved that more should be done to arm the Irish Volunteers and Thomas Lundon raised the possibility of armed men being needed to enforce home rule in the event of an RIC mutiny.[43] On 25 May, when the home rule bill passed its third reading in the House of Commons (meaning that its enactment into law seemed imminent), thousands celebrated at the O'Connell monument at the city's Crescent. The killing of Dublin civilians by British troops on 26 July in the aftermath of a failed attempt to seize the rifles outraged nationalist Ireland. The Limerick Board of Guardians termed it a 'Cromwellian massacre'.[44] Once Redmond realized that the maturation of the Volunteers meant he could no longer discount them as a threat to his hegemony, the Limerick MPs rowed in with organizational efforts.

Cumann na mBan, the republican women's organization, grew alongside the Volunteers. A Limerick city branch was established on 5 June 1914 with over 100 women joining. The Daly sisters, Kathleen and Madge, dominated. The closeness of the relationship between Cumann na mBan and the Volunteers was demonstrated by the fact that all correspondence was to be sent to 1 Hartstonge Street, Volunteer HQ. In May 1915 the *Irish Volunteer* described Limerick's Cumann na mBan branch as one of the most 'flourishing' in Ireland.[45] The comments of local Volunteer organizer, Robert Monteith, on Cumann na mBan applied throughout the revolutionary period:

> Not only did the women learn to use firearms, but they showed a lead to the men in many ways. They organised an efficient Red Cross service, collected funds, were active recruiters, and relieved the monotony of hard work by social affairs, dances, outings etc. In fact, without their help the Volunteer movement could never have been the success it was. These women did not theorise, they did practical work. At Limerick they accompanied us on all field work in order to train the Red Cross section … they knew what should be done, they knew how to do it, and they did it.[46]

While Cumann na mBan saw itself as an auxiliary to the Volunteers, women such as Madge Daly often dictated to male colleagues and on at least one occasion, during the IRA attack on Kilmallock RIC barracks in May 1920, Limerick members of Cumann na mBan engaged in combat.

In March 1914 Roger Casement wrote a series of letters to John Daly requesting him to introduce a German journalist, Oscus Schweriner, editor of the *Vossische Zeitung* of Berlin, the paper of record, to the 'true nationalists of Limerick, not the Shoneens'.[47] Casement believed that

> his influence on the continent will count for much, and it is essential the liars should not get him but that he should understand that, at bottom Ireland is still Ireland – today shall be as yesterday. The red blood flows in Ireland still. Show him the Fianna and if possible the Volunteers … What you tell him may help much to give the truth to Europe – to Germany at any rate.[48]

Schweriner never visited, but Casement and Daly were clearly thinking in terms of assistance for an Irish rebellion from allies in Europe and Limerick's prospective role. Their accurate anticipation of international war was not the norm, however. The home rule crisis had dominated Irish political life from 1912 to 1914. Nationalist Ireland, including the majority of Limerick Volunteers, were thinking more in terms of civil war in defence of home rule against Ulster unionism. This seemed a likely outcome of the extra-parliamentary means that had been widely adopted over the previous two years. Limerick unionists' Theatre Royal protest of October 1912, instead of being a curtain-raiser to a long-running show of strength, ended up as more of a finale. And if Limerick's unionists did not feel isolated enough already, it had become abundantly clear that their Ulster counterparts would not be joining them in any home rule Ireland. When frantic political efforts to find a compromise foundered on the question of Ulster's exclusion in July 1914, the imposition of home rule, violent Ulster resistance and civil war seemed probable. All changed utterly, however, when Britain declared war on Germany and Austria-Hungary on 4 August. Home rule, indeed Ireland generally, was relegated from the top of the political agenda. In new circumstances, the IPP had nothing new to offer. Revolutionaries like Limerick's Daly family sensed weakness.

3 'It is England's war, not Ireland's': Limerick, 1914–16

On 14 August 1914, 1,000 men of the 2nd Battalion, York and Lancaster Regiment departed Limerick railway station for the war. They were cheered off by excited crowds.[1] Men from Limerick city and county joined the army at a rate of ten a day for the first three months of the war, reporting to the recruiting centre at the Strand Barracks.[2] The families of reservists who rejoined were supported by a fund instituted almost immediately by the Limerick Chamber of Commerce.[3] Limerick's MPs, civic authorities and newspapers, but not its Catholic clergy, committed themselves to the war effort in expectation of a swift and glorious triumph. But as soldiers' obituaries started to appear with greater frequency in the *Chronicle*, enthusiasm waned. This was much the same plot that played out countrywide. About 4,000 Limerick men joined the British armed services between 1914 and 1918. Over 1,000 Limerick men and six Limerick women who were working in the services were killed. Seven civilians from Limerick died when the RMS *Leinster* was torpedoed outside Dublin Bay in October 1918. Michael Joyce was on board but survived the mass drowning.[4] Twenty-two men from Coonagh, a village on the banks of the Shannon and near the Clare border with a population of 200, went to war. Half of them were killed, apparently giving Coonagh the dubious honour of having the war's highest death toll per head of population.[5]

The war had a transformative economic effect on both the city and county, but its impact was uneven. Profits soared in agriculture and industry and the dynamics of the employer–employee relationship had to be recalibrated. The volume of cash in circulation surged but so too did inflation, negating many benefits of the boom. Politically, there was a dramatic swing in the IPP's fortunes. Home rule was officially entered on the statute book on 18 September 1914 to popular acclaim. Redmond was nationalist Ireland's hero of the hour. There were joyous celebrations around Limerick.[6] But home rule, suspended for the duration of the war, would never be implemented. And Limerick's republicans saw the war as an opportunity for rebellion. By mid-1916, less than halfway through the war, the political landscape looked dramatically different than it had two years earlier. Limerick, with its Catholic bishop to the forefront of the anti-war campaign and its secret cabals working feverishly in the background, played a major role in this change. Redmond's instinctive reaction to the war was that Irishmen should be entrusted with the defence of Ireland, rather than fighting on foreign fields. On 20 September, however, to demonstrate home rule Ireland's loyalty, he called on Volunteers to join the

army. The movement was sundered apart. The majority remained under the
Redmondite banner, and became known as the National Volunteers. The
minority, under Eoin MacNeill, retained the title of Irish Volunteers. The RIC
estimated the strength of the Volunteers in Limerick in September 1914 as
8,235 members in eighty-two branches. This translates to fifty-eight members
of the Volunteers per thousand of population in Limerick at the time. The
comparative figure for Clare was forty-nine.[7] Of 1,250 men in the Limerick
City Regiment, more than 200 went with MacNeill but only 100 were active
subsequently.[8] The fall-off was partly due to businesses warning employees to
desist from 'Sinn Féin' activities.[9] The split in the Volunteers had repercussions within Cumann na mBan. When the Redmondite faction failed to gain
access to funds that had been raised for the Volunteers prior to the split, they
resigned en masse and formed the National Volunteers Ladies' Association, an
organization unique to Limerick but which soon faded away. The several hundred pounds concerned was provided to MacNeill's Irish Volunteers to fund
the purchase of arms.[10] Limerick Corporation, like much of the country,
believed that home rule would be applied after a quick and triumphant war
and adopted a resolution 'heartily approving' of Redmond's stance, with only
two members dissenting. One was John Dalton, a member of John Daly's old
Labour coterie.[11] The county council adopted a similar position. The proposal
of Councillor Anthony Mackey, one of the leading IRB men in Limerick, that
half of the council's credit balance should be used to purchase arms for the
Volunteers, a call which had the support of Bishop O'Dwyer, was rejected by
members in early September.[12]

The eagerness of the civic authorities did not translate into enlistment,
however. Measured in these terms Redmond's endorsement of the war was
not greeted with enthusiasm in Limerick, though Councillor McGrath of the
Customhouse ward enlisted.[13] Attendances at drilling declined substantially
after the outbreak of war because Volunteers believed that they would be
required to join the army if they continued to parade. Even after the split, the
National Volunteers showed no increased desire to enlist.[14] A suggestion that
the 8th Royal Munster Fusiliers should have the title 'Limerick Battalion' was
rejected by Lieutenant-General Sir Lawrence Parsons of the 16th (Irish)
Division because he deemed the initial enlistment rate of the Limerick
National Volunteers to be unsatisfactory.[15] There was also an element of discontent among members of the National Volunteers who were dissatisfied
with the foisting of ex-officers with strong unionist views on them by the central leadership in Dublin.[16] The *Leader* lambasted republicans for manipulat-
ing the Volunteers, and elicited strong support from respondents who
declared that the 'despicable tactics', absurd and inane doctrines, and 'theo-
rizing and vapourings of the small Sinn Féin element have disgusted the
rank-and-file of the City Volunteers'. In early September the *Leader* referred

to Seán Mac Diarmada as the 'pro-German editor' of *Irish Freedom*. Mac Diarmada drafted a reply but, on discussing the matter with John Daly, decided that it would be 'unwise to go into correspondence with such a man'.[17] Daly was not afraid to take a public stand when he judged it warranted, however. At the outbreak of war in August the military sought to commandeer four of the nine horses used in the family bakery. Daly threatened to shoot all of the horses rather than surrender one. The army, in consultation with the local Crown prosecutor, James Gaffney, feared the effect that the shooting of the animals by the Fenian would have on public opinion.[18] Daly was the only merchant in Limerick who kept all his horses.[19]

Between city and county, approximately 940 Limerick men had enlisted by the end of January 1915. Recruitment propaganda increased in the local press. In March 100 men apparently enlisted over two days in Limerick.[20] From early 1915, however, the rate of enlistment declined all over the country. According to the RIC, 1,776 men from Limerick joined the army during 1915, with at least 586 known to be National Volunteers.[21] The registrar general recorded 19,728 men of military age in Limerick on 15 August 1915. Some 7,994 of them were in indispensable labour, 4,367 were physically unfit and 6,551 were available for military service, of which 3,177 joined up between the start of the war and 15 August 1916, but only 816 of them joined between 15 August 1915 and 15 October 1916.[22] In May 1916 the *Leader* reported that between 400 and 500 National Volunteers from Limerick city were serving in the army.[23] Recruiting was most successful among the city's working class. It was universally unpopular in agricultural areas, farmers needing all the hands they could muster to reap the benefit of the huge demand for their goods.[24] The difference in the number of recruits to the Irish Volunteers and the army must be interpreted in the context of financial incentives and the collective communal pressures involved in working–class recruitment, but also the greater risk to life and limb inherent in service on the Continent. Propaganda resources were also vital. The army did not just rely on newspaper advertisements and public posters; Colonel Sir Charles Barrington, provincial sub-director of recruiting for Limerick, Clare and Kerry, sought to employ the latest technology and to use local cinemas to mythologize Limerick war heroes.[25]

At the end of 1914 there were approximately 7,000 National Volunteers and 450 Irish Volunteers in Limerick.[26] In April 1915 the Irish Volunteers formed an insurance society, An Cumann Cosanta, to protect members 'against victimisation, the possibility of which we have learned through experience'.[27] The victimization that they were most likely to face was loss of employment.[28] On 23 May 1915, Whit Sunday, Irish Volunteer companies from Dublin, Cork and Tipperary joined their Limerick colleagues to parade through the city. They encountered considerable antagonism, particularly in areas where there were a high proportion of 'separation wives'. One Volunteer recalled getting 'an awful hiding' and being barraged with bottles, iron bars and full chamber pots.[29] Dan Breen of Tipperary was 'sorely tempted to open fire on the hostile crowd'.[30] Some Volunteers fired shots into the air and one bayoneted an assailant but without doing much harm. As with the riots of October 1912, it was the influence of Fr Mangan rather than the police that was decisive in restoring calm.[31] The only consolation the Volunteers could possibly have taken from the day's events was that they had maintained their discipline in the face of formidable provocation. A sanguine Patrick Pearse 'felt that the great bulk of the people in the city were sympathetic and that the hostile element was small, though noisy. Personally, I found the whole experience useful.'[32] Whit Sunday was not an isolated incident. When the West Limerick Volunteers paraded in Newcastle West on Saint Patrick's Day 1916, they were assailed by soldiers' wives and families who hurled not only verbal abuse, but also rotten eggs.[33] Up to early 1915 troops passing through the city on their way to the front, as well as recruiting parties, routinely met with warm receptions. As the lists of dead and injured grew longer, however, official attitudes seemed to change. The visit of the Irish Guards band to the city in April drew no welcome from any civic representative. After thirty Limerick men died fighting with the Royal Munster Fusiliers at Aubers Ridge on 9 May, the Irish Guards band was shunned again in July.[34] In August a proposal that Limerick Corporation should address the lord lieutenant during his visit to Limerick was only carried by thirteen votes to ten.[35]

Also in August 1915, at the request of Tom Clarke, Irish Volunteer instructor Robert Monteith left Limerick and made his way to Germany, where he was to act as drill officer to Roger Casement's projected Irish Brigade of prisoners of war.[36] Monteith was a serious loss to the Limerick Volunteers. The Defence of the Realm Act (DORA) was originally designed to suppress political dissent during the war, but was regularly implemented in Ireland until the 1921 truce. It was used to curb freedom of the press, freedom of speech and public meetings. Republicans were arrested, imprisoned and deported without recourse to civil law. Newspapers were shut down, organizations like the Gaelic League and the Gaelic Athletic Association (GAA) were banned and social gatherings like fairs were prohibited. DORA also allowed for the imposition of martial law. In July 1915 Ernest Blythe was served with a DORA order to leave Ireland. Clarke and Daly regarded this as a test case and urged non-compliance. Limerick Corporation condemned the affair, which won the Volunteers much sympathy.[37] Blythe was imprisoned in Belfast but returned to Limerick in November 1915. He found it 'much easier to get visible results' in Limerick than in Clare between then and his arrest in Athea and deportation just weeks before the Rising. He did not return to Limerick again until the summer of 1917.[38] Coupled with the earlier departure of Monteith, the loss of Blythe at crucial times undermined the Limerick Volunteers on an organizational and operational level. But they were well-regarded by their colleagues nationally. In the summer of 1914, before the split, *Sinn Féin* described the city corps as 'the best drilled in Ireland'.[39] In February 1915 Pearse wrote

> Is dóigh le'n a lán gurab é cath Luimnighe an cath is treise dá bhfuil againn. Tá fir maithe in a gceannais, fir nach bhfuil a sárugad in Éireann, ar dílseacht, nár ar calmacht, nár ar stuaim.[40]

> [There are many who think the Limerick Battalion is the best we have. There are good men in command, men whose loyalty, courage and precision are not surpassed in Ireland].

At the same time an inspector from the Volunteer executive identified Limerick as perhaps the most efficient unit in the provinces and as leading Dublin in some respects. A year later, thanks to the competence of its leaders, Limerick was still the best organized urban area outside Dublin.[41] Circumstances in Dublin, however, were radically different to those in the rest of the country. Dublin communications were better, it was easier to concentrate forces there and the Dublin Brigade was better drilled and armed. Dublin officers were more closely informed of the intentions of the Military Council of the IRB and, consequently, were better prepared for the Rising.

By early 1916 the National Volunteer movement in Limerick existed only in name. The Irish Volunteers, meanwhile, were increasing in strength. There were 689 members in seventeen branches in February and 872 members in twenty-two branches in June according to the police.[42] Blythe was occasionally successful in encouraging National Volunteers to secede, particularly where he had the support of the Catholic clergy, and in recruiting farmers' sons of military age. According to the police, farmers' sons believed that membership of the Irish Volunteers would protect them from conscription.[43] The threat of conscription, according to Blythe, 'made it as easy to form Volunteer Companies as it had previously been difficult.' But his experiences around Limerick suggested to him that it was not just fear for personal safety that had men flocking to the Volunteers. Rather, the conscription issue had led to 'rising National spirit'.[44] This was a generous interpretation of the motivations at play.

The UIL enjoyed a renaissance around Limerick in 1915. Redmond, speaking in Limerick in December 1914, had stressed the continuing need for a strong UIL and urged its revitalization. The *Leader* understood how people were 'deluded into the notion' that the League had outlived its usefulness, 'the Home Rule Cause having been at long last successful'.[45] In response to Redmond's plea, a concerted drive was made to rejuvenate the UIL in

Limerick. There were eighty-eight UIL meetings in the county in 1915, twice
as many as in 1914, and thirty of these were reorganization meetings. The
League had not been as active since 1907. The Ahane branch, where the
League had not been present for four years but where there had been strong
branches of the AOH and Irish Land and Labour Association, reorganized in
January.[46] By the end of the month three new UIL branches had affiliated in
the west Limerick division since the last executive meeting the previous
November.[47] In July Ballyhahill UIL was reorganized after a six-year lapse.[48]
While it was not uncommon for meetings of political associations to be held on
Sundays, these UIL reorganization meetings took place almost invariably after
Mass on Sunday morning in the local Catholic church. They were occasionally
held in the churchyard. Besides the obvious convenience of a ready-made
crowd, this suggests close clerical involvement in the movement. The real motivation behind this renewed activity was anti-conscription sentiment. At one
meeting, P.J. O'Shaughnessy referred to critical comments made by Mayor
O'Donovan about the National Volunteers' response to the war and said that
'they required no certificate of courage from his Lordship and that whatever
faults Irishmen had they were not cowards'.[49] At another meeting, Thomas
Lundon pledged that he would shed his blood to resist conscription.[50] When
the IPP gave its implicit support to a new coalition government including a
number of die-hard unionists in May 1915 it was, for the first time, subject to
explicit criticism from nationalist Ireland. Such criticism was conspicuous by
its absence in Limerick, however. The local press and UIL were unstinting in
their praise of Redmond's decision to decline a cabinet position while ignoring
the loss of influence involved.[51] In June, however, CI Yates observed that 'the
people on the whole are not very keen about the UIL as they believe that it is
principally for election purposes it is being re-organised'.[52]

SF, in its most successful pre-1917 initiative in Limerick, orchestrated an
anti-recruitment campaign. It involved disruption of rallies, assaults on army
personnel and materials, and the distribution of propaganda. SF returned
forms with the details of men who were purportedly prepared to enlist, but
who in reality had made no such commitment. This created some confusion,
though hardly chaos, for local recruiting committees.[53] One of the SF spokesmen was James Dalton, who was also a founder of the Volunteers in
Limerick. In the knowledge that his words were being noted by detectives
from the RIC Special Branch, he delivered a colourful address to a Volunteer
rally in Shanagolden in September 1915. He condemned the war and those
who enlisted:

> I don't give a damn who is listening and I am prepared to take the
> consequences. We the Irish Volunteers are meant to defend Ireland but
> if we are asked to defend England then to hell with England and if we

are asked to fight for Germany to hell with Germany ... Those who
have volunteered or would volunteer to fight with England are only
traitors, cowards and prostitutes.[54]

The anti-recruiting campaign, as well as the anti-conscription campaign,
received significant Catholic clerical support. Six Limerick clergymen came
to the attention of the RIC during 1915, 'owing to their disloyal language or
conduct'. This was the third-highest number in Ireland.[55] The rogue priests
had the blessing of Bishop O'Dwyer, who was a staunch opponent of the war.
In November 1915 he engaged Redmond in the press. He wrote that 'it is
England's war, not Ireland's', declaring that the war would ruin Ireland and
that home rule would never be implemented. Limerick Corporation supported
the bishop. The police believed that O'Dwyer's 'notorious letter' offered
'immense assistance' to 'seditious writers' and estimated that it was circulated
in pamphlet form 'by the thousand'. Augustine Birrell deemed it 'one of the
most formidable anti-recruiting pamphlets ever written'.[56] It lent respectability to clerical involvement in anti-war demonstrations and, by extension,
Volunteer activities. Charles Barrington responded to O'Dwyer by calling a
rally in Pery Square on 20 November. Vice-Lieutenant of County Limerick
since March, 65-year-old Barrington had spent the previous four months
driving his personal ambulance in France; he had only returned to Limerick
in late October.[57] Redmond, a distant second-best to O'Dwyer in November,
won a significant victory in securing Ireland's exclusion from conscription
after it was imposed on Britain in early 1916, and the *Leader* declared
Limerick's unyielding fealty.[58]

Meanwhile, southern unionism seemed to be gradually waning. On 25
January 1916 a land agent and farmer in Limerick admitted that local unionists were 'practically submerged. Hardly a hundred now on the Register. If
the issue [Home Rule] was raised again, very hard to say if [unionists] would
bow to the inevitable'.[59] On the same day, however, Stephen Quin, a unionist, was elected mayor in the hope that he would be able to attract industry,
in the shape of munitions factories, to Limerick. In anticipation of Quin's
election, Councillor John Dalton, a brother of James, had proposed a resolution that the new mayor should not act in a manner 'that might be likely to
lower the national dignity of our city'. Nine out of thirty-seven members of
Limerick Corporation, who, to use Councillor Matthew Griffin's expression,
considered Quin a unionist 'flunkey', supported Dalton's resolution.[60] This
represented a significant shift in the political equilibrium of the corporation
since August 1914, when only two members opposed Redmond's call for
Irishmen to join the army.

Quin's election pointed to the importance of the economic spin-offs of the
war, and its economic influence was all-encompassing. In July 1914 efforts to

establish a branch of the Irish Transport and General Workers' Union (ITGWU) in Limerick 'completely failed'.[61] Wartime inflation forced workers to organize and the frequency of strikes, number of strikers, and volume of workdays lost due to strikes increased annually in Ireland from 1915 to 1918.[62] As the demand for labour increased and supply decreased, high profits in certain sectors meant that wage demands could be accommodated. Between 10,000 and 15,000 Limerick workers marched to celebrate Labour Day for the first time on Sunday, 5 May 1918.[63] Such a turnout in a city of 40,000 people reflected Limerick labour's organizational and industrial strength. Limerick port suffered badly during the war. Due to German naval activity, sea journeys to Britain were longer and more hazardous from Limerick than from the east coast, so strategic and economic concerns meant a huge decline in traffic and cargo tonnage through the port. In March 1916 a ship carrying bacon from Limerick to Glasgow was sunk by a German submarine.[64] The docks were in difficulty in any case: they were under-financed and under-mechanized compared to rival ports. As casual, non-contracted labourers, dockers were always particularly vulnerable. They worked only when a ship docked, and in hazardous conditions. Many enlisted or found alternative employment, so that a scarcity of labour became another problem for the harbour to contend with. Coal merchants wanted to erect a crane but Limerick United Trades and Labour Council argued that it would be 'a betrayal of the 500 quay labourers who are at present fighting in France and the other fronts'.[65] Flour mills, dependent on American wheat, suffered shortages. A biscuit factory in the city cut 100 jobs in the middle of 1916.[66] There were strikes and industrial sabotage at the docks in late 1917 and early 1918 (a lorry-borne crane was dumped into the Shannon) but there was a remarkably swift upturn as soon as the war ended. Within weeks the *Leader* was reporting a 'gratifying stir in shipping activity ... giving employment and helping to stimulate local trade.'[67]

In agriculture, there was a boom as demand in Britain for Irish animal meat and dairy produce soared and prices obtained by farmers followed suit. Limerick's pig-buyers and cattle-dealers did well on the back of the farmers' wartime bonanza. Shopkeepers thrived and bank deposits multiplied. For working-class people, however, the war brought little benefit. Heavily limited coal imports meant sharp rises in coal, gas and electricity prices. Daily staples increased steeply. Sugar rose from 2½d. per pound to 6d.; butter from a 1s. per pound to 1s. 6d.; flour increased by 20 per cent, bacon by 25 per cent. Most beers became twice as expensive. In general, the cost of living increased by about 50 per cent from 1914 to 1916, and the upward trend continued thereafter.[68] In November 1916 the *Leader* urged readers to donate as much as possible to the local Fuel and Blanket Fund. In May 1917 police had to ration sugar to women who besieged a city shop. Some of the city's poor relied on a Cooked Food Depot.[69] Limerick's bacon barons had mixed fortunes. While Denny's won army contracts, most of the profit in pigs resided in England. Curers were left without material as 57,000 pigs were exported in 1914, 100,000 in 1915 and 145,000 in the first eight months of 1916.[70] The Limerick Pork Butchers' Society decried the fact that in just the fifteen weeks before mid-January 1918, 60,000 pigs were sent to England.[71] It was not until well into the 1920s that Limerick's bacon industry returned to its former glory. Not much of the farmers' wartime windfall trickled down to farm labourers, although the Agricultural Wages Board set minimum labourer rates at 19–24s. per week in 1917. This was around double what labourers had earned on average in 1911. But as with industrial labourers, there was no guarantee of employment from one week to the next and the new rates still failed to keep pace with inflation. The 1917 Corn Production Act guaranteed minimum prices. When it was repealed in 1921, prices slumped and wages spiralled downwards.[72]

The families of many of the Limerick men who went to war were better off than they had been beforehand due to receipt of separation allowances granted to the wives and families of recruits.[73] They were designed as an incentive to volunteer, and to compensate financially for the absence of the bread-winner. A flat rate of 9s. per week was awarded with supplements based on rank and number of children. Privates in the army earned 7s. per week, half of which went directly to their wives if they were married. This amounted to £18 a year if they survived that long. So, for instance, if a man with a wife and three children volunteered, the family at home had a guaranteed income of over 22s. per week, and no adult male to feed.[74] The separation allowance, however, was viewed in some quarters as a system that facilitated, if not encouraged, excessive consumption of alcohol. A number of soldiers' wives were brought before the City Petty Sessions in September 1915 and it was claimed that 'something should be done to put an end to the drinking habits prevalent among these women ... which, to say the least, constituted a grave scandal'. One magistrate proposed that some form of supervision be imposed on soldiers' wives in receipt of separation allowance so as to direct their spending.[75] Despite such condescending and sexist interventions, the appeal of the separation allowance is obvious, particularly for those who previously subsisted on a low, irregular income.

Limerick's separatists, however, were indifferent to the economics of the war. Their focus was on the potential for rebellion that it created while the government was distracted by events elsewhere. In December 1915 the police learned from an informant that 'prominent extremists and Irish Volunteers recently met at Limerick to discuss the proposal to strike a blow for Irish Independence'. This may have been the same informant who, a year earlier, was reporting to Constable James O'Mahony of William Street barracks on

John Daly's correspondence. O'Mahony also had 'other sources' of information on the Dalys. The intelligence garnered from Daly's letters was limited. The informant was 'afraid to be inquisitive fearing they might become suspicious, for he says they are aware that letters coming through the post are under observation'. Censorship of Daly's post began in November 1914 but it quickly became obvious to the police that he operated an alternative system for sensitive communications.[76] Seán Mac Diarmada and Tom Clarke spent Christmas 1915 in the Daly home. Con Colbert spent time with them also. This was Colbert's last visit home, and he made it a productive one, swearing his brother into the IRB. He also took the opportunity to put the Athea company through a series of drill exercises.[77] The Royal Commission on the Rising found that Clarke and Daly were at the centre of the 'inner circle by which the plans for insurrection were no doubt matured'.[78]

The first Limerick fatality of the revolution occurred on 16 January 1916 when John Wright, a member of a Volunteer company at Killoughteen, near Newcastle West, was killed by an accidental gunshot during drill exercises.[79] Michael Colivet was the senior Volunteer officer in the Limerick Command at Easter 1916. A full strength battalion should have had 500 Volunteers but none of the eight battalions under Colivet (including four in Clare) ever mustered much more than 200 men, not all of whom were armed. It had been only days before Easter that Colivet learned of Roger Casement's anticipated German arms landing in Kerry. News of the failure of this plan reached Limerick on Easter Saturday morning. The fiasco involved the deaths of three Volunteers, including Donal Sheehan of Templeglantine, west Limerick. The men drowned when the car in which they were travelling to meet Casement went off Ballykissane pier, Killorglin, County Kerry. On the Sunday Colivet took the City Battalion on its usual march to Killonan. Having received a series of contradictory messages through Sunday and Monday, he chose a course of inaction. The Crown forces in the city alone consisted of 800 infantry, a battery of artillery, and 100 constabulary. Within hours of the rebel proclamation of the Irish Republic in Dublin on Easter Monday, 24 April, 2,000 infantry with two batteries of artillery had taken complete charge of Limerick city, holding all roads and bridges.[80] On 25 April Colivet convened a meeting of the local leadership which decided that nothing could be done. On 5 May as the British were set to raid for arms, the Limerick Volunteers, through Colivet, and with Bishop O'Dwyer as facilitator, surrendered their guns to Mayor Quin and he passed them on to Colonel Sir Anthony Weldon, commander of the British forces in Limerick.[81] If the surrender of arms was partly an attempt to pre-empt arrests and deportations, it was largely successful, although Colivet informed the Volunteer executive that 'contrary to common report, no engagement whatsoever was given, or sought, that there would be immunity from subsequent arrest.'[82] Most of the fifty people who were arrested in Limerick after the Rising were released within a few days.[83] Events were equally shambolic elsewhere in Limerick. In the Galtees, for instance, Commandant Liam Manahan mobilized before being issued with Eoin MacNeill's countermanding order half-a-dozen times. He dismissed his men on Sunday evening. An attempted remobilization during the week petered out.

In early 1917 the executive of the Volunteers authorized an inquiry into the response of the Limerick units (as well as Cork and Kerry) during Easter Week. Having investigated dispatches allegedly received by Limerick from Dublin urging action, they submitted their qualified findings in March 1918:

> Some of these dispatches, [Limerick] did not, in our opinion, receive at all and those they did receive were so conflicting that we are satisfied no blame whatsoever rests on the officers and men of Limerick. With regard to the surrender of arms, it is to be deprecated that at any time arms should be given up by a body of men without a fight.[84]

Colivet demanded a direct verdict as to whether or not the surrender of arms was justifiable in the prevailing circumstances but none was forthcoming. The influential Daly sisters were not slow to question his competence and willingness to fight, however.[85] Ernest Blythe's poetic assessment of Colivet's performance was also less than complimentary:

> The non-combatant Colonel of the non-combatant corps,
> Was a drilling of his Battalion down by the Shannon shore,
> Parading all the city streets dressed in his jacket green,
> And saying in a martial tone the things he didn't mean.
> A fight broke out in Dublin and the Colonel's courage shook,
> He said 'I don't believe in fighting and I think we've done enough,
> We'll beat the whole world at this noble game of bluff'.[86]

The reality is that Colivet's options were severely restricted. Events made existing plans redundant. Not only were communications inadequate but the IRB's subterfuge, necessary as it was to maintain secrecy, had severely compromised the Volunteer chain-of-command. Even with the most generous of estimates the Volunteer forces in Limerick, in terms of both numbers and arms, were far below what was required to carry out any of Colivet's orders.

On 27 April 1916, in its 'The War' column, the *Chronicle* reported the attempted landing of arms under the heading 'German Descent on Irish Coast'. The importance of the German connection was widely exaggerated at the time. On 5 May the *Leader* described the number of casualties as 'appalling' but did not use such exercised language when referring to the catastrophic death tolls on the western front. The climate in Limerick was very much one of staunch support for the IPP. The *Leader* claimed that the country was 'unquestionably behind the Irish leader' and identified a choice facing nationalists between 'futile revolution and disaster' or 'constitutionalism and success'. Its editorial of 10 May did, however, warn against tensions being exacerbated by vindictiveness on the part of the military authorities.[87]

This followed the executions of Limerick men Con Colbert and Ned Daly, and Seán Heuston and Tom Clarke, who also had Limerick connections. P.J. O'Shaughnessy, recognizing the groundswell of sympathy for these men and perhaps responding to demands in his West Limerick constituency, raised Colbert's case in the House of Commons. He questioned 'what grounds there were for [his] execution ... whether his youthful age was taken into account before sentence ... and whether he had the ministration of a priest before death'. Political demonstrations were banned, so a leading manifestation of the growing public compassion for the executed men was the phenomenon of memorial Masses. They had started in Limerick even before the last executions. An apocryphal story quickly circulated about the priest who gave the last rites to Colbert having a special religious 'intention' granted after the martyr's heavenly intercession on his behalf.[88] This is an example of how the spiritual credentials of the rebels were emphasized in concert with the sacred nature of their cause.

CI Yates was not impressed by such tales. He commented that the insurrection was 'generally denounced as an insane act ... done by those getting German money and that these people had to show something for what they got' but he did note an undercurrent of fellow feeling with the rebels. IG Sir Neville Chamberlain identified Limerick as one of the places where that sympathy was most pronounced.[89] Limerick County Council, while restating its confidence in Redmond, expressed 'regret that the military authorities should have acted so severely' and appealed to the government to deal leniently with 'our misguided fellow countrymen'. The council also congratulated Bishop O'Dwyer on his defiance of General Sir John Maxwell's demand that disciplinary action be taken against two Limerick priests for their nationalist activities.[90]

Maxwell had arrived in Ireland on 28 April as military governor of the country, with plenary powers under martial law. The final arbiter of whether death sentences imposed on rebels were commuted or implemented, he literally assumed the power to determine life or death for a spell.[91] O'Dwyer was one of the first prominent figures to voice publicly what was to become the popular attitude to the rebels and the executions. While most of the IPP, newspapers and Catholic hierarchy condemned the rebels, O'Dwyer praised the 'purity and nobility of their motives ... and splendour of their courage'. He labelled Maxwell the 'military dictator of Ireland', his reaction to the Rising as 'wantonly cruel and oppressive ... an abuse of power as fatuous as it is arbitrary', and his regime as 'one of the worst and blackest chapters in the history of the misgovernment of this country'. O'Dwyer was correct in assuming that he was giving voice to a widespread grievance and sense of injustice: 'Personally, I regard your action with horror and believe it has outraged the conscience of the country.'[92] Newspapers carrying the bishop's response sold out. It was also widely distributed in America and Australia.[93] On 6 June Prime Minister Asquith told his cabinet that O'Dwyer's letter to Maxwell was one of the key factors in generating sympathy for the rebels and raising anti-British fervour.[94] The Limerick RIC shared this opinion:

> the consequence of the rebellion and the subsequent executions have been an increase of disloyalty and disaffection and a more bitter feeling against England and the British Government than has ever before been experienced. The R.C. Bishop and some of the clergy have to some extent voiced the feelings of the people in this respect.[95]

The number of UIL branches affiliated in Limerick increased significantly in the twelve months before the Rising and there were twenty branch meetings in Limerick in 1916 before Easter, but hardly half that number during the rest of the year. The Rising also sounded the death knell for already moribund provincial home rule bodies in counties such as Clare and Longford.[96] Charles Barrington's recruiting rallies had been regular events in Limerick for the previous six months but there was none between the Rising and the end of the year.[97] To the consternation of Limerick nationalists, the only real outcome of summer negotiations on the future of home rule was the cementing of Ulster unionists' singularity.[98] There was a perception among Redmond's Limerick supporters that Lloyd George, secretary of state for war, had duped him into the concession of the six north-eastern counties. The *Leader* damned the 'base betrayal' of the IPP and its leader by the coalition cabinet and Asquith, which 'disgraced and discredited British statesmanship in the eyes of the world'.[99] In the changed political circumstances after the Rising, Redmond's actions – in September 1914 when he promoted volunteering, in May 1915 when he accepted coalition ministries alongside Unionists, and in mid-1916 when he compromised on partition – were seen as a betrayal. The IPP won the five Westminster by-elections that were contested between the outbreak of the war and the Rising, as well as retaining two non-contested seats. All conquering in 1914, and even though the ostensible achievement of home rule lost its shine as the war dragged on, the IPP was still in pole political position before the Rising. While the possibility of an all-island home rule Ireland had always been a slender one, it was consigned to history after the Rising. Republicans seized the initiative at Easter but the IPP remained intact, if badly shaken. The debacle of the talks with

Lloyd George shattered the party's morale, however, and it fell into a stupor, making no attempt to consolidate until the new year, by which stage it faced the challenge of a vibrant republican movement.

The war overshadowed all else from 1914 to 1916. Mass recruiting and mass casualties were only one part of the ferment in Limerick. The agricultural and industrial consequences of the war had an immense impact on economic and social life throughout the city and county. Amplified demand for Irish produce, from both land and factory, together with army allowances for families and army contracts for manufacturers, meant that farmers and labourers, employers and workers all gained. And even though Limerick's unionists were struggling under the weight of the war, the desire to extend the economic boom was such that a unionist was elected as mayor of the city in 1916. Limerick did not rise in 1916 but Limerick's revolutionary cabal, led by John Daly, had been key architects of the rebellion. The war, rather than uniting nationalists and unionists, drove a deeper wedge between them and accentuated the divisions within nationalism. The local press and municipal authorities, together with Limerick's parliamentarians, stood by Redmond and his policies but their loud declarations of support were starting to ring hollow. Bishop O'Dwyer had engineered public disputes with the most senior political and military figures in the country and stage-managed them so that his anti-war and anti-execution arguments left Redmond and Maxwell exposed. While Redmond had been fêted in Limerick in 1914, it was a fitting marker of how much things had changed in two years when Limerick Corporation granted his adversary O'Dwyer the Freedom of the City in September 1916.

4 'A centre of turbulence and rioting': from Rising to soviet, 1916–19

> When I reached Limerick ... the first thing I noticed was a wall bearing the shining message in white paint: 'Vote for De Valera, the Dublin Hero'. It was the day of the [1918 general] election, and the town was in a ferment of excitement. The steep central street leading down to the river – William Street – was crowded with people and vehicles. Ford cars covered with dust and filled to overflowing with gesticulating young men, dashed here and there.[1]

Journalist Douglas Goldring arrived in Limerick on 14 December 1918 to be greeted by the sight of Sinn Féiners at full throttle, the city bedecked with green, white and orange tricolours. Peripheral before the Rising, SF was the most powerful political machine in the country before the end of 1917. This transformation had its genesis in the Volunteer split of September 1914, after which the Redmondite *Freeman's Journal* carried a disparaging account of the first meeting of the 'Sinn Féin' Volunteers (MacNeill's minority) in Limerick.[2] From the summer of 1915, 'for convenience', IG Chamberlain dubbed a range of 'extreme Nationalists' as 'Sinn Féiners'.[3] Post-Rising Irish politics was in a state of flux and this popular and official mindset that lumped the Volunteers, IRB and other Irish-Ireland groups under the one label and erroneously termed the Easter insurrection 'the Sinn Féin Rising' meant that SF received much credit that it did not strictly deserve. Bishop O'Dwyer's endorsement of the party carried considerable weight locally and nationally. O'Dwyer resumed his attacks on Redmond and made a significant contribution to a series of critical SF by-election victories around the country in 1917.

There was change afoot in Limerick politics also. In January 1917 Stephen Quin was re-elected as mayor by twenty-five votes to ten.[4] Quin's promise to attract munitions factories to Limerick did not materialize, although the Rising and subsequent growth of the Volunteers would have discouraged the authorities from opening munitions works in areas where the material could fall into the wrong hands. Neither was there any rush to industrialize the south, particularly not when soldiers were needed for the army and workers required for factories in England. Opposition to Quin grew. From July 1917 former supporters, fearful that he was in favour of partition, objected to him representing the corporation at the Irish Convention on the status of home rule.[5] Quin was officially registered as a 'Nationalist' at the convention but he did vote with the Unionists on at least one occasion.[6] The convention was boycotted by SF and therefore became a futile exercise. The suggestion that it would introduce devolution and conscription simultaneously led to its collapse in March 1918. Quin was defeated for the mayoralty in January 1918 by Alphonsus O'Mara, a former home ruler and the first Sinn Féiner to hold the office. O'Mara's election by twenty-three votes to thirteen exemplified how fundamentally the Irish political climate had transformed from Redmondite support of the war in 1914 to widespread rejection of British rule.[7] The new mayor was the political antithesis of his predecessor. He refused to take the oath of allegiance to the Crown, and he suggested the use of 'armed opposition' to conscription.[8]

Local MPs were in an invidious position, albeit one of their party's devising: they had to encourage recruitment, which was ever more unpopular, while railing against the spectre of conscription. The IPP quickly became irrelevant before being dispatched to oblivion at the 1918 election. SF took all three seats in Limerick, only one of which was contested. The protracted nature of the war meant that Limerick continued to reap the economic benefits of sending meat to England but there were no political or social rewards for sending men to fight in France. And while SF made a giant leap forward during these years, it was actually outstripped at times by the labour movement in Limerick. The relentless demands of the war economy altered the balance of power in industrial relations. There was little excess labour available to farmers and factory owners so unions were in a stronger bargaining position. The ITGWU flexed its new muscle to impressive effect but there was little corresponding growth in the political status of the Labour party. However, for two weeks in April 1919 Limerick's striking workers exercised an unprecedented level of control over the city when they led rather than followed SF and Labour, and raised a significant challenge to British militarism.

The compliance of the Limerick Volunteers at Easter 1916 meant that the authorities' reaction was restrained. While the surrender of arms rendered the Volunteers impotent, most leading republicans in Limerick escaped police attention altogether. Their structures remained in place and the police were aware of immediate efforts on the part of the 'Sinn Féin revolutionary movement' to build subversive momentum at underground meetings and through the Irish National Aid Association and Irish Volunteers Dependents' Fund.[9] Cumann na mBan, led by the Daly sisters, administered the Volunteers Dependents' Fund in Limerick from June 1916. Madge Daly gave jobs in the family bakery business to two Dublinmen, Peadar Dunne and Peadar McMahon, on their release from Frongoch in December 1916. Dunne and McMahon were central to developments in Limerick in 1917. In August 1916 CI Yates referred to the frequency of meetings of 'Sinn Féiners'. He suggested that 'but for martial law they would be more active than before the Rising' and he found it necessary to request the cancellation of special trains to Limerick 'to avert the danger apprehended from a monster Gaelic Athletic Association meeting' on 24 September. That meeting was followed by a parade through the city featuring the flag of the Irish Republic and rebel songs. The police did not have enough manpower to disperse a 'seditious demonstration' near William Street barracks. Attempts to revive most Volunteer units around the country did not begin until early 1917 (after some internees returned under a Christmas amnesty), whereas the Limerick City Battalion mobilized in September 1916. At a September meeting attended by Michael Joyce, the National Volunteers pledged loyalty to Redmond and vowed to resist conscription. Joyce stated that he and his party colleagues would fight conscription by every means in their power. Lundon organized two branches of the Anti-Conscription League in the county.[10] By November forty to fifty Volunteers were regularly drilling in the Fianna hall. Some 350 people attended the Manchester Martyrs commemoration in Limerick on 26 November. Eighteen of the twenty-one marches held around the country were 'orderly and rather poorly attended'.[11] Limerick was one of the exceptions. The parade marked the first public display of the city battalion since Easter but the Volunteers were dispersed by a police baton charge.[12]

East Clare Volunteer leader Michael Brennan was released from internment in early 1917. He contrasted his departure from Limerick, when the wives of British soldiers hurled insults at him, to his return, when a crowd of 'thousands' chaired him through the streets. For Brennan, 'it made it clear that the Rising had already changed the people'.[13] At a Town Tenants meeting on 21 January 1917, at which MPs Joyce, Lundon and O'Shaughnessy were in attendance, Sinn Féiners disrupted the proceedings and rushed the platform. Lundon sustained injuries which necessitated eight days in hospital. He was targeted because of a speech he had made criticizing the Volunteers.[14] As republicans were emboldened, the authorities increasingly resorted to DORA. Hugh O'Brien-Moran, a solicitor who was president of the Tom Clarke SF club, protested that while the legislation 'had a very high sounding name', it was actually applied to 'every two pence ha'penny case': 'At the present time if a policeman heard the word Kaiser, Kingdom, Dublin, Rebels or Volunteers uttered his feathers immediately became ruffled and he brought a case under the Defence of the Realm Act.'[15]

There were frequent arrests for petty offences such as shouting 'Up the rebels' or 'To hell with the king'. Anyone wearing a uniform of a military character, carrying a sword or taking part in movements of a military nature was liable to arrest. When Volunteers were tried and sentenced by a court-martial for such offences, public admiration for them increased. Police and military correspondence reveals a great deal of uncertainty about how to react to the republican revival. However, reports by the senior British military officers in Limerick, namely Lieutenant-Colonel N.B. Grandage and Colonel

Weldon, indicate that during a personal conversation in January, Colivet had
assured Weldon there would be no further drilling. As Yates pressed for
Madge Daly to be court-martialled for allowing her premises to be used by
the Volunteers, Weldon recommended tolerance. According to Weldon,
Colivet had discontinued drilling in an effort to avoid 'unnecessary trouble':

> I have no reason to disbelieve this gentleman's assurances as he has
> consistently kept his undertakings with me, as indeed have the other
> leaders of the Sinn Féin body here (note that he was mainly instru-
> mental in getting in arms last May without my having unnecessarily to
> employ the military to seize them).[16]

Colivet's conciliatory attitude would soon give way to a more aggressive
approach among Limerick Volunteers. On 22 February 1917 Colivet himself
was found in possession of reconnaissance reports on the military defences of
Limerick and making recommendations for attacks.[17]

The fallout from 1916 involved a number of debilitating internal wrangles
in the Limerick Volunteers. In the Galtee Battalion, Liam Manahan vied for
influence with an IRB element led by Donnchadh O'Hannigan. The ill-feel-
ing ran so deep that two brothers led two rival companies in the square mile
of the townland of Lissard, between Emly and Galbally.[18] General Headquarters (GHQ) attempted to resolve the impasse (and exert some measure of
central control) by dissolving the battalion. The companies in Cork and
Tipperary fell in with formations in their respective counties and Seán Wall
of Bruff was appointed O/C of the new East Limerick Brigade. The split had
a negative effect on organization, discipline, morale and unity and remained
an issue through the War of Independence and Civil War. Acrimony between
the city's old 1st Battalion and the new 2nd Battalion, formed in 1917, was
rooted in the non-event of Easter 1916. The surrender of arms was the
sharpest sticking point.[19] The Daly sisters drove the dispute.[20] There was 'bad
blood' and 'Whisperings, underhand rumblings and all these things were
taking place to blacken the character of the Executive of the 1st Battalion'.[21]
Richard Mulcahy, chief of staff of the Volunteers from March 1918, facilitated a meeting between the two groups in 1917 but Colivet refused to work
with Peadar Dunne, commandant 2nd Battalion, on the basis that he was 'a
man of peace'. This was a strange attitude for a senior leader in a revolutionary army to take. Another Dublin-led attempt to solve the problem involved
the appointment of Michael de Lacy, a neutral figure, as leader of both
groups. De Lacy did not command the respect of either battalion, however:
he was dismissed by a member of the 1st as 'a damn poor man' and a
member of the 2nd as 'the laziest man I ever met'.[22] Efforts to reunite the
contending factions were not successful until the spring of 1921.

That the city Volunteers fell out after the Easter Rising was not unusual. Peter Hart made the case that the split was not merely personal or political, but also based on social class. Hart demonstrated that IRA units were often formed around a particular workplace, but that any kind of stratification or segregation between companies was rare.[23] Importantly, he identified Limerick city as an exception. Hart was not the first to point to this apparent anomaly. During his interviews with his erstwhile IRA colleagues in the late 1940s and early 1950s, Ernie O'Malley 'noticed that there was a good deal of working men in the 2nd Bn and I think this was a kind of distinction between these 2 Bns'.[24] Peadar McMahon suggested that the 'white collar' 1st Battalion 'didn't like' the 2nd Battalion because of this peculiarity.[25] The standing of rugby men in the 1st Battalion reflected a continuation of the status quo. The nucleus of the five companies which comprised the 2nd Battalion were five hurling teams that had formed after the Rising: all were linked to SF clubs. This was indicative of the developing radicalization of the GAA, along with the Gaelic League, as an outlet of republican activism and defiance of British authority which filled the vacuum created by government repression in the months after April 1916. The GAA and the Gaelic League were the most active organizations in Limerick for an extended period after the Rising. The greatest challenge that Blythe faced in organizing training for the new units, however, was that 'between Sodalities and Confraternities there was not so much as one night in the week in which everyone was free.'[26]

Seán Ó Muirthile of the IRB Supreme Council worked with the Gaelic League in Limerick after the Rising. For IG Brigadier-General Sir Joseph Byrne, Ó Muirthile was 'probably the most dangerous Gaelic league organiser'. CI Yates regarded the GAA, and the Gaelic League particularly, as 'powerful means for propagating hatred of England and the Empire' and as being 'at the root of all the disloyalty' in Limerick.[27] The GAA facilitated symbolic gestures of civic defiance and the articulation of popular support for the Rising. In January 1917, for instance, Hugh O'Brien-Moran successfully defended James Ryan, secretary of Limerick GAA County Board, on a charge of refusing police admission to a hurling match without payment. Both were imprisoned, however, for refusing to reveal the origin of the documents used in evidence. In early 1917 a Volunteer conference in Limerick was attended by delegates from the six Munster counties. The police learned from an informant that reorganization was to be conducted by local activists in conjunction with and under cover of the Gaelic League.[28] Republicans were happy to capitalize on and exploit trends of popular mobilization which were developing autonomously. SF in Limerick had already been able to wrap itself in the veneer of middle-class respectability provided by Bishop O'Dwyer but the Gaelic League provided another nexus through which non-militarist separatists and middle-class moderates, including former home rulers, were assimilated into the republican movement. The GAA, on the other hand, acted as a route of blue collar mobilization in Limerick. That elements of the working class in Limerick were hostile to the Volunteers had been made clear on Whit Sunday 1915. The new hurler-Volunteers of 1917 had a more pronounced plebeian complexion.

The social composition of the republican movement in Limerick city certainly changed after the Rising but the portrayal of the 1st Battalion–2nd Battalion split as purely a blue collar–white collar division is a false dichotomy. There were more tradesmen than clerks in the old 1st Battalion and not all of them joined the new corps. Friction between the two battalions was based on differences over the performance of the old unit in 1916 as much as it was on social tension, but it also reflected the increasing involvement of Limerick's working class in militant nationalism from 1917 onwards. Unskilled and semi-skilled workers became increasingly prominent in the ranks of the city Volunteers, *vis-à-vis* the previously dominant skilled workers and middle classes.[29] The 2nd Battalion was 'manned largely by young fellows who had not anything to do with Bn 1', according to 1st Battalion member James Gubbins.[30] Recruits to the Volunteers were more likely to join a new, vibrant unit rather than a stagnant and discredited one. So, while class divisions did not cause the split they may have been a factor in prolonging it.

Despite these unwelcome diversions, the Limerick Volunteers were successful in bringing disorder to the streets of the city and, to a lesser degree, the towns and villages of the county. Token gestures of resistance such as singing rebel ballads, waving tricolours, wearing SF badges, and having Masses said in honour of the 1916 martyrs were commonplace. Until 1920 violence between republicans and Crown forces rarely involved shooting and usually took the form of rioting. Orchestrated public disturbances, especially anti-police and anti-military riots, were a principal tactic in what, by the end of 1917, was the successful renewal of the Volunteers in Limerick. Vigorous anti-conscription activity in Limerick in 1918 facilitated the further expansion of militant republicanism. Republicans became increasingly bellicose towards the RIC. On 23 March 1917, to mark the return of Hugh O'Brien-Moran from imprisonment, a 'Sinn Féin mob' attacked two police patrols in the city, firing a number of revolver shots.[31] This was the first time that the Volunteers had fired at Crown forces in Limerick. Although there were no injuries, it represented a significant escalation, news of which travelled quickly on the republican grapevine. Imprisoned in Lisburn, Ernest Blythe was happy to hear that 'Limerick is becoming a centre of turbulence and rioting'. 'Was it true that some people in the crowd fired at the police the other night?', inquired Blythe hopefully.[32]

As seizures of soldiers' rifles became more frequent and were accompanied by increasing violence, Captain J.H.M. Staniforth complained to his parents

about the intimidating atmosphere in which he and his army colleagues operated in Limerick:

> There's a lot of 'dark doings' over here now, and the authorities are
> getting wind up about the forthcoming Patrick's Day and Easter Week.
> This town in particular is a nest of Sinn Féinery, and our men won't
> go through the riverside streets after dark unless there are two or three
> of them together. Officers who have been out in the country riding or
> motoring all day come back late at night with stories of lonely barns
> and stables by the roadside full of people talking and planning and that
> sort of thing; and the town is swarming with men of all ages sporting
> the Sinn Féin rosettes or buttons.

He returned to this theme in another letter home:

> This city has a population of 32,000 and about a third of them are
> brawny young hooligans parading the streets shouting 'Hoch der
> Kaiser!', 'To hell with King George!', 'Down with the Army!', 'Up the
> Germans!', and other such pleasantries, and throwing half-bricks when
> they see a soldier by himself. And the women are worse.[33]

On the first anniversary of the Rising an 'unlawful assembly' of Sinn Féin
members in the city resulted in a confrontation with the RIC and rioting. A
republican flag flew briefly over the town hall on the morning of 25 April,
copies of the Proclamation were displayed all over the city and county and
Masses were said in memory of the 1916 martyrs but a bulked-up police presence ensured that the anniversary of the Rising and the executions passed
without major incident in Limerick.[34] The victory of SF's Joe McGuinness in
the South Longford by-election on 17 May, however, was celebrated by 'seditious and turbulent demonstrations' in which republicans threw stones and,
in one instance, an open razor at the police.[35] On 6 June, while escorting
Volunteer prisoners from Galbally courthouse to the barracks, several of the
100 armed policemen on duty received head wounds from stones and bottles.
Revolver shots were again fired at the RIC.[36] The fact that the Volunteers
were able to use the cover of angry mobs shows that they were at the head of
a growing and increasingly radical popular movement.

SF's support base was also expanding significantly during this period and
its separatist policies were crystallizing. But there were radical social leanings
among sections of the party and SF clubs were involved in incidents of agrarian unrest around the county.[37] The IPP continued to engage in such agitation also, though only occasionally. Outside of counties where electoral
contests took place during 1917, Limerick had the fourth-highest ratio of SF

members to population in the country.[38] Between May and September 1917
over seventy SF clubs sprang up around Limerick, with at least a dozen
clergy presiding at organizing meetings or being elected to leadership positions. At the end of the First World War the police counted fifty-nine clubs,
named for the martyrs and heroes of 1916, and 4,637 members.[39] The chief
secretary's intelligence files for 1918 noted that SF 'clubs have found their
way into every village in the County [of Limerick], and all, except some of
the older people, are Sinn Féin to a man'.[40] A single Liberty League club was
active in the city for a time around September 1917, but this was as much
progress as Count Plunkett's ill-fated challenge to SF made in Limerick.[41]

The Irish Nation League broke away from the IPP during the summer of
1916. It attracted support in those parts of nationalist Ulster which were to
be excluded from home rule, but it did not gain much favour in Limerick
(despite the presence of Michael O'Callaghan in its ranks) or neighbouring
counties. Instead, it was subsumed by SF in September 1917. The emergence
of several such splinter groups was a symptom of the IPP's disarray. Most of
these groups quickly disappeared but the Nation League further undermined
the UIL by siphoning away members who might have helped the party to
reorganize. The Nation League also smoothed the transfer of some IPP members to SF.[42] The separatist press regularly carried reports of officials of the
UIL and AOH severing their connections with those organizations and apply-
ing for SF membership in Limerick during 1917–18, but the magnitude of
such transfers may have been exaggerated for propaganda purposes. None of
those UIL leaders, for instance, who represented Limerick at the National
Directory for more than a decade before the Rising switched allegiance. The
subsequent influence of some of the individuals involved, however, was critical. Fr John Fitzgerald, former chairman of the west Limerick executive of
the UIL, was a driving force behind the growth of SF around the county in
1917. Michael Colivet was initially a Hibernian. The O'Maras, one of
Limerick's leading bacon processors, were key converts. As well as Alphonsus
O'Mara, others who went from home rule councillor to SF mayor during the
revolutionary period included Alphonsus's brother Stephen, Michael
O'Callaghan and Bob de Courcy.

The release of the Rising prisoners in June 1917 further energized an
already buoyant republican movement. The esteem in which released prisoners were held gave them the authority to lead the charge. On 23 June, for
instance, Con Collins (who had been due to meet Casement in Tralee at
Easter 1916), Richard Hayes (who had fought in the battle of Ashbourne
under Thomas Ashe) and Éamon de Valera were greeted at Limerick train
station by a crowd of over 1,000 people, along with two Volunteer companies
and a band. On 24 June Collins's appearance at Newcastle West was the catalyst for the renewal of the local company.[43] He said that people were sick of

oratory and wanted guns and bullets, and he advised every young Irishman to get rifles and ammunition.[44] The message was clear: there would be no reversion to solely constitutional means. SF was now an emphatically separatist political party rather than the broadly defined, catch-all nationalist group of pre-1916. At a de Valera rally in Clare in June 1917, James Dalton of Limerick declared that 'We must have a revolution and this country will run red with blood.'[45] Diplomacy and discretion were not Dalton's strong points, and his comments were among the most extreme made by any Sinn Féiner from an election platform at the time. De Valera duly won his by-election in East Clare on 11 July. Armed Volunteer units from Limerick attended polling stations.[46] These activities helped to forge closer contacts between the Volunteers in Limerick and elsewhere that would come to fruition in the shape of joint operations in the following years. De Valera's success was brought home to Limerick people with great immediacy by the Tivoli cinema on Charlotte's Quay, which showed film of the day's events.[47] W.T. Cosgrave's election in Kilkenny in August maintained the political momentum. A series of cultural festivals held under the auspices of the Gaelic League or local SF clubs acted as vehicles for popular mobilization. Three thousand people attended at Doon on 24 June. Twice that number gathered at Ballylanders on 22 July. Large bodies of Volunteers marched despite the presence of extra police.[48] Prominent Sinn Féiners, including de Valera and Cosgrave, attended Bishop O'Dwyer's requiem Mass in Limerick following the bishop's death on 19 August. There were no representatives from the IPP.[49] O'Dwyer's successor as bishop, Denis Hallinan, lent his support to SF on the condition that it did not endorse armed rebellion. Hallinan understood the SF principle to be self-reliance rather than collusion with secret societies and resort to violence.[50] He was naïve in this regard.

In another escalation, on the night of 16 September three Volunteers armed with revolvers confronted two RIC men armed with rifles at Ballinacurra. The attackers fled when the police resisted the attempt to seize their weapons. Volunteer Edward Punch was arrested and court-martialled. He had keys to three city police stations and one military barracks. Various military manuals and a rudimentary hand grenade that had been manufactured at a factory in Limerick were found in his house.[51] Demonstrations to mark the death of Thomas Ashe took place around the county in September. Yates lamented the fact that, just as the 'suppressed feeling of political excitement' that prevailed around Limerick was gradually decreasing, Ashe's death had provided 'a good excuse for inflaming public opinion again'.[52] De Valera was appointed as the president of Sinn Féin and as the president of the Volunteers in October 1917. One of his first speeches in this new capacity was in the Theatre Royal in Limerick on 2 November. Their aim, he claimed, was clear: 'to free their country from the grip of the British Empire … to get recognition as an independent republic'.[53] The political and military wings of the republican movement were, at least superficially, united. This apparent harmony was sufficient to maintain cohesion until the summer of 1921, despite the fact that the political wing of the movement had little real control over the military wing.

The Volunteers showed their strength through more regular public drilling. In December delegates representing twenty-four clubs in east Limerick alone attended a regional SF convention.[54] Police records indicated the presence of fifty-six SF clubs in Limerick at the end of 1917 with a membership of 3,828.[55] The RIC were faced with increasingly hostile and secretive populations and in the absence of solid information were prone to speculation and supposition. There were eighty SF-affiliated clubs in Limerick on 17 December 1917 and 110 in Cork, eighty-five in Kerry, seventy-five in Tipperary, seventy-three in Clare and twelve in the Redmondite stronghold of Waterford.[56] The Volunteers' policy of selective public drilling in 1917 and 1918 meant that while some units avoided police scrutiny, others received close attention. In January 1918 the average strength of the Limerick companies known to the police was sixty-eight, whereas in April 1916 it had been forty. There were similar rates of increase in neighbouring counties over the same period: from forty to seventy-four in Clare, forty-two to seventy-two in Cork, and fifty-eight to ninety-two in Kerry.[57] By the end of 1917 Volunteer recruitment was promising, morale was high and formal training and leadership structures were in place locally and nationally. In early 1917, for instance, the membership of the Patrickswell company was in single figures; by December it had sixty men and had joined a battalion with four neighbouring companies.[58]

A number of new newspapers published in the city heightened republican fervour in 1917–18. The *Factionist* first appeared in January 1917. Circulated privately among republicans, it proudly claimed the title of 'the smallest paper in the world' and, for the first few issues, the editor sarcastically declared that 'As we are kept up by "German Gold" we can afford to distribute our Official Journal free'. The characteristic tone of the *Factionist* was a mixture of humour and acerbic invective directed against all non-republicans. It threatened to name anyone who associated with the police.[59] This was part of the process of ostracizing the RIC from local communities. Servants in police stations were the subject of most cases of boycotting in Limerick. The level of intimidation in Tournafulla in south-west Limerick was such that the military had to intervene to ensure that the police were able to obtain basic supplies from shopkeepers.[60] The *Factionist* exhibited pious Catholicism; yet, on a dock labourers strike in May, it commented that 'We do not like to advocate syndicalism but we do think Jim Larkin is needed in Limerick'. Its attitude to violence was unambiguous: when the police 'severely batoned several people' at a republican demonstration in the city, the paper recommended that

> the police could be well taught a lesson, that they would not forget for some time, and we suggest that in future if any crowd of young men feel inclined to demonstrate they ought to come prepared to meet the peelers at their own game.

It declared that 'The way to Freedom is a sword-track through our enemies.'[61] The *Factionist* gloried in the failure of the authorities to suppress it and defied the 'imitation detectives and fat-headed peelers of Limerick to locate us'.[62] However, the last of the thirty-two issues of the *Factionist* was published on 6 September 1917. The *Weekly Observer* and *Southern Democrat* newspapers were suppressed in April 1918.[63] At least four other underground separatist papers were printed in Limerick during 1917–19 but there were not more than a few editions of each.

Growing political and trade union consciousness was expressed by the publication of Limerick's first working-class newspaper, the *Bottom Dog*, on 20 October 1917. A branch of the ITGWU was established in the city in October 1917. It affiliated with Limerick United Trades and Labour Council. By the end of 1918 the ITGWU claimed to have over 3,000 members in Limerick city and a wave of farm labourers' strikes had built up membership in the county.[64] The 'bottom dog' was anyone oppressed by nation, class or sex and the paper's aim was 'hastening the day of the Bottom Dog'.[65] It continued for forty-eight editions until 1 November 1918, around which time Ben Dineen, the paper's editor, city baker and Trades Council secretary, succumbed to influenza. The epidemic claimed 300 lives in the city and 551 in the county in 1918.[66] The *Bottom Dog* concentrated almost exclusively on issues such as housing and work conditions, food prices and rates of pay. It blended its idiosyncratic socialism with nationalism, pious and sectarian Catholicism and anti-Semitism, while ignoring the war and the Bolshevik revolution. It regarded Cumann na mBan as a fair target for criticism. When a 'Woman's Day of Protest' against conscription was held in the city on 6 June 1918, the paper suggested that it did not involve a procession because this would have forced its middle-class members to walk through the slum areas of the city and to be accompanied by women from such areas.[67] The majority of members of Cumann na mBan, certainly those in leadership positions, came from wealthy merchant families and were well educated. The *Bottom Dog* had a wide circulation, including in rural Limerick, but its influence in developing a radical socialist consciousness among Limerick workers is unquantifiable.

The first issue of the *Soldier Hunter*, on 23 February 1918, detailed its plans, including the use of physical force, to guard against the moral corruption of young Limerick women by the British garrison: 'We are out to clean up the town. Social Hygiene, if you will, is our objective.' The paper published a letter from a city priest about a military chaplain who had been assaulted by a Welsh Fusilier when he tried 'to protect a girl of sixteen years of age against the lustful passion of this low clodhopper'. The priest called on 'the support of the young men of Limerick for the parish clergy in their efforts to uphold public morality'. An article described khaki-clad 'demons in human form', one of whom had allegedly tried to take advantage of a young girl by offering her drugged chocolates. In early March 1918 there were violent clashes in the city involving soldiers of the Welsh Fusiliers. The *Leader* pinpointed the conduct of soldiers in relation to young women as the source of the tension. The military were confined to barracks for three nights after the clashes, during which at least one soldier and two policemen were seriously injured.[68] The notion of social hygiene was closely linked to social order and to the control of public spaces in the city. The violence, however, may have had more to do with the Volunteers' lust for guns than with protecting women.[69]

British forces on the Western Front were creaking under the weight of German pressure in the spring of 1918. Three successive by-election victories at the start of the year seemed to indicate that the IPP had regained the impetus from SF but the government's April move to extend conscription to Ireland decisively reversed that trend. IPP MPs vacated Westminster to make common cause against conscription with their rivals. When the Catholic Church lent its weight to the anti-conscription movement, it grievously undermined the moral writ for British rule in Ireland. Priests administered an anti-conscription pledge around Limerick. Before the pan-nationalist Mansion House Conference of 18 April, at which SF placed itself firmly in the vanguard of the anti-conscription campaign, Limerick County Council had protested vigorously against conscription.[70] The Limerick Board of Guardians used such strong anti-conscription language that thirty-three of them were summoned on various charges of unlawful assembly and sedition.[71] The conscription crisis pushed moderates into the arms of SF and propelled the party forward ahead of the general election. Several thousand people attended an anti-conscription protest at the Crescent in Limerick city on 14 April. As many as 10,000 protested in Newcastle West on 15 April. After the arrest of a Volunteer in Newcastle West the police came under such heavy attack that they were forced to open fire. The telegraph wire had been cut to prevent them calling for assistance, showing that the operation was conducted with a degree of sophistication. CI Yates reported that 'the whole city and county are seething with hatred against the government for passing conscription. This is egged on by the Sinn Féiners whose movement has swallowed all others.' On 21 April between 15,000 and 20,000 protesters gathered again at the Crescent. The general strike of 23 April was an anti-conscription protest and it received full backing outside of the north-east. The magnitude of a trade union rally in Limerick on the day is illustrated by the fact that it took the marchers twenty-five minutes to pass a given point. Protesters marched behind a banner bearing the slogan 'Death Before Conscription' and a portrait of James Connolly.[72] Farmers protested that any further loss of agricultural labour would have a devastating effect on the harvest and result in the loss of crops on which both Ireland and England depended.[73] Limerick Corporation voted eighteen to two to strike Lord Dunraven off the Roll of Freedom of Limerick for advocating conscription (he was restored to the Roll in 2007).[74] A side effect of the conscription crisis was a significant step in the radicalization of the Volunteers from a public movement into a secret revolutionary army; as the government adopted more draconian measures, only the most dedicated and radical activists remained committed. An associated development was an increase in organized raids for arms by the Volunteers, who planned to resist conscription by force if necessary. The numbers in most Limerick companies ballooned with an influx of temporary recruits but deflated again when the tide of the war turned and the crisis passed in August.[75]

By 1918, it was eight years since the last general election and the profile of the electorate was very different. The Representation of the People Act (1918) extended the franchise to all men over twenty-one and, for the first time, awarded women the right to vote – provided they were over thirty and owned £5 worth of property or were married to a man who did. In 1910 700,000 Irish people had the vote. In 1918 it was two million. Nobody under the age of twenty-nine had voted in a general election before. Their political consciousness was formed against the background of the war and the Rising. They had seen the IPP atrophy and SF thrive. The British made every effort to suppress the SF election campaign: three successive directors of elections were among hundreds of party activists imprisoned, meetings were dispersed and leaflets, posters, and literature were seized. However, this harassment generated favourable publicity for the party and gave it 'the halo of martyrdom'.[76] Sinn Féin's election manifesto committed to achieving a republic 'by any and every means available to render impotent the power of England to hold Ireland in subjection by military force or otherwise'.[77] When set in the context of the type of aggressive rhetoric being employed by candidates like Con Collins, it seems quite clear that an implicit, and sometimes explicit, part of SF's election programme was the conditioning of its supporters for a campaign for independence in which the use of violence would potentially be a primary method.

On 5 September 1918 Limerick Corporation decided to confer the Freedom of the City on de Valera, Eoin MacNeill and Kathleen Clarke, as representatives of the proscribed SF, Gaelic League and Cumann na mBan organizations.[78] On 6 September Volunteer Tommy Leahy of Tournafulla fired on policemen near Abbeyfeale, wounding one constable.[79] This was the first time that a Volunteer had shot a member of the Crown forces in Limerick. On 11 September Con Collins was selected as the SF candidate for West Limerick. The self-nomination of a Patrick O'Connell was rejected as illegal after an objection from Collins's solicitor.[80] In mid-September, Michael Colivet, while interned in England, was announced as the SF candidate for Limerick City. In mid-October P.J. O'Shaughnessy announced that he would not be standing for re-election in West Limerick on health grounds (his last speaking contribution in Westminster had been in April 1917).[81] On 13 October Thomas Lundon was selected as the IPP candidate for East Limerick.[82] But despite his best efforts – engaging in agrarian agitation locally and speaking in parliament in stout defence of the GAA and against conscription – he had been something of a lame duck for more than a year. As early as October 1917, Kilmallock Urban District Council (UDC) passed a motion calling on Lundon to resign his parliamentary seat because he no longer represented the nationalists of the constituency. Almost simultaneously, SF proposed Richard Hayes as its preferred candidate in East Limerick.[83] Like Colivet, Richard Hayes, the SF candidate for East Limerick, was interned in England. Canvassing and rallies took place around the city and county in November. On 2 November the police in Broadford dispersed a crowd that had assembled to celebrate the release from prison of three Cumann na mBan members. Fr Tomás Wall, one of the two priests at the centre of the post-Rising duel between Bishop O'Dwyer and General Maxwell and a member of the SF national executive, was happy that the confrontation had occurred:

> The peelers … were so frightened by the magnitude of the turnout that they telephoned for military to Newcastle West … A mess was made of the crowd, the peelers using the butt-ends of rifles and batons. The military did nothing except march up to where I was and fix bayonets … But the peelers, wherever they came on an isolated group around the village, they batoned fiercely …. The whole incident will do good and has done good already. The village was one of those places overrun and bossed by police and police pensioners.[84]

MacNeill received the Freedom of Limerick on 8 November but while de Valera and Clarke were in prison. Michael Joyce was confirmed as the IPP parliamentary candidate for Limerick City on 21 November but subsequently withdrew. There was an almost complete absence of nationalist organization in the constituency, but Joyce had also been pressurized by Colivet's supporters. He cited 'the opposition we would be faced with both inside and outside the polling booths … the knowledge we had that many respectable citizens were afraid to sign a nomination paper for me' and a desire to preserve 'the peace and harmony of the city'. On 23 November the authorities prevented the Manchester Martyrs commemoration from taking place in the city. In less than a month, from early November to the start of December, at least eight priests spoke at meetings in support of Colivet.[85] Bishop Hallinan and his clergy had lost faith in the IPP. They feared for Ulster Catholics in a partitioned Ireland and became alienated from the party when it appeared to consent to such a settlement. Furthermore, the Catholic Church saw little to fear in SF's 'Irish-Ireland' philosophy, and backing a flourishing movement was pragmatic. CI Yates stated that SF was 'dangerous, perfect, and kept well together by certain RC curates ... continually inculcating a doctrine of hatred against England'.[86]

Colivet and Collins, both unopposed, were declared elected on 14 December. Republicans held celebratory torchlight processions. On 15 December Hanna Sheehy-Skeffington addressed a meeting in the city to demand the release of Colivet, Hayes and all political prisoners.[87] Hayes defeated Lundon by 12,750 votes to 3,608. The SF campaign in East Limerick was so well managed by John Lynch of Kilmallock that even some of the dead rose to vote for Hayes! Lundon's campaign was timid and he 'did not dare to hold an open-air public meeting'.[88] That the Volunteers assumed police duties on polling day illustrated that the republican movement was not only preventing the existing government from exercising its functions, but beginning the process of providing an alternative.

In January 1919 Yates reported 'a strong undercurrent of discontent and disloyalty' in Limerick and suggested that the 'outlook for the future is not good' because the 'whole aim of the SF movement is to promote disloyalty, to bring the law into contempt, and to foster hatred against the servants of the Crown.' SF diligently pursued its aims as outlined by Yates during the first quarter of 1919 while the Volunteers were largely inactive.[89] On 10 March Michael Colivet was fêted at Limerick station by between 4,000 and 5,000 people on his return from internment. He had been co-opted to Limerick Corporation as well as elected to parliament while incarcerated.[90] As SF peaked, Limerick's labour movement also approached its highest point. In December 1918 the police estimated that there were 3,433 ITGWU members in Limerick, equivalent to about 74 per cent of the SF membership. By January 1919 the ITGWU was overshadowing SF.[91] On 6 April an IRA attempt to rescue imprisoned Volunteer Bobby Byrne from Limerick Workhouse Hospital led to two deaths. Byrne and Constable Martin O'Brien were both fatally wounded.[92] As many as 20,000 people attended Byrne's funeral on 10 April.[93] Limerick had been proclaimed a 'Special Military Area' the day before in an effort to prevent rioting. This was tantamount to a proclamation of martial law. Permits were introduced to regulate movement into and out of the city. These measures may well have been introduced simply to hinder republicans but were too crude and sweeping to be effective, only serving to inconvenience workers. Two of the city's largest factories, Cleeve's Condensed Milk Company at Landsdowne and Walker's Distillery in Thomondgate, were on the north side of the Shannon, which marked the northern boundary of the Special Military Area. Many residents of Thomondgate, going the opposite way for work in the city, were equally discommoded.

The ITGWU members at Cleeve's went on strike on 12 April. The Trades Council called a general strike on 13 April, in which 14,000 workers participated from 14 April. The strike committee of the Trades Council became known as the 'Limerick soviet'. John Cronin was president of the Trades Council and chairman of the strike committee. 'Yes, this is a soviet', he told visiting American journalist Ruth Russell: it was a protest against the injustice of having to seek military permits 'to earn our daily bread.'[94] That there were over 100 'soviets', basically local strikes involving the occupation of creameries or factories, in 1919 and 1920 indicates the vitality and revolutionary potential of the Irish labour movement.[95] The Limerick soviet was unique in scale and influence, however. While the strike committee had local sovereignty, this depended to an extent on the toleration of the British army which chose to avoid any further escalation. The aim of the strike was not to foment social revolution but to remove the military permit order. Labour's stance, however, went beyond opposition to restrictions on civil liberties. In proposing the Trades Council's resolution of sympathy to Byrne's mother, Cronin made it clear that he, for one, identified with the dead man's republican politics:

> [Byrne] was murdered by the minions of English tyranny here in our midst. But whilst condoling with Mrs Byrne I must also congratulate her in having reared a son of such a heroic disposition, whose name will be handed down in generations to come as an example of what an Irish man should be.[96]

Aided by the Volunteers, Na Fianna and farmers who made a patriotic virtue out of necessity, the soviet collected and distributed food at fixed prices (the cost of eggs fell by one-third and milk by more than half according to Cronin),[97] published a daily news-sheet called the *Worker's Bulletin*, and printed its own money. Some unions failed to issue strike pay and a shortage of cash precipitated the printing and circulation of soviet banknotes, which were all redeemed. Shops opened only with the strike committee's permission. Skeleton staffs maintained gas, water and electricity facilities and other essential services such as bakeries. The strike involved many functions that were not usually associated with work stoppages and achieved more than most of the subsequent factory occupations which were labelled as soviets. In terms of socialist theory, however, the strike was not a soviet. It had a distinctly Catholic hue and there was no takeover of private property. While Bishop Hallinan and Mayor O'Mara condemned the proclamation of the city, they were uneasy at the display of trade union power and were influential in convincing the Trades Council to abandon the strike. Within a fortnight, disappointed in its expectation of outside support, the soviet collapsed. The military proclamation was lifted a week later. O'Mara and Hallinan had struck a deal with army commander General C.J. Griffin.[98] The employers of the city would operate the permit system in place of the military. They had offered this alternative at the outset of the dispute but Griffin had opted for the heavy handed approach before waiting the crisis out. May Day was not observed in Limerick.

The *Worker's Bulletin* presented the soviet as an anti-imperial labour protest:

> the strike is a worker's strike and is no more Sinn Féin than any other strike against tyranny ... our fellow Trade Unionists in khaki [British soldiers] are refusing to do the dirty work which is only fit for such invertebrates as the RIC ... Tommy [the British soldier] is not our real enemy and we wish him to understand he is merely the tool of his Imperialistic, Capitalistic Government.[99]

Many of those employed at Cleeve's were members of SF, as were the ITGWU leaders.[100] The police hinted to the media that SF agents at Cleeve's orchestrated the strike.[101] Batty Stack, who had led Byrne's rescue, worked at Cleeve's and did not welcome the prospect of being questioned by the military four times daily as he went back and forth. Stack suggested that the staff of the 2nd Battalion engineered the strike.[102] While East Clare IRA leader Michael Brennan was not a member of any trade union, he was on the strike committee. This was a practical decision – it acknowledged that there was a need for IRA involvement while sidestepping sensitivities between the two feuding city battalions. Brennan's farming background also created a link with the conservative rural hinterland that might not have been as forthcoming with material and moral support otherwise. Neither the national leadership of the republican movement, which was perturbed at this display of trade union power, nor that of the labour movement, which was unenthusiastic about purely nationalist political strikes, inspired the soviet. Local SF officials had condemned socialism as a distraction from the national struggle ahead of the 1918 general election and the soviet's fusion of nationalism and syndicalism discomfited both republicans and trade unionists. That the strike committee, with the grudging cooperation of business leaders, shopkeepers and clergy, could run the city, had shocked the British political and military leadership.

The Republic, another subversive Limerick newspaper, was bitterly critical
of 'the nincompoops who call themselves "the Leaders of Labour"' and who
had 'bowed the head in shameful submission to the Army of Occupation'.[103]
Organized labour, however, except perhaps for a small minority of the most
radical socialists, did not intend to overthrow the state. Its more radical man-
ifestations, such as the Limerick soviet, were short-lived and localized. The
impressive organizational achievements of the soviet are suggestive of long-
term ideological socialist planning. In reality, the origin of the soviet was both
industrial and political. It was the immediate result of an intensification of
nationalist feeling sparked by the shooting of Bobby Byrne combined with a
spontaneous defence of the rights of labour in the face of the restrictions
imposed on local workers by British militarism. The soviet should not be
viewed in isolation. Its remarkable accomplishment was not replicated elsewhere, but the frequency of strike activity, particularly involving the
ITGWU, had increased dramatically during the early months of 1919. In the
aftermath of the soviet, local labour militancy increased. There were thirty-
seven strikes and lockouts in Limerick in 1919, nearly twice as many as in
1918.[104] At the end of 1919 the ITGWU had 7,478 members in forty-four
Limerick branches. Its expansion peaked in June 1920 with 7,738 members in
forty-five branches.[105] The increasing intensity of the military campaign took
its toll on ITGWU organization and activity from that point on.

That the radicalization of Limerick labour went only so far is evident in
its dealings with the local Catholic hierarchy, which was critical of socialism.
During the course of the First World War, various labour bodies regularly
expressed their allegiance to particular clerics and Church organizations in
resolutions printed in the press. Even when politics occasionally intervened,
declarations of dutiful fidelity still took priority. In the wake of the Rising,
and Bishop O'Dwyer's exchange with General Maxwell, the main concern of
the Bread Vanmen's Society was to condemn 'in the strongest manner possible the action of any military officer who thinks fit to interfere in the eccle-
siastical duties of our clergy' and to 'uphold his Lordship in every way in our
power'.[106] Influential but conservative elements within the local labour movement occasionally invited members of the clergy to involve themselves in
trade union matters. O'Dwyer had acted as an arbitrator in local industrial
relations disputes in 1916 and 1917 to avert strikes. His successor, Bishop
Hallinan, resolved a strike in 1918.[107] This phenomenon meant that one of the
soviet's defining features was its notably Catholic interpretation of communism. Ruth Russell of the *Chicago Tribune* observed some of the nuances of
Limerick's brand of Bolshevism: the poster on the back of a donkey card
rolling around the streets read 'Working Under Order of the Strike
Committee: GOD AND MAN'; the red-badged guards of the soviet standing and blessing themselves at the Angelus bell; the SF mayor explaining that

there would be no support for communism because 'There can't be. The people here are Catholics.' 'Isn't it well that communism is to be Christianized?' said the bishop of Killaloe.[108]

Between Easter 1916 and Christmas 1918 there was a seismic shift in Irish nationalist politics from the IPP's home rule constitutionalism to SF's radical republicanism. Pre-Rising politics had revolved around electioneering. After the Rising, as resort was more frequently made to DORA, commitment to republicanism carried the risk of arrest (and from 1920 a risk of death). The common enemy of the UIL and all other provincial political associations had been public apathy but SF became a popular front. Announcing his resignation from parliament in the weeks before the 1918 general election, long-time Limerick City representative Michael Joyce explained his decision to the electorate: 'a new generation has arisen in Ireland, who are determined to carry out their ideas and ideals by other ways and other means'.[109] Cowed by the challenge of SF, the veteran was neither willing nor able to stand in the way of the new politics that he sensed enveloping the constituency. While there was certainly some replication of pre-war nationalist strategies by SF during the revolutionary period and some continuity in personnel, there was a pronounced difference in the generational background of the mass of activists that contributed to the break from the IPP. Police reports regularly referred to the spirit of sedition that existed among young men and women and to the influence of young curates in that regard. The presence of clergymen in SF clubs, usually in senior positions, gave the party a valued decorum.

The slow demise of the IPP since earlier in the century accelerated after the false dawn of home rule in 1914; each dead and maimed soldier was another stark reminder of its failed war policy. Its disintegration in the 1918 general election was almost total. Its presence on local councils was strongly diluted once voters had the opportunity to express their wish for change there too. The IPP's Limerick organization had been stagnating for the better part of a decade, passing pro-Redmond resolutions and engaging in the odd agrarian dispute, but even its fundraising efforts were lethargic. Its constituency workers were daunted by the steely idealism and energy of SF activists. Sitting MPs, tainted by recruiting and enfeebled by the conscription crisis, were no match for heroes who had fought or been imprisoned for Ireland. But IPP local structures did provide the basic blueprint for SF's growth spurt in 1917–18 and many Limerick home rulers deserted their sinking ship for a place in SF during these years. Even the *Limerick Leader* jumped on the republican bandwagon after the 1918 election.

SF reached its apogee with the general election victory of December 1918 and the establishment of Dáil Éireann in January 1919. Having routed its foe, however, SF now found itself in a situation similar to that faced by the IPP after the theoretical attainment of home rule in 1914: it had no meaningful political opposition outside of Ulster. The threat of conscription ceased with the end of the war, and with it went much of SF's momentum. The party faded into the background as the IRA assumed the mantle of leadership. The military movement stepped into the vanguard of the independence struggle. Proscription and the violence of 1919–21 drove the party underground and hindered political activity. In the absence of elections and political competition, club meetings in Limerick and elsewhere ground to a halt. SF, in a certain sense, had outlived its usefulness: it had served its purpose by facilitating advanced nationalism's defeat of moderate nationalism and the establishment of republican central government. The Dáil assumed the functions of SF. The party wilted in the shadow of the republican parliament and army but its members continued to perform vital revolutionary functions as the administrators of local authorities and republican courts, nowhere more so than in Limerick city and county.

Like the general election, the Limerick soviet illustrated that SF had nothing to fear from the Labour party. The strike achieved removal of the military permit order but Labour was pushed further to the periphery of national politics. The workers of Limerick showed that they were powerful agents in their own right, however. Significantly, the actions of the police in particular provoked deep resentment and made republican violence against them more acceptable to the public. The soviet suggested that separatism had gathered wider support, and that the level of disaffection among the civilian population was now sufficient to provide support for a guerrilla war. In challenging the imposition of British militarism, the soviet threatened to undermine a central strategy of British rule and provided a further fillip to those who supported the use of violence and who were asserting their leadership of the republican movement in the early phase of the War of Independence.

5 'We are the government of the country': the republican counter-state, 1919–21

Whereas the IRA are celebrated in story and song, their less glamorous bureaucratic counterparts in Dáil courts and SF-controlled local authorities have never fired the popular imagination. The psychological power of guerrilla warfare often exceeded its military meaning, shaping popular perception and shrouding the Volunteers in heroic legend: 'Every one of our little fights or attacks was significant', wrote Ernie O'Malley, 'they made panoramic pictures of the struggle in the people's eyes and lived on in their minds.'[1] The management of grants, property rates, malicious injuries claims, taxes, public wages and programmes of rationalization, and adjudicating on mundane matters concerning livestock, grazing rights, land title and right of way lack the romance of tales featuring freedom fighters. But as this chapter demonstrates resistance to British rule took many forms.

Local government elections had not been held in Ireland since 1914. In January 1920 SF won control of 72 out of 127 urban councils in the country and took shared control of another 26. In June SF won a majority of seats on 28 of 33 county councils, 182 of 206 rural district councils and 138 of 154 poor law boards.[2] Republican forces now controlled the apparatus of local government in the south of the country and in much of the north. In Limerick, the IPP had been largely defunct since 1917–18 but a home rule rump managed to retain influence on the corporation even after January 1920. The party was strongest in rural areas and took a clean sweep of seats on Limerick County Council in June 1920. Public opinion had swung more firmly behind the separatist policies and strategies of the republican movement. By August 1920 republican courts were functioning in every county bar Antrim.[3] Outside of east Ulster and Dublin the British justice system was largely obsolete. In July 1920 Lord Monteagle of Foynes wrote of Limerick that 'the Sinn Féin courts are steadily extending their jurisdiction and dispensing justice even-handed between man and man, Catholic and Protestant, farmer and shopkeeper, grazier and cattle-driver, landlord and tenant'.[4] Limerick's republican administrators won a battle of wits and wills against their Crown counterparts to ensure that the local counter-state survived and indeed thrived to an extent.

Dáil Éireann met thirteen times between its first assembly in January 1919 and its suppression the following September, and only eight more times from then until the truce of July 1921. It operated under severe financial and logistical constraints. Thus, the republican counter-state had to be highly localized and decentralized. The Dáil's immediate concern with local government was constituency organization with a view to the municipal elections of 1920.[5] Michael Collins, as minister for finance, oversaw the Dáil loan, which accumulated a staggering £371,000. Successful fundraising required public support and solid constituency structures. East Limerick was a shining light nationally and benefitted to the tune of £35,000, while west Limerick secured £20,000 and Limerick city £10,000.[6] The Dáil sought to wrest the administration of justice away from the old order and into a rival republican legal structure. The authority, efficiency and morale of the RIC and Crown courts had already been undermined by extensive boycotting and intimidation. SF-established arbitration courts became widespread in the west of the country as land disputes and agrarian agitation flared from late 1917. In 1919 the Dáil established local parish courts, district courts and a national circuit court. In 1920 apprehensive that arbitration courts were being used to pursue factional interests rather than republican principles, the Dáil attempted to assert central control. The chaotic circumstances of the day, however, meant that Austin Stack, minister for home affairs, had little influence over the courts until after the truce. Local IRA units were granted police powers to implement the jurisdiction of the courts.

Agrarian issues provided the impetus for the development of the republican justice system in west Limerick.[7] The first reference to a 'Sinn Féin court' in the Limerick press was made in August 1919.[8] On 14 July 1920 delegates representing SF, the Farmers' Association and various labour bodies met in Limerick city. Richard Hayes presided and local courts were formed for every Catholic parish in the county.[9] The west Limerick SF executive posted notices on church gates on 9 May 1920, informing the public that it had established arbitration courts to deal with all 'reasonable and legitimate claims'.[10] Some disputes, not necessarily any more or less reasonable and legitimate than others, were concluded outside of the courtroom. The IRA's influence was often evident. On 13 May 1920, for instance, Thomas Atkinson of Adare and his tenant received letters warning them to relinquish a property from which a widow had been evicted or they would 'get the lead'.[11] SF warned the owners of grazing ranches that 'Compulsion is coming. It is better for them to settle any fair demand on equitable terms now, and live in peace and harmony with their neighbours than to face the uncertain future.'[12] The estate of Mountiford Westropp of Mellon, Kildimo was seized in June 1920, and his agent shot and seriously injured. He received no further income from his land until March 1922, when he was forced to sell the 628 acres concerned to a committee of farmers at 'their own price' for local redistribution.[13] Workers on Westropp's land in Adare, who had previously received threatening letters, were visited by armed men in July 1920 and forced to leave their jobs and withdraw their stock. Again, the motive was to render the estate unworkable and compel its sale for division.[14] In early 1921 the Irish Land Commission, under the provisions of the Soldiers and Sailors Resettlement Acts, granted allotments of twenty to thirty acres to a number of ex-servicemen at Bottomstown, near Knocklong. Subsequently, the East Limerick Brigade gave notice to individual tenants that they were to be evicted because the commission had no authority to make such grants. But the order did not 'prejudice' claims provided they were 'made to the proper authority namely – the Minister for Home Affairs, Dáil Éireann'.[15]

Between 2 and 16 May the roofs of several farm buildings at Bottomstown were torn off.[16] In June and July fences and gates were knocked, the land was turned into commonage and livestock were grazed. If ex-soldiers did not immediately vacate their plots on receipt of the eviction notice they were threatened with being shot. Both the RIC and the Land Commission were unsympathetic. DI Adam Sanson suggested that 'the IRA only wanted to be recognised as being the governors of the country.' The Land Commission continued to charge some of the ex-soldiers rent after they had been dispossessed. Revealingly, several of those expelled from Bottomstown in 1921 returned to their allotments in May 1923.[17] This development coincided with the end of the Civil War and was most likely facilitated by the IFS government as part of its conservative reaction against the social radicalism of the period.

The number of cases of 'ordinary crime' before the regular Crown courts declined to the extent that Limerick Petty Sessions only had to sit for a number of minutes and there were no indictable cases at Limerick Assizes in March 1920.[18] Meanwhile, military tribunals established under DORA and the Restoration of Order in Ireland Act of August 1920 (ROIA) to hear political cases became increasingly busy. As the vulnerability of the RIC forced them to abandon routine policing (map 5 illustrates their retreat), the republican police and IRA increasingly assumed that role. The republican police, in the East Limerick Brigade area at least, were recruited from the ranks of those Volunteers 'unsuitable for military duties for one reason or another'.[19] The 6th Division of the British army regarded the republican police in Limerick as less than heroic:

> the activity of the Sinn Féin police usually consists of a couple of men sneaking up to a Public house door, hastily informing the proprietor that the Commandant orders them to close at such and such an hour and when this has been done these Stalwarth [sic] Police of the Irish Republic run away as fast as their legs can carry them as they have no desire, apparently, of coming into contact with either the Military or Police.[20]

Volunteers found themselves dispersing looters, investigating bank and post-office robberies, burglaries and cattle-stealing, and enforcing the licensing laws, as well as dealing with land disputes.[21] Two cases concerned alleged breaches of promise of marriage were brought by the fathers of young women against young men. Another young woman requested that a Volunteer compel a young farmer to marry her because he was the father of her unborn child.[22] In May 1920 there were several armed robberies of livestock and farm produce committed around Shanagolden in the name of the IRA. The culprits were identified as farmers' sons, none of whom were Volunteers. The Shanagolden company seized their arms and gave them a warning.[23] The perpetrators of a series of robberies around Kilmallock did not get off so lightly, however, and were exiled for two years.[24] Abbeyfeale Volunteers made a number of arrests at the town fair at the end of June for breaches of the peace and 'tramps and undesirables were obliged to retire early'. On 26 June the Murroe Volunteers closed down a shebeen in the Clare Glens.[25] The republican police were particularly active in Limerick city, where they fined youths who had damaged a pony trap, recovered stolen money and bicycles, regulated the opening hours of public houses, and curbed the menace of hurling on the roads. Individuals who were found guilty of drunken disorder were ordered to take the total abstinence pledge. The republican justice system also extended into the area of family law: a court in Limerick city ordered a husband to make increased support payments to his wife and child.[26] On more than one occasion in Limerick a Volunteer fell foul of his colleagues in the republican police. On 20 September 1920 a number of Volunteers who had been found on a licensed premises after hours were tried at Castlemahon court, fined and reprimanded.[27] In October 1921 Galbally parish justice John Casey sought counsel from the minister for home affairs, Stack, on how to try an IRA man caught committing a robbery. Stack decided that if the Volunteer was on duty at the time of the offence he should face a court-martial. If not, he should be tried before a Dáil court.[28]

There was popular acceptance of (or at least compliance with) the new legal regime. Most participants were satisfied to abide by republican decisions rather than seek redress from the Crown. Public opinion was one consideration and the likely intervention of the republican police another, more pressing one. If a court order or fine was ignored, the republican police might seize livestock until the subject conformed. Individuals who were anything but sympathetic to republicanism participated in the republican justice system. Lord Dunraven, who acknowledged that the system worked 'very well', apparently brought a case relating to building plans for Adare Manor to a republican court, which found in his favour.[29] In June 1920 the Irish Situation Committee, which reported to the British cabinet on the collapse of its administrative structure in Ireland, was informed by a Limerick unionist that

'Sinn Féin rules the County and rules it admirably': it was just as well that the republican police and courts were impartial and efficient because they were 'the only authority in the County'.[30]

Colonel Williamson, resident magistrate for Limerick, made it clear to the Irish Situation Committee that Crown officials were 'terrorized' and that there was no alternative to the republican system.[31] Williamson was targeted by the IRA because he 'dished out very severe sentences for only minor offences. He also had the reputation of having prisoners roughed up.' He narrowly avoided an IRA ambush on 2 December 1920, as he left Stephen Quin's home at Castleconnell.[32] Mayor O'Callaghan choreographed a meeting of Crown city magistrates on 29 July at which seven justices resigned, apparently 'as a protest against the present methods employed in governing Ireland' and in the belief that 'peace and civil order will not be restored until Ireland is governed in accordance with the wish of the Irish people'.[33] The county council likewise pressurized magistrates to resign. The IRA targeted all tiers of the British legal body. For instance, on 14 July 1920 John Kelly, a civil bill officer, was warned not to serve another writ or ejection order and duly resigned.[34] The Crown solicitor for Limerick made a point of going and returning from court by different routes. He occasionally travelled with an armed police escort.[35] Volunteers further interfered with the operation of the Crown courts by denying accommodation to visiting judges. In June 1920 Justices Moore and Samuels had to stay in the county courthouse until Lord Dunraven offered them beds in Adare Manor.[36]

Arbitration courts were not illegal and RIC IG Sir Thomas Smith regarded the 'toleration extended to republican courts' as the key factor in their success.[37] According to the RIC Divisional Commissioner, Brigadier-General Cecil Prescott-Decie, the head policeman in north Munster, the police had complete knowledge of all Dáil courts records, where they were held, who attended, who conducted them, and the places in which convicted prisoners were held. Prescott-Decie was confident that the RIC could easily suppress the republican courts if so ordered.[38] British procrastination may have been in the expectation that the courts would fail, thereby discrediting the Dáil. There was a dramatic change in attitude once the government came to realize that the republican courts were instrumental in undermining its authority in Ireland. The admission of CI Patrick Marrinan (Yates's successor) in July 1920 that the courts had 'struck a strong blow at British prestige' and 'placed a very considerable portion of the county under the control of that organisation' was applicable to most of the country. Marrinan's claims about his success in dealing with the courts, however, were derided as 'rubbish' by senior colleagues.[39] From June the government fell back on coercion. This involved the introduction of the Auxiliaries, the enactment of the ROIA and the suspension of grants to SF-controlled local councils. Republican

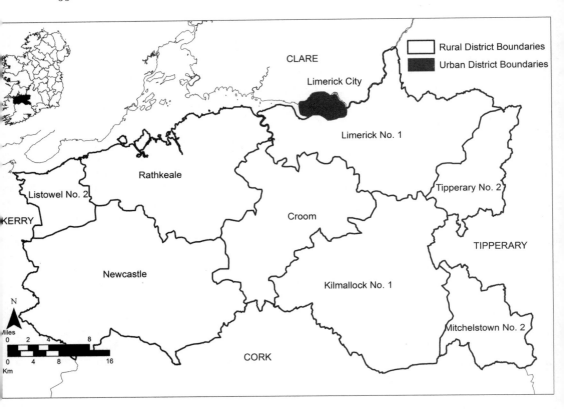

CLARE

Rural District Boundaries

Urban District Boundaries

Limerick City

Limerick No. 1

Rathkeale

Tipperary No. 2

Listowel No. 2

KERRY

Croom

TIPPERARY

Newcastle

Kilmallock No. 1

N

Miles
0   2   4   8

0   4   8   16
Km

Mitchelstown No. 2

CORK

4 Local government divisions

courts were driven underground. Notice of sittings was curtailed and many
people wanted cases adjourned in the hope that they might never be heard.[40]
Still, in the latter half of 1920 of the forty-nine cases that were listed for hearing in the west Limerick district court, forty-five were heard.[41] Bar one, all
the decrees in the thirty cases dealt with between February and June 1921
were implemented.[42] In September 1920 the courts continued to sit regularly
in nine counties, including Limerick, but the RIC were able to enforce the
ordinary law more strictly and bring more cases before the Crown courts
towards the end of 1920.[43] The Dáil courts were more successful in east and
west Limerick than in the city due to the greater concentration of Crown
forces there and detailed RIC intelligence.[44]

After the truce, Stack acknowledged that the court system had temporarily broken down in much of the country owing to the pressure exerted by
Crown forces but he paid 'a special tribute to a few districts', including east

Limerick, 'which never for a day ceased to carry on their work'.[45] The courts were soon working more regularly and more efficiently all over the county. CI John Regan noted in October that they were flourishing.[46] The courts remained, at least in theory, restricted to arbitration functions. While the RIC was empowered to check that these limitations were observed, its attempts to restore the standing of the Crown courts largely failed. At the start of December 1921 Fr David Fitzgerald of Abbeyfeale parish court wrote to Stack about RIC interference. Fitzgerald declared that 'We would not violate the Truce one iota if we considered we were committing a breach of it.' He told Stack: 'Your Department can hardly sanction the probable violation of the Truce in every Parish Court in Ireland', to which Stack replied: 'We are the government of the country and as such are entitled to try all kinds of cases in our Courts.'[47] Stack's claim that 'We are the government of the country' contained much truth. While republican courts had to be veiled in secrecy and intrigue, the cases they heard were typically humdrum disputes about money and property. But even trivial matters attained revolutionary significance in Dáil courts.

Extensive impersonation at the municipal elections in Limerick city on 15 January 1920 explains a turnout of up to 97 per cent in several wards.[48] SF received 63 per cent of first preferences.[49] The new Limerick Corporation consisted of twenty-six Sinn Féiners, five Labour members, and nine independents, who were mostly former home rulers. Eleven of the fourteen sitting members who went forward were re-elected, and of the other twenty-nine members, seven had served before the last election in 1914. This was a striking level of continuity (45 per cent) among personnel in municipal representation more than a year after the seismic shift of the 1918 general election. Most of these councillors, however, had never practised political monogamy and would rarely have been members of the UIL or any other political body exclusively. Eleven of the twenty-six SF representatives were trade unionists.[50] Among the Labour representatives were John Cronin, James Carr and James Casey – the Trade Council's three most prominent spokesmen. All three had been involved in the management of the 'Limerick soviet'. Casey topped the poll, as did Labour's Patrick Walsh and James McInerney in their respective wards. There was a republican/Labour pact in Newcastle West where eight Sinn Féiners and seven Labour candidates, all of them ITGWU members, were unopposed for the fifteen available seats.[51]

For the first time, a woman, Emily Crowe of SF, was elected to Limerick Corporation.[52] A second woman, Máire O'Donovan, a member of Cumann na mBan and SF, was co-opted as a councillor on 7 April 1921 to replace SF Mayor George Clancy, who had been assassinated by Crown forces the month before. O'Donovan (neé Murphy), was a sister of Professor Kate O'Callaghan, wife of Michael O'Callaghan, who was killed on the same night as Clancy and in the same circumstances. Mrs O'Callaghan was elected to the Dáil in May 1921. O'Donovan became the first woman to act as mayor of Limerick, when she deputized for Stephen O'Mara from May 1921 until January 1922. SF, unlike the UIL, did not exclude women from membership. There were women members in eighteen of the sixty SF clubs in Limerick at the time of the truce in July 1921, when nine per cent, or 401 out of a total membership of 4,698, of Limerick Sinn Féiners were women.[53]

While remnants of IPP influence clearly endured in the city in early 1920, Michael O'Callaghan was unopposed for the mayoralty.[54] The *Leader* was hopeful that the new corporation would 'devote itself more to practical and constructive work than to mere showy futilities or gallery acting'. It warned 'against the horrid and paralysing evil of corruption' and reported favourably on the official advice from SF to local councils, urging them '"to see that the old and evil system is completely swept away"'.[55] This reflected the contempt for the perceived corruption of local authorities that was widespread among republicans.[56] SF was strongest in rural areas and took a clean sweep of twenty seats on Limerick County Council in June 1920. Of the thirty-six candidates originally nominated, only three were outgoing councillors. IRB man Anthony Mackey was the sole outgoing member returned. Withdrawals meant that sixteen members of the new council had been unopposed. The four contests that took place were in Kilmallock. Each of the four SF candidates polled more than 1,000 votes, while the fifth-placed candidate received 492 and a former councillor received only seventy-two. The high rate of withdrawals was not just down to chance. Independent councillor Michael Ryan of Pallasgrean was informed that his candidature would be taken as support of British government and betrayal of the principles for which his Fenian grandfather was imprisoned in 1867. John McMahon withdrew his candidature in Castleconnell 'in consequence of a request made by the Sinn Féin party'.[57] CI Regan reported with resignation that:

> It would have been useless for any person in this County to have opposed the Sinn Féin candidate at the recent elections. The gunman rules the politician in these instances and any prospective candidate not to their liking would need to live in a Police or Military Barracks.[58]

Regan had informed the previous council that the RIC would be unable to assist at the elections and the Volunteers assumed their duties at the polling booths.[59]

Republican local government began with a series of gestures that had been prearranged with the Dáil.[60] The corporation, with the independents dissenting, and the county council both pledged allegiance to Dáil Éireann as the rightful government. The county council also pledged its 'moral and material support to the men who are now engaged in what may well be described as the final stage in the struggle against British militarism'.[61] At this stage the Dáil's Local Government Department (DÉLG) had no clear plan beyond continued financial reliance on the Local Government Board (LGB), a body which it repudiated.[62] The British denial of belligerent status to the IRA meant that the cost of damage inflicted on people and property by the IRA or Crown forces came under the provisions of the Criminal and Malicious Injuries Act and was charged to property rates. From July 1919 both Limerick County Council and Corporation disregarded malicious injuries decrees. From June 1920 they did not defend claims in court.[63] The vast majority of councils in the south did likewise. In July 1920 Hibernian Insurance informed Limerick County Council that it would not cover Malicious Injuries damage to council property and instructed the council to seek redress from the British government.[64] In April 1921 the corporation applied to the government for compensation for damage done to a footpath during an official reprisal by Crown forces, namely the burning of the Daly family's furniture. The claim was denied.[65]

The funding stand-off was brought to a head in July 1920 when the LGB issued an ultimatum that unless councils undertook to submit their accounts for audit and to adhere to its rules, grants would be diverted. Republican delaying tactics had proved effective – the British appeared responsible for the withdrawal of funding. On 10 August the Dáil instructed all councils to sever their connection with the LGB and to organize their finances according to a method whereby officials, acting as trustees, would conduct the financial business of the council through their personal accounts.[66] The withdrawal of grants and suspension of the payment of rates on government property made bankruptcy a pressing threat. Limerick County Council officials responded with ingenuity, operating up to ten different bank accounts to conceal what cash they had from the prying eyes of the LGB.[67] T.H. Brett, manager of the local Munster and Leinster Bank branch, was as indulgent as possible.[68] The council prioritized economy and full collection of rates. The legal status of rate collection was shrouded with uncertainty. The LGB held collectors liable for lodgements to unauthorized accounts while the Dáil could dismiss them for disloyalty if they followed LGB guidelines, but the Dáil pledged to indemnify collectors against any financial loss they might incur as a result of implementing republican procedures.[69] Nevertheless, the result of this double-jeopardy scenario was that many rate collectors chose a course of inaction, while many ratepayers capitalized on an excuse to do the same.[70]

None of this changed in revolutionary Limerick. Because of the financial woes it inherited and the stringent conditions under which it operated, the corporation was unable to undertake public works of any significance or improve road surfaces during 1920–1. It was hardly able to light the city.[71]

Royal Welsh Fusilier Robert Graves, commenting on the poverty he observed in the city during the winter of 1918–19, compared peace-time Limerick to a 'war-ravaged town', with 'holes like shell-craters' in the streets and many buildings seemingly about to crumble.[72] At its first meeting, in June 1920, the new Limerick County Council expressed dissatisfaction with rate collection. It resorted to temporary overdraft facilities and warned that 'drastic measures' would be taken against defaulters. In August a report on the wages paid to workers on the Direct Labour Scheme voiced the ITGWU grievance that 'the present wages of the roadmen in County Limerick seem to be among the lowest in the country.' A raise was awarded but this was the last council response to labour demands for some time.[73] In September Constance Markievicz, minister for labour, admonished the council for hiring non-union workers.[74] In late 1920, as part of cuts in expenditure, the county surveyors were directed not to employ additional road workers without express direction from the council. Preference should be given

> to married men with young helpless families, or to a man who is the support of a family but that employment be not given to more than one man in each family, or more than one animal hired from one family.[75]

Unmarried men were dismissed as a result and the council failed to implement the Unemployment Insurance Act.[76] Payment of wages to labourers was regularly deferred. All road works were suspended before the truce and only resumed in August because of dirty streets. In September Thomas Meany, chairman of Murroe ITGWU, advised the DÉLG that

> As the financial position of the Council is worse than ever now it seems there will be no road work this winter … the peace outlook is bright, so for God's sake do not let us follow the example of Russia and let penury be the first fruits of the victory that seems to be at hand.

In December the council ordered that road workers absent for IRA training should not be paid.[77]

As well as encouraging thrift, the Dáil formulated reform plans. In October 1920 the DÉLG suggested the amalgamation of poor law unions.[78] On 25 February 1921 the county council agreed to centralize services in a hospital at Croom and a home for the aged at Newcastle West. The Trades Council protested to the Dáil on behalf of the working classes of Limerick city who found it difficult to visit people in Croom and would also face dramatically increased funeral expenses if a relative died there.[79] Another correspondent elaborated on the transport problems: 'The relatives of patients are not riders on motor cars: the jolly donkey cart or even Shanks mare are far more likely to be their mode of progression.'[80] The chief resistance to amalgamation came from the city. SF protested against the proposed 'dismemberment' of Limerick Union as an unbearable burden on citizens and a disgrace to the party. The claims made by the corporation to have the hospital in the city were discounted largely because the union had been so costly. The DÉLG believed that there was no possibility of consensus because of 'an absence of the cordial relations which ought to exist between the different local authorities in the city and county of Limerick'.[81] The question of employment in the new institutions also generated strife. When the amalgamation committee appointed nuns to the county home but lay staff to the hospital, prominent Limerick republican Fr John Lee attempted to exert spiritual pressure on minister for local government W.T. Cosgrave, advising him that the situation was 'a test of your faith and of the religion of Sinn Féin'. He beseeched Cosgrave not to consent to 'the scandal of expelling the nuns from the care of the sick and dying poor and replacing them with lay people'. Cosgrave's concession was that nuns would be appointed as vacancies arose: 'Medical opinion coincides with my own that the presence of nuns would be advantageous.' The compromise also satisfied Bishop Hallinan, who withdrew his opposition.[82] The county hospital was ready to receive patients by October but no savings had been made before the truce. Republican administrators in Limerick did not attempt to oversee a social revolution but they did at least begin a scheme of modernization.

Local appointments were a contentious area in which the IRA began to interfere more regularly following the truce. Brigadier Liam Forde of Mid Limerick was condemned by minister for defence Cathal Brugha for attempting to have one of his staff appointed as medical officer in Croom. Councillor Micheál Ó hAodha had written to the DÉLG warning that there was unease about a creeping return to the cronyism that had sullied the reputation of the public bodies that had preceded it. Michael Colivet, as well as the Manister SF club, had also written to the Dáil complaining about the appointment of Drs Lane and James Brennan, brother of Michael, the East Clare brigadier, and the non-appointment of Dr Hederman, who had been working and living in Croom for seven years. The two doctors appointed lived respectively at some distance, which increased the cost of employing them. The situation caused great local dissatisfaction. At government level, O'Higgins wrote to Brugha to complain of IRA pressure. Forde was subsequently 'instructed that his action was not justifiable and that in accordance with instructions already in his hands he must not interfere in matters of this kind in future'.[83] Stressing that the main reason he had recommended Brennan was a military one, he justified his action to IRA chief of staff Richard Mulcahy on two counts. The first was that the IRA 'adopted the practice general in all counties of exercising their influence on behalf of the candidate who served in the

war as against the candidate who did not'. Brennan had been a member of the
IRA since 1917 and had offered his services to the East Clare and Mid
Limerick Brigades since then. Second, Forde argued that it was important to
have a sympathetic doctor in the position in case hostilities resumed. Mulcahy
understood Forde's thinking but also the bigger issues. He criticized the
explicit violation of orders that prohibited interference in matters of civilian
administration and was anxious about ill-will against the IRA.[84] In November
Limerick County Council informed the Dáil that the situation in regard to
Hederman and a storekeeper who found himself in similar difficulties had
been rectified.[85]

Republican local authorities were not proscribed, but as the lure of grants
failed to secure their fidelity, the Crown turned to repression. The primary
tactic of obstruction involved raiding offices and removing documents. Both
Limerick County Council and Corporation withheld all paperwork from the
LGB when it attempted to audit their accounts in October 1920. On 18
November their minute books and financial records were seized.[86] Several
members of local authorities in Limerick served in a dual capacity as administrators and Volunteers. Public officials were more easily identifiable than
Volunteers. Five were killed: Councillor John Lynch of Kilmallock (who was
not a Volunteer); Volunteer Tim Madigan of Shanagolden, who was a
member of Rathkeale UDC; Mayor George Clancy, who was a Volunteer;
Michael O'Callaghan, Clancy's predecessor as mayor, who was not a
Volunteer; and Seán Wall, chairman of the county council and brigadier of
the East Limerick IRA. Despite these trying conditions, the local authorities
in Limerick managed to maintain a solid rate of activity. The average attendance at the nine county council meetings held in the year prior to the June
1920 election was seventeen.[87] From its first meeting in June 1920 until after
the truce, the council was an underground body, meeting secretly, at different venues and at irregular dates. The average attendance at its fifteen meetings between June 1920 and the end of 1921 was sixteen.[88] The SF council,
then, met slightly more regularly than its predecessor and had only a slightly
lower rate of attendance. The average attendance at the sixteen meetings of
Limerick Corporation held between 30 January and 3 November 1920 was
twenty of its forty members. Only once did it fail to reach a quorum.[89]

Inquests into violent deaths were controversial. Dr James Barry, a former
mayor, had been appointed city coroner in 1909. In May 1920 he led the
inquest into the notorious killing of James Dalton, a member of the 1st
Battalion, Limerick City IRA, by members of the 2nd Battalion.[90] Barry
resigned in June 1920 when his position was debated in Westminster. It is not
clear if he answered to the Commons or the Dáil. The ROIA replaced coroners' inquests with military courts of inquiry which were not required to
include a legally-qualified member and were usually conducted without

republican representation.[91] On 10 September Cosgrave wrote to local authorities that this was 'an attempt to strike at a most important safeguard to the lives of Irish citizens' and should therefore be ignored, coroners continued with inquests as before. In October the council dismissed P.J. Cleary of Kilmallock as coroner when he refused to hold an inquest.[92] Apart from limited cases of ineptitude and disloyalty among rate collectors and unwillingness to pay rates among council employees, Limerick seems to have been relatively free from the degree of corruption experienced by some councils. There was a suggestion, however, that one rate collector had misappropriated funds.[93] Limerick was dutiful in implementing DÉLG directives. The council supported the request of the Dáil Department of Labour to find employment for British servicemen who resigned. After sectarian disturbances in Belfast in July and August 1920 the resolution of the General Council of County Councils calling on people not to trade with Belfast merchants and others imposing religious and political tests was adopted unanimously by both Limerick Corporation and County Council. The corporation further called on the citizens of Limerick to withdraw their money from Ulster Bank as part of the Belfast boycott.[94] After the truce, Michael Colivet was criticized by some of his colleagues in the Dáil because Limerick had applied the boycott to the whole of the six partitioned counties rather than just to areas where attempts had been made to drive nationalists out.[95]

The financial situation of local authorities in Limerick, although far from exemplary, was not as dire as councils elsewhere, such as those in Clare, Kerry, Sligo and Leitrim. It was not unknown for SF to lose control of local authority bodies as happened with Longford UDC.[96] Crucially, Limerick's local authorities and IRA enjoyed a good working relationship. SF's shrewd financial manoeuvring and preservation of control over all subsidiary bodies, along with the survival of the Dáil courts, meant that Limerick's republican counter-state was a broad success. This was a powerful demonstration of the Irish capacity for self-government and the credentials of the claim to self-determination. It was also a clear illustration of the importance of local initiative and leadership to the revolution. The judicial and administrative counter-state was instrumental in undermining British authority and making the republic a tangible reality. And its low-level functionaries were also rebels, if not in quite the same way as active IRA and Cumann na mBan members. The counter-state was a democratic coup in which Limerick was a standard-bearer. The city and county were also leading military theatres during the conflict between the IRA and the Crown forces.

6 'Prepare for death': IRA versus Crown forces, 1919-21

Not all of the people or places in Ireland participated uniformly in the insurgency of 1919-21. But Munster was the frontline of what IRA GHQ termed the 'War Zone'.[1] And Limerick, both city and county, as well as consistently being among the most prominent regional theatres of radical political activity, was also to the fore in republican military operations. In Limerick and other highly active areas, the confrontation between the IRA and Crown forces developed in several broad phases.[2] The first encompassed low-intensity operations against the RIC from 1917 until the winter of 1919-20. The RIC was a logical target for the IRA because of its detailed intelligence on local circumstances and personalities and as a potential source of ordnance. The police retreat from hundreds of untenable rural outposts around the country to consolidated urban barracks surrendered large swathes of territory and much moral authority to the IRA. The 56 RIC barracks in Limerick in early 1919 had reduced to 21 by the time of the truce in July 1921 (see map 5). There were 37 barracks in Tipperary on 1 January 1919 but only 22 two years later. The number in west Cork dropped from 40 to 19, while no fewer than 54 barracks closed in Clare.[3] In the second stage of the war, during the first half of 1920, the IRA destroyed evacuated barracks and other government buildings and also attacked occupied stations. Such operations provided many Volunteers with their first experience of military engagement. Physical assaults on Crown officials and property were also of symbolic importance. The further militarization of the RIC in response only served to advance the republican agenda by discrediting whatever remained of the force's image as a civil police. The third phase of the campaign played out against the backdrop of the coercive ROIA of August 1920, which extended the provisions of DORA and granted Crown forces a high degree of immunity from the civil law. Amplified pressure forced unprecedented numbers of Volunteers to go on the run as full-time revolutionaries. While never more than a small minority of the IRA, they formed elite mobile fighting formations and maintained a standing force in the field for the first time. They became known as 'flying columns' or, more properly, Active Service Units (ASUs). Successful IRA attacks grew more destructive between the autumn of 1920 and the spring of 1921, inflicting heavier casualties, though their frequency did not increase dramatically. Crown reprisals outraged public opinion. Finally, from the spring of 1921, as the augmented British military presence and perennial arms shortages undermined the capacity of the IRA to perform demanding operations such as barracks attacks and ambushes, the focus returned to low-intensity operations such as the felling of trees or digging of trenches to block roads. In the prelude to the truce, the war had seemed to reach a dead end.

'Uneventful ... A meeting once a fortnight or so, and a lecture was read out to us'.[4] Ahane IRA Volunteer Joseph Graham's experience of the start of the War of Independence was pretty typical. Much of the time, nothing happened. IRA guerrillas spent long periods lying in wait for the enemy, usually without result, and longer periods again studiously avoiding them. There was one non-fatal shooting of a policeman in Limerick in 1918. The Soloheadbeg ambush of 21 January 1919, an autonomous enterprise by the South Tipperary Brigade, unauthorized by GHQ, has traditionally been considered the opening action of the War of Independence. Soloheadbeg assumed historical meaning because it had political resonance, coinciding with the first sitting of Dáil Éireann, and because of its deadly outcome, two constables being killed. The ambush did not herald the general intensification of hostilities anticipated by its abettors but it did have a direct sequel. On 13 May 1919 two policemen were killed at Knocklong in Limerick during the rescue from Crown custody of Seán Hogan, one of the Soloheadbeg ambush party. Immediately following Soloheadbeg, the attackers were censured by GHQ, condemned from the pulpit and widely scorned. Popular resentment quickly refocused on repressive state measures, however, as witnessed in Limerick following the deaths of Volunteer Bobby Byrne and Constable Martin O'Brien in April. In the wake of Knocklong, 'Rory of the Hills', righter of wrongs in the agrarian conflicts of the 1870s, issued a proclamation which featured a hand-drawn coffin bearing the name Peter Wallace, the sergeant fatally wounded at Knocklong:

> Informers, [company] keepers and all persons caught talking to Peelers will be shot without further notice and girls who go meeting Peelers will be hanged. This is no mock notice, what is said is meant so beware you do not get a dose of the Knocklong cordial. Wallace thought he was monarch of all he surveyed but he got the lead all right so beware you do not get the same.[5]

CI Yates observed that there was 'an utterly callous feeling throughout the county ... no sympathy has been expressed with the serg[ean]t's widow or the deceased const[able]s relatives'. IG Byrne reiterated that local people

> remain perfectly callous and give no assistance in tracing the murderers ... 'Knocklong Aboo!', 'Up Knocklong', 'Wallace bowled over, RIP', was chalked on the streets, and the Sergeant's [Wallace] widow was jeered at on her way to Mass.[6]

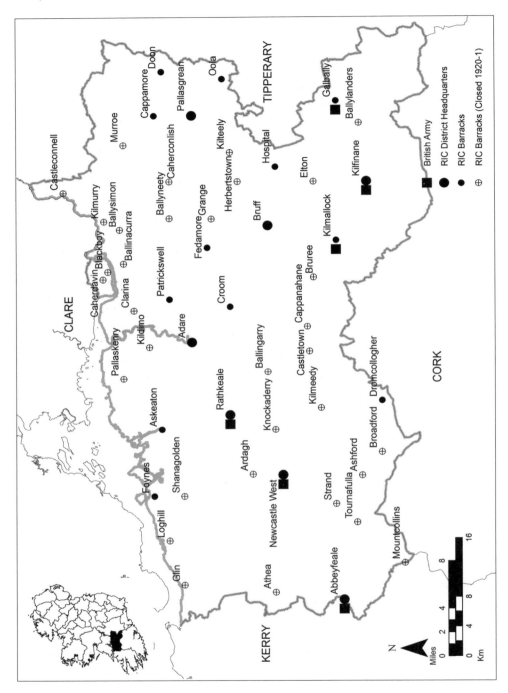

5 Distribution of the Crown forces

Jane Gallagher, a civilian who tended to the injured policemen at Knocklong, fled the country.[7]

By mid-1919 the morale of the Limerick RIC was sinking and the capability of the force as an anti-republican agency had been greatly diminished.[8] There was another military lull in store, however. While the Limerick IRA had been fundamental to the gradual intensification of the armed campaign in the first half of 1919 and continued to fulfil a central function in its evolution thereafter, there was no politically related violent death in Limerick for nearly eight months after Knocklong and the IRA was not responsible for another fatality until March 1920. Most of the fighting took place in the eighteen months before the truce, the frequency of killing increasing dramatically as events progressed.

In April 1920 the RIC was restructured. Divisional Commissioners were appointed. They were often high-ranking military figures, including Brigadier-General Cecil Prescott-Decie in Limerick. Yates was replaced as CI by Patrick Marrinan in June. Marrinan was then quickly replaced by John Regan, who had come to Limerick in April as a DI and staff officer to Prescott-Decie. Regan and Prescott-Decie were at one in implementing the martial policy promoted by General Sir Nevil Macready, new commander-in-chief, Sir Hamar Greenwood, the chief secretary, and Major-General Sir Henry Hugh Tudor, the police adviser. Prescott-Decie earned a singular rebuke from Macready for believing 'that martial law means that he can kill anybody he sees walking along the road whose appearance may be distasteful to him'.[9] At the start of 1919 Yates had 357 men at his disposal. At the start of 1921 there were 545 men serving under Regan. The high rate of resignations and retirements among existing RIC members, worn down as they were by IRA attrition, and their replacement by temporary cadets meant that 332 of the 544 policemen serving under Regan in February 1921 were Black and Tans.[10] On 18 April 1921 the twenty-four functioning stations in Limerick were staffed by 475 men, which was 116 below proposed levels.[11] There were only twenty-one barracks operating in Limerick at the time of the truce (see map 5). Barracks were maintained or shut based on physical capacity rather than strategic location, ceding further advantage to the IRA, and sometimes creating rather than solving problems for Crown forces. Pallaskenry barracks, for instance, was closed in the autumn of 1919 and the garrison transferred to Kildimo, but the courthouse remained in Pallaskenry. On 18 March 1920 the IRA twice ambushed policemen returning to Kildimo from Pallaskenry Petty Sessions.[12] The final reorganization of the RIC in Limerick was characterized by a number of incongruities. Seventeen constables reported to one sergeant in Askeaton while there were seven sergeants in Newcastle West but only thirteen constables. DI Adam Sanson was responsible for a cluster of barracks in Doon, Oola, Pallasgrean and Cappamore. He was also responsible for Fedamore barracks, which was twenty miles away from the other four.[13] The IRA capitalized on this imbalance in February 1921 when ambushing Sanson's convoy at Dromkeen, near Pallasgrean, as it returned from Fedamore.

As well as the police, various British military units were stationed in Limerick. The 18th Infantry Brigade of the 6th Military Division was head-quartered at the New Barracks, garrisoned by two battalions of Royal Welsh Fusiliers, a detachment of the Royal Army Service Corps, and a specialist armoured car unit. On 27 May 1921, between the men in the New Barracks, the battalion of the Royal Oxford and Buckinghamshire Light Infantry Regiment in the Strand Barracks, and the artillery batteries and engineering units based at the Ordnance Barracks, there were approximately 2,000 army personnel in the city, including about 200 officers. The Warwickshires had a further nineteen officers and 367 men spread between Newcastle West, Abbeyfeale and Rathkeale. The 1st Battalion of the Machine Gun Corps, had six officers and ninety men in both Kilmallock and Kilfinane.[14] There were platoons posted in Bruff, Cappamore, Croom, Hospital and Pallasgrean for a month or more at various stages. In the period approaching the truce, then, no more than 150 full-time Limerick IRA Volunteers faced, at a conservative estimate, 3,000 members of the Crown forces. Large concentrations of military in Tipperary town and an Auxiliary company in Killaloe, County Clare, also both regularly took the field in Limerick. In Cork, around 450 men did the bulk of the fighting. Kerry ASUs could call on 125 or so Volunteers, Clare on 85, and Waterford on 75. In Tipperary, the numbers were quite pro-portionate to those in Limerick with 100 IRA men taking the war to 1,000 Crown forces.[15] Guerrilla tactics were designed to compensate for the associated discrepancies in numbers, armaments, and technology.

The RIC's 'Daily summaries of reports on outrages' recorded ninety incidents in which Crown forces came under fire in Limerick between May 1920 and July 1921. Such bare statistics do not tell the whole story, but spiralling resignation figures indicate shattered morale. Policemen received letters warning them to 'Prepare for death. You are doomed.' Wives and children were evicted and houses wrecked.[16] Volunteers raided homes 'to frighten families having sons or brothers in the RIC into using their utmost efforts to get their kinsmen to resign'.[17] During the summer of 1920 IG Smith worried about the possibility of mass indiscipline:

> no body of men can be expected to support indefinitely the conditions under which the police in many places are forced to live, boycotted, ostracised, forced to commandeer their food, crowded in many instances into cramped quarters … every man's hand against them, in danger of their lives and subjected to the appeals of their parents and their families to induce them to leave the force.[18]

The strain showed not just in resignations. In May 1920 a constable was arrested for firing revolver shots at a colleague during a dispute in Hospital barracks.[19] In December one constable accidentally shot and killed another in Cappamore barracks.[20] The following April a Black and Tan stationed in Pallasgrean committed suicide by shooting himself when he was found in possession of property stolen during a house search.[21] The Limerick IRA killed another twenty RIC men, seventeen Black and Tans, nine soldiers and one Auxiliary during the War of Independence. RIC veterans could choose between loyalty to the uniform or self-preservation, two competing instincts. RIC officers cooperating with the rebels did not broadcast their behaviour, and so remained in danger from the IRA at large. Two such collaborating policemen were killed in IRA ambushes in Limerick in 1920.[22]

IRA GHQ officially sanctioned attacks on barracks in January 1920. The first such operations in Limerick, at Murroe on 25 January and at Doon on 7 March, were unsuccessful due to faulty explosives and Volunteer inefficiency: 'We had no training. We didn't know the requirements of the bomb'.[23] The first successful barracks attack in Limerick was led by Tomás Malone at Ballylanders on 27 April. Michael Collins sent Malone to East Limerick in 1919 with instructions to ease the damaging residual tension from the post-1916 Manahan-O'Hannigan IRA–IRB split. Ballylanders was targeted because Malone judged it 'a reasonably easy task' but it also served as an opportunity to reunite the brigade. When the factions gathered, however, 'one side threatened to shoot some of the other side'. The attack was a success, nonetheless. The barracks was set alight and its seven-man garrison surrendered. The IRA seized weapons and ammunition which 'put us on the pig's back', Malone recalled.[24] Still, some Volunteers had limited skills. Seán Meade's rifle jammed at Ballylanders and he admitted that he 'knew little about how to manage it'.[25] Dave Hennessy doubted the accuracy of his colleagues: 'most of our fellas wouldn't be able to shoot a haystack.'[26] The capture of the barracks arsenal was vital because the raiders expended much of their existing cache. Growing in confidence and experience, the Volunteers confronted a ten-man garrison in the heavily-fortified Kilmallock barracks on 28 May. Led by East Limerick, over 100 Volunteers from the three Limerick brigades, East Clare, Tipperary and North Cork, mounted one of the biggest operations of the war.[27] The attack started after midnight and continued until the IRA, almost out of ammunition, withdrew at around 7 a.m. Two RIC men and one Volunteer were killed. Much of the barracks was engulfed in flames but Sergeant Tobias O'Sullivan refused to submit. A Cumann na mBan contingent 'used a rifle and kept the kettles boiling as occasion demanded'.[28] While members of Cumann na mBan provided safe houses, food and clothing for men on the run, were frequently involved in the care of wounded men, distributed propaganda, officiated in the republican justice system, raised funds, gathered intelligence and acquired arms, it was rare for them to engage in combat operations. Kilmallock was not an unqualified success for the IRA. Malone received a reprimand from IRA Adjutant General Gearóid O'Sullivan for the excessive expenditure of precious ammunition. Planned attacks on Newcastle West and Rathkeale barracks did not ensue, apparently because of the unsustainable drain on resources. A stronger deterrent, perhaps, was the armoured car positioned outside Newcastle West barracks after Kilmallock.[29] From the British perspective, Kilmallock had not been an unmitigated disaster. The police had mounted a heroic defence and reports described Tobias O'Sullivan leading his men out of the burning barracks at dawn with fixed bayonets.[30] O'Sullivan would not survive the war.

In early April 1920 seventeen barracks were burned in Limerick and there were raids on the income tax office and the custom house in the city as part of a countrywide campaign. Seven more police stations were destroyed in Limerick in May. This prevented evacuated barracks from being reoccupied by the military or by the new police recruits arriving in Ireland. Seven Limerick Volunteers suffered fatal injuries while burning government property in 1920–1: lack of training in this type of activity was probably a factor. Two of the largest mansions in the country, Mount Shannon, Annacotty, and nearby Lord Massy's Hermitage, Castleconnell, were burned down in June 1920. The RIC had withdrawn from the area and acknowledged that local Volunteers believed the military were about to establish bases in both houses. The burning of several other houses in Limerick occurred in similar circumstances.[31] Property burning was not only the preserve of the IRA, however. Creameries, which were at the heart of many rural communities, and often employed Volunteers, were a popular target for reprisal attacks by Crown forces. There was a spate of at least seven creamery burnings in east Limerick in April 1920.[32] By the end of October there had been thirty-five attacks on creameries nationally, the majority of them in Limerick and Tipperary.[33] The burning of creameries became the subject of much British propaganda. It was common for police statements to blame rival republicans or competing creameries.

After Kilmallock the IRA focus switched to ambushes on convoys and patrols. The new tactic reflected the unsustainability of consuming large volumes of ammunition in laying siege to well-defended strongpoints. The East Limerick ASU emerged even before the introduction of the ROIA. East Limerick soon seized more rifles from the enemy than it had members. Ordinary Volunteers who were not members of columns concentrated mainly on arms raids, mail raids, road trenching, bridge demolition, cutting telegraph and telephone wires, billeting and guarding columns, and administration of local government and justice. As one Volunteer recalled, 'I am not pretending that I ever did anything spectacular – I didn't – nor wasn't asked.'[34] If

men were not known to the authorities, they continued in their usual employment. It was not until 4 October 1920, by which stage the East Limerick unit
had been in the field for four months and the West and Mid Limerick counterparts were also operational, that GHQ directed the formation of ASUs.[35]
The proliferation of the concept and the almost universal adoption of its tactics was an entirely practical response to prevailing local circumstances. The
largely self-sufficient nature of the ASUs only served to make them even less
amenable to central authority.

In the city, a pattern developed whereby IRA actions were followed by
indiscriminate police reprisals. Prescott-Decie was concerned about the 'tick-
lish' problem of poor police morale: 'They have been very near throwing up
the sponge'.[36] Part of his recommended remedy was systematic harassment of
civilians. In summer 1920 the *Leader* reported that owing to the stress caused
by Crown violence in the city, there were an elevated number of patients with
'nervous complaints'.[37] Beatings in the streets and the destruction of homes
and businesses were almost nightly occurrences. The unenviable position of
veteran RIC members was most poignantly illustrated by their difficulty in
obtaining coffins and hearses for fallen comrades, and on one occasion
Catholic clergy apparently refused to officiate at a police funeral.[38] John Regan
confirmed that 'they felt it very keenly when the clergy turned hostile'.[39]
Patrick Marrinan received a personalized death threat when he was CI. Regan
credited him with revitalizing flagging spirits. Marrinan was not trusted by
his superiors but he was satisfied that repressive measures had 'reduced the
IRA to a hunted, cowardly gang of assassins, harried and sleepless'. In July
there had been fifty-seven indictments in Limerick for offences including
murder, armed riot, firing at police with intent, disarming of police and soldiers, arson, raids for arms, robberies of mails, and sending threatening letters, but only thirty-three in August. Marrinan had seemingly 'got rid of the
majority of the old useless men who were not pulling their weight against the
rebels and the latter now feel that we will stand no nonsense'. The 'old useless men' referred to by Marrinan were presumably long-serving members
whose ability or will to perform their duties was undermined by the fact that
they and their families were well known. He encouraged those who had
achieved pensionable service to retire.[40]

Marrinan was less concerned about rampant indiscipline than about the
increasingly antagonistic ITGWU, which he described as a 'Bolshevist–Sinn
Fein organization that was a danger to the state'.[41] As a DI, he had refused
to answer questions at a coroner's inquest into the police shooting of a civil-
ian in the city in May.[42] The police continued to run amok with fatal results.
On 15 August Temporary Constable Cyril Nathan was killed outside Edward
Street barracks. He was almost certainly shot by inebriated fellow Black and
Tans as they engaged in reprisals.[43] As many as 100 houses in Carey's Road

were badly damaged. An ex-soldier, Edward Paget, suffered a fatal beating at the hands of policemen in the nearby People's Park. Marrinan commended his men for their 'discipline and forbearance in a very difficult and exasperating situation'.[44] A meeting of ex-servicemen in the city on 21 August sympathized with Paget's widow and expressed dismay that 'they sacrificed everything ... to crush German militarism and kultur, but that militarism and kultur ... was allowed to be carried on in their own city at the present day.'[45] Government-sanctioned reprisals from late 1920 represented an acknowledgement that discipline had broken down. This attempt to reassert control over police actions backfired spectacularly in respect of propaganda. IRA activity was hampered by the increased numerical strength and transport resources of Crown forces in Limerick at the end of the year. A substantial number of Volunteers were either killed or in custody. The proclamation of martial law on 10 December curtailed the 'street gunmen' of Limerick and weekly police dances helped to improve morale.[46] Generals Tudor and Macready along with Joint Under-Secretary Sir John Anderson were particularly impressed with Regan's performance as CI and with the state of affairs in the city.[47]

The case of Thomas Huckerby reveals Regan's *modus operandi* when dealing with Black and Tans. In William Hall's application to the IGC he described himself as 'an ex-member of the RIC, one of them that had to leave and will not be able to return again'. A policeman in the village of Foynes in west Limerick, Hall had envisaged retiring to nearby Shanagolden and taking a share in his wife's family's grocery shop. Instead, on the disbandment of the RIC in 1922 he fled Ireland in fear of his life. He was relocated to Chadwell Heath in Essex, which was part of the largest public housing estate in the world in the 1920s (at least one other family settled in Chadwell Heath after being boycotted in Limerick).[48] Hall was a central character in some of the most harrowing incidents of the War of Independence in Limerick. On 26 August 1920 Huckerby accompanied Hall from Foynes to Shanagolden, where Crown forces had attempted to burn the creamery the night before. Recklessly, both were unarmed. They were waylaid by Volunteers, then stripped and paraded through the village in their bare feet and underwear before being released. That night, they returned to Shanagolden to restore their honour, reinforced by colleagues from Foynes. Huckerby shot dead a 60-year-old villager. Regan later excused such reprisals as inevitable in view of the experience undergone by Hall and Huckerby.[49] Huckerby was immediately transferred to Abbeyfeale.

On the night of 18/19 September 1920 the West Limerick ASU ambushed a police lorry on the outskirts of Abbeyfeale. Huckerby, the prime target, was not on duty but two other constables were killed. During a spate of Crown reprisals, an 11-year-old girl was shot in the ankle.[50] On 20

1 The Church Lads Brigade forms up in Pery Street, adjacent to the Church of Ireland diocesan hall, *c*.1900. In the background is the Dominican Catholic church, with the chimney of Matterson's bacon factory looming behind it and, to the right, Tait's clock, a tribute to Scottish entrepreneur Peter Tait, owner of the adjacent Limerick Clothing Company and former mayor of Limerick.

2 (*above*) Limerick Young Men's Protestant Association, 97 O'Connell Street, probably around the time of the coronation of Edward VII as king on 9 August 1902. **3** Michael Joyce, MP for Limerick City, 1900–18, during his mayoral term, 1905–6.

4 Labourers at Limerick docks, many of them covered in coal dust after unloading a shipment for use in Bannatyne's mill. Two Royal Navy sailors and a RIC constable stand on the extreme right.

5 (*below, left*) Lord Dunraven. 6 (*below, right*) Notice of the anti-home rule unionist meeting that preceded the riots of October 1912. *Limerick Chronicle*, 8 October 1912.

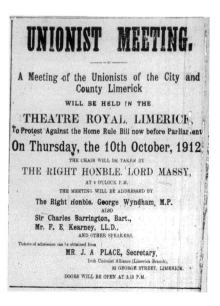

UNIONIST MEETING.

A Meeting of the Unionists of the City and County Limerick

WILL BE HELD IN THE

THEATRE ROYAL, LIMERICK,

To Protest Against the Home Rule Bill now before Parliament

On Thursday, the 10th October, 1912

THE CHAIR WILL BE TAKEN BY

THE RIGHT HONBLE. LORD MASSY,

AT 4 O'CLOCK P.M.

THE MEETING WILL BE ADDRESSED BY

The Right Honble. George Wyndham, M.P.

ALSO

Sir Charles Barrington, Bart.,
Mr. F. E. Kearney, LL.D.,

AND OTHER SPEAKERS.

Tickets of admission can be obtained from

MR. J. A PLACE, Secretary,

Irish Unionist Alliance (Limerick Branch),

92 GEORGE STREET, LIMERICK.

DOORS WILL BE OPEN AT 3.15 P.M.

7 The Barrington family in the grounds of their Glenstal Castle home, *c*.1915. *Left to right*: Charles Jr, Winnie (who was accidentally killed in an IRA ambush in 1921), Lady Mary Rose, Fitzwilliam and Sir Charles.

8 At Na Fianna Éireann hall, 15 Barrington Street, Limerick, *c*.1913. Standing, from left, Joe Halpin, Joe Dalton, unknown, Con Colbert, Seán Heuston, Jack Dalton, Ned Fitzgibbon. Seated, from left, Patrick Whelan, John Daly, James Leddin.

9 (*Above*) A physical culture class at Na Fianna Éireann hall, *c*.1913.
10 (*Below, left*) Irish Volunteers Michael Colivet, Robert Monteith and George Clancy in uniform.
11 Cumann na mBan programme cover for a fête in the Markets Field, Garryowen, 2–3 July 1914.

12 Limerick City Irish Volunteers and Cumann na mBan, *c*.1915. *Front row, left to right*: Mrs Bermingham, Mary Clancy, Miss Downey, Mrs MacCormack, Eileen Crowe, Eileen O'Donoghue, Siún O'Farrell, Madge Daly, Carrie Daly *Back row, left to right*: Ned O'Toole, James O'Driscoll, Alphonsus O'Halloran, John Grant, James Ledden, Liam Forde, George Clancy, David Hennessy, Jimmy Kirby, James MacInerney, Stephen Dineen, Michael Colivet, James Dalton, Patrick Walsh, Robert Monteith.

13 Nine Limerick City Irish Volunteers who camped at Killonan on the night of Easter Sunday/Easter Monday 1916. Judging by his armband and the fact that he is the only one not holding a wooden imitation rifle, the first man on the left may be a medic. Third and fourth from left, with the 'x' marked over their heads, are John MacSweeney and Frederick Kenny. The River Mulkear runs across the background.

14 The Daly family in mourning following the executions of Edward Daly and Tom Clarke, Kathleen Daly's husband, for their roles in the 1916 Rising. Back (*left to right*): Madge, Catherine (mother) and Agnes. Front (*left to right*): Laura, Nora and Carrie.

15 Early February 1917. Limerick people, 'separation wives' probably among them, watch on as the Duchess of Connaught's Own Irish Canadian Rangers march by (out of shot).
16 Early February 1917. A civic welcoming party awaits the Duchess of Connaught's Own Irish Canadian Rangers at City Hall, Limerick. Stephen Quin, centre, with his hands clasped, wears the mayoral chain and ceremonial cocked hat.

17 IRA Volunteer Bobby Byrne's tricolour-draped coffin as his funeral procession turns from William Street on to O'Connell Street, 10 April 1919. Contemporary reports suggested that 20,000 took to the streets to pay their respects. Note the soldiers under 'The Household Bazaar' sign saluting the coffin.

18 (*Bottom, left*) Limerick soviet currency was printed in three denominations: one shilling, five shillings, ten shillings. They carry the inscription around the edges: 'General Strike Against British Militarism. Limerick April 1919', and in the centre: 'The Workers of Limerick Promise to Pay the Bearer [amount] for The Limerick Trades and Labour Council'. They are signed by the chairman and treasurer of the strike committee, John ('Jno') Cronin and James Casey. They are validated by an oval purple 'Mechanics Institute Limerick' stamp with a shamrock at its centre.

19 Con Collins, Sinn Féin TD for West Limerick, 1918–21, and Kerry–Limerick West, 1921–3.

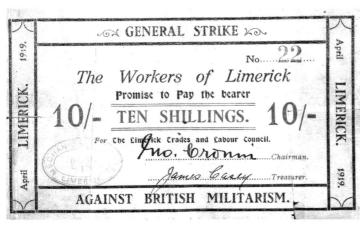

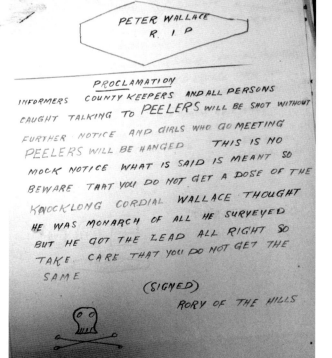

PETER WALLACE
R I P

PROCLAMATION
INFORMERS COUNTY KEEPERS AND ALL PERSONS
CAUGHT TALKING TO PEELERS WILL BE SHOT WITHOUT
FURTHER NOTICE AND GIRLS WHO GO MEETING
PEELERS WILL BE HANGED THIS IS NO
MOCK NOTICE WHAT IS SAID IS MEANT SO
BEWARE THAT YOU DO NOT GET A DOSE OF THE
KNOCKLONG CORDIAL WALLACE THOUGHT
HE WAS MONARCH OF ALL HE SURVEYED
BUT HE GOT THE LEAD ALL RIGHT SO
TAKE CARE THAT YOU DO NOT GET THE
SAME
(SIGNED)
RORY OF THE HILLS

20 IRA Volunteers, Limerick, 1919.
21 An example of IRA intimidation – a public proclamation issued as part of its campaign against the RIC and warning civilians against any association with the police. The hand-drawn coffin bearing a name was originally a sinister Land War motif. Peter Wallace was one of the policemen killed at Knocklong in May 1919. 'Rory of the Hills' was a righter of wrongs in agrarian conflicts in the 1870s. This type of signature had the effect of making the IRA seem omnipresent.

22 Joint RIC–military patrol in Limerick, 1920.
23 The Royal Welsh Fusiliers band and regimental mascot, a white goat, parading outside The Crescent Post Office on Quinlan Street (between O'Connell Avenue and the Crescent), in the direction of the Crescent, 1920.

24 (*Above, left*) Constables Fred Palmer, Harry Beard and Fred Halls, Black and Tans who served at Kilmallock. This photo was obtained by IRA intelligence and the subjects identified.

25 Sinn Féin's Michael O'Callaghan, killed by Crown forces on 7 March 1921.

26 Volunteers arrested by Crown forces at Piggott's safe house, Milltown, Croagh, June 1921. *Left to right*: Michael John Neville, Croagh; farm labourer Bill Sheehy who worked at Piggott's (Sheehy was not a Volunteer and was released soon after this photograph was taken); Timmy Hartigan, Croagh; Jack Neville, Croagh; Jack Farrell, Adare; Jack Hickey, Adare; and Jack Horgan, Adare. These men were released after the truce of 11 July.

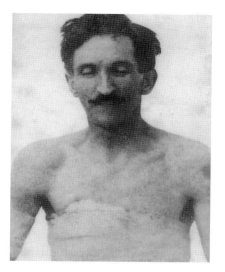

27 (*Above, left*) On 6 May 1921 Seán Wall, brigadier of the East Limerick IRA, chairman of Limerick County Council, was captured by Crown forces and then killed by a shotgun blast while in custody. This photograph of Wall's body was publicly displayed in an effort to establish his identity. 28 (*Above, right*) Seán Wall memorial, Bruff.

29 *Left to right*: Kathleen Clarke of Limerick's Daly family and widow of executed 1916 Rising leader Tom Clarke, Constance Markievicz, who later threatened to turn the IRA on striking Limerick workers, and Professor Kate O'Callaghan, widow of Michael O'Callaghan, on the steps of the Mansion House Dublin after their election as Sinn Féin TDs in May 1921.

30 Banner that read: 'Bruree Workers Soviet Mills – We Make Bread Not Profits', August 1921.

31 'Looting at the Ordnance Barracks. Limk. 7.22.' captures a moment post-ATIRA withdrawal and the burning of the barracks. Looking along Mulgrave Street to the barracks entrance at left; between the entrance and the three youths facing the camera, there is a cart laden with wood; on the extreme right is a man sitting on the shafts of a horse and cart laden with what appears to be a cast iron stove and a machine with a large wheel handle.

32 Post ATIRA–withdrawal, three soldiers and four civilians pose in a breach blasted in the wall of Strand Barracks by NA artillery on 20 July 1922.

33 ATIRA prisoner under guard, County Limerick, 22 July 1922.

34 Injured NA soldier attended to by Red Cross, County Limerick, 25 July 1922.

35 NA troops on the move, early August 1922. A civilian vehicle has been pressed into service (indicating the inadequacy of NA transportation resources), hauling the 18-pounder field gun that was crucial in the opening phase of the Civil War. It appears as if an unsuccessful attempt has been made by the ATIRA to sabotage the bridge.

September Huckerby killed Pat Hartnett and Jeremiah Healy in Abbeyfeale; neither was a Volunteer nor had any political affiliation.[51] Huckerby's rampage bears out Peter Hart's suggestion that 'For a member of the Crown forces seeking a target, almost any young Catholic man might do'.[52] Hartnett was a government employee – a postman – and his mother had been a servant in the local RIC barracks for eighteen years until she was intimidated out of the job that summer. The Hartnetts' subsequent application for financial support from the British state claimed that Huckerby 'left the town that evening to avoid a stronger manifestation of resentment'.[53] Unusually, the military court of inquiry into the killings named Huckerby.[54] There was no hiding behind standard terminology such as 'justifiable homicide' or 'in the course of duty'. Huckerby was transferred to the city 'after getting into trouble', as Regan put it, 'in order that he would be under our eye.' He proceeded to attempt to drown a man in the River Shannon.[55]

In October Huckerby appeared at Limerick Quarter Sessions to seek compensation for the injuries inflicted on him at Shanagolden on 26 August. The 'moral damage' of being publicly degraded had 'a very serious effect' on Huckerby, according to the Crown solicitor. He was awarded £100 compensation.[56] Regan eventually transferred Huckerby back to the police depot in Dublin just days after two civilians had been shot outside Limerick. In November, only hours after ex-soldiers James O'Neill and Patrick Blake were acquitted of killing a Black and Tan in the city in July, O'Neill was blindfolded and shot four times in the head, and James Blake was killed by bullets intended for his brother Patrick. Like Hartnett and Healy, neither had any republican affiliation. Huckerby fitted the physical profile of the ringleader.[57] He resigned from the RIC on 26 December, before unspecified disciplinary charges were pressed.[58] Regan's willingness to tolerate reprisal killings was palpable. Huckerby might well have been 'a public school type ... [with] excellent manners', as Regan described him, but it did not stop him killing at will.[59]

Even after Huckerby departed the scene, this particular cycle of violence continued to run. Tim Madigan was killed by Crown forces near Shanagolden in December. His brother, Willie, was arrested. William Hall was one of the raiding party. He knew the Madigans had been among the IRA who accosted himself and Huckerby in August. Willie later confirmed Hall's account that Tim was shot 'while trying to escape'.[60] In February 1921 the IRA unsuccessfully attempted to hold up a train on which Hall was travelling to Limerick to testify at Madigan's court-martial. Hall claimed that a note found on Brigadier Seán Finn's body in March stated that he (Hall) 'should be shot at sight'. Regan then brought Hall into the city. His wife was left behind in Foynes, where she fell into 'a nervous state of health'. Disbandment did not offer Hall any relief as his life was apparently still under threat.[61]

During 1920 the conflict increasingly assumed a dirty war character. The 'Anti-Sinn Féin Society' announced itself in the press from late summer and claimed responsibility for various attacks, primarily in Cork, but with cameos elsewhere, including Clare, Kerry, Tipperary and Limerick. It presented itself as a secret loyalist society. In reality, the moniker was employed by Crown forces as a cover for unofficial reprisals.[62] On 21 July Limerick city Volunteer Michael Hartney's property was destroyed in an explosion which fatally wounded a civilian. The motive was the false suspicion that Hartney had been involved in the killing in Cork of Divisional Commissioner Lieutenant-Colonel Gerald Smyth, Cecil Prescott-Decie's counterpart in south Munster. A note claiming responsibility read: 'These reprisals against the property and members of the IRA are taken by order of the President of the ASFS', the Anti-Sinn Féin Society.[63] The so-called 'Anti-Murder Gang', another Crown cover, terrorized republican communities with summary killings, such as those of Mayor George Clancy, ex-Mayor Michael O'Callaghan and Volunteer James O'Donoghue in Limerick city on 7 March 1921. On 31 May 1920 the 'Brothers of the Faithful Circle' warned O'Callaghan to 'call the rats off', or they would take 'retribution and vengeance of a drastic measure'.[64] The 'All-Ireland Anti-Sinn Féin Society' convened in Limerick on 13 October 1920. The 'Supreme Council of the Limerick Circle' announced plans to escalate reprisals: for every member of the Crown forces killed, they would kill two Sinn Féiners or three 'sympathisers'.[65] O'Callaghan received a second death notice on 15 October, the source of which his wife Kate convincingly argued was Dublin Castle.[66] Brigadier-General Frank Percy Crozier, who resigned as head of the Auxiliaries in protest at the latitude afforded by senior British officials to his men to commit atrocities, concluded that Clancy and O'Callaghan were 'murdered by the police acting under orders as part of a plan to "do away with" Sinn Féin leaders and put the blame on to Sinn Féin'.[67] George Nathan, an Auxiliary intelligence officer and reputed member of what republicans termed the 'Murder Gang', was the leading gunman. In July the Mid Limerick Brigade requested GHQ to ascertain his whereabouts: they were plotting revenge.[68]

It is likely that extrajudicial killings were unofficial political policy. Prescott-Decie certainly took a cavalier attitude to the use of force that had been approved further up the chain of command.[69] Just weeks later Divisional Commissioner Smyth, in the presence of General Tudor, head of the RIC, and speaking in anticipation of the coercive ROIA, urged the policemen of Listowel, County Kerry, to abandon restraint:

> You may make mistakes and innocent persons may be shot but that cannot be helped and you are bound to get the right parties some time. The more you shoot, the better I will like you, and I assure you no policeman will get into trouble for shooting any man.[70]

Smyth and Tudor were ejected from the barracks. Smyth was subsequently killed by the Cork IRA. The army's senior figure in Limerick, General R.P. Cameron, attempted to hold his subordinates to a higher standard. Three officers – Major Gray, Captain Davis and Lieutenant Loup – were arrested in relation to the death of civilian Richard Leonard at Caherconlish on 31 December 1920. Cameron was satisfied that Gray and Davis (who killed Leonard) were intoxicated during the episode. While the military court of inquiry found that Leonard was fired at to prevent his escape, Cameron concluded that 'There seems to be no reason why, under ordinary circumstances, Leonard should have made a dash for liberty, knowing what the risks would be. I think he must have been affected by his treatment when arrested.'[71] This verdict may well have been applicable to many of those shot 'while trying to escape'.

Police violence continued unchecked but it occasionally caused serious embarrassment for the government. The killings of Clancy and O'Callaghan in Limerick received international attention. Then, on 17 April 1921 Auxiliaries and Black and Tans engaged in a shootout in a Castleconnell hotel. One of each was killed, along with the hotel owner. A witness told the military court of inquiry that the hotelier was put up against a wall and shot. The anti-war activist and Conservative peer, Sir Charles Cripps, Lord Parmoor, highlighted the shootings in Westminster. His brother had been staying in the hotel and witnessed the Auxiliaries rampaging 'like demented Red Indians'. The Lords glossed it over and the military court found no breach of discipline. Commander-in-chief Macready concluded that such situations occurred in war from time to time. The comments of one of his adjutants were even more revealing, and are pertinent to the broader question of the role of ancillary policemen, both Auxiliaries and Black and Tans, in the War of Independence:

> They all had the wind up, blood up, and did what they used to do in the trenches in France. In the circumstances you cannot hold them criminally responsible, but they are not fit to be policemen – but are any Auxiliaries?[72]

December 1920 and January 1921 were disastrous months for the Limerick IRA, during which twelve Volunteers died. In response, eleven policemen were killed at Dromkeen on 3 February. East and Mid Limerick conducted the operation, with Donnchadh O'Hannigan in command. It was second only to Tom Barry's Kilmichael ambush in November 1920 in terms of the number of fatalities suffered by the Crown forces. Whereas three of Barry's men were killed, there were no IRA losses at Dromkeen. The attackers capitalized on detailed intelligence regarding police movements. A convoy of two lorries under DI Sanson travelled from Pallasgrean to Fedamore and back on the same day each month with pay and supplies. Unwisely, it always took the same route. On the day of the ambush, the lorries disregarded another standard procedure by driving closely together and were trapped in the firing zone.[73] The assault was ferocious and swift. The medical evidence from the court of inquiry makes for grisly reading and false rumours circulated that some of the corpses had been mutilated.[74] Heavy firing and bombing resulted in a scene of terrible carnage. When the bodies were searched, some of their bandoliers had to be cut off because they were 'immersed in human flesh'. In preparation, O'Hannigan apparently urged his colleagues to 'Kill them without pity, without mercy'.[75] Maurice Meade may have killed as many as seven men at Dromkeen, two of whom he shot in cold-blooded execution-style killings. Volunteer Thomas Moynihan described hearing one man plead for his life and O'Hannigan reply 'Dead men tell no tales'.[76] Visceral emotion dictated that there would be no reprieve, only vengeance.[77]

In the wake of the devastating Christmas and New Year period, Dromkeen came at a vital juncture for the Limerick IRA. To an even greater extent than barracks attacks, the psychological effect of successful ambushes exceeded their military significance, profoundly affecting the public consciousness. The vast majority of intended attacks simply failed to materialize, mostly due to the non-appearance of the Crown forces, faulty intelligence or flawed technique. Bad luck could also be a factor: civilians might stumble into a prepared ambush site forcing abandonment. An effective operation resulted in an influx of troops into the locality, thereby neutralizing the potential for further guerrilla activity. Ambushes became more difficult to accomplish as British counter-measures improved. Journey times and routes were varied; cycle and single-lorry patrols were abandoned in favour of heavily armed convoys; hedges and trees that might have provided cover for ambushers were removed, and hostages were used as deterrents. Crown forces in Limerick carried both civilians and Volunteers as human shields from December 1920 to March 1921.[78] The IRA, on the other hand, was rarely in a position to hold prisoners for extended periods. As well as putting safe houses at risk, it was not convenient for a guerrilla army to expend time and manpower on guarding and moving subjects. Brigadier-General C.H.T. Lucas, for instance, was captured in June 1920 in the North Cork Brigade area. The most senior Crown officer to fall into the hands of the IRA, his month-long detention was a propaganda coup. According to his own staff, no music-hall programme in London was complete without a joke at his expense.[79] Lucas's custody, however, was a major burden. He was passed between brigades in Cork and Clare, as well as the three Limerick brigades before he was deliberately presented with the opportunity to escape.[80]

The West Limerick Brigade killed six members of the Crown forces between March and September 1920, but the failure to seize arms ruled out large-scale actions. In the city, four policemen and one soldier were killed in

1920. Mid Limerick had also been involved in four barracks attacks with mixed results. Outside of the city, no member of the Crown forces was killed in Mid Limerick territory. Four barracks attacks yielded mixed results. Eleven members of the Crown forces were killed in East Limerick, which also suffered the highest number of fatalities. This pattern continued in 1921. In January brigades from Cork and Tipperary met with the East Limerick Brigade to discuss the formation of a divisional unit. The inactivity of Limerick city, 'where possibly 400 rifles are lying idle', was noted. There was seething discontent in East Limerick about the perceived ineptitude of Mid and West Limerick. East Limerick even contemplated raiding Mid Limerick 'for the big number of guns which they never lent to us ... they were never used.'[81] Jack MacCarthy, claiming that Mid and West Limerick were 'a danger to us in our operations', suggested to Seán Wall that several of their battalions be co-opted into East Limerick and GHQ considered such a move.[82] O'Hannigan and Malone divided the expanding East Limerick ASU into two. In March, under orders from GHQ to go to West Limerick 'to put things going there', O'Hannigan's fifty riflemen rendezvoused with Seán Finn's unit of twenty-five. From the start of 1921 it was rare for small Crown patrols to venture outside garrisoned towns. Finn, whose leadership credentials were questioned in some quarters, needed assistance to confront any bigger force because his unit only had eighteen rifles, nine of them outdated Lee Enfields.[83] East Limerick saw an opportunity to divert attention from its own territory but Finn was killed on 30 March and most of the West Limerick ASU spent the next six weeks in East Limerick, hiding from enemy sweeps. The pressure under which the columns were operating was revealed when O'Hannigan's prohibition of alcohol was infringed on the return march to east Limerick. One drunken Volunteer even managed to shoot himself in the foot.[84]

After Finn's death, there was disquiet among East Limerick veterans about whether mixing ASUs was good practice, but deadly mistakes were repeated.[85] On 1 and 2 May an unwieldy East, Mid and West Limerick conglomeration incurred eight fatalities. The British army *Gazette* lauded 'the finest show in Ireland up to date' but the incidents also highlighted shortcomings in IRA leadership. Amid much recrimination, Ernie O'Malley suggested that Liam Forde was 'not fit' to command an ASU.[86] Belatedly, many Volunteers were instructed to return to their localities.[87] Combined with incessant enemy pursuit, a scarcity of ammunition and the logistical difficulties inherent in housing, feeding and coordinating large numbers, the events of early May copper-fastened the decision to stand-down brigade ASUs in favour of battalion ASUs. This involved fundamental changes in organization, tactics and operations. The intention was to facilitate simultaneous attacks in different areas but the smaller units were poorly coordinated and prone to factionalism. Neither did they have the resources necessary for engagements.

There was no reconciliation between the feuding city IRA units before Richard Mulcahy officially suspended the 1st Battalion in 1919; in reality it had ceased to function long before. Relations reached a nadir when members of the 2nd Battalion shot and killed the 1st Battalion's James Dalton as a spy in May 1920. When Forde became brigadier of Mid Limerick in February 1921, he remonstrated with Mulcahy about manpower shortages and formed the mistaken impression that he earned GHQ's 'good will and respect'.[88] The two city battalions eventually amalgamated in the spring of 1921. Discord then emerged in the 4th Battalion, however, after Commandant Richard O'Connell was captured in March.[89] In June an East Limerick Brigade report noted that the organization of O'Connell's battalion remained 'deficient, and will continue so until it is found possible to transfer suitable officers from the other B[attalio]ns'.[90] These tensions flared fully on his release after the truce when Mid Limerick's non-city battalions pledged to form an independent brigade if the fight resumed. Eoin O'Duffy, the investigating officer from GHQ, concluded that disaffected non-city officers were attempting to undermine the city battalion staff. The core issue seems to have been dissatisfaction with the performance of the city before the truce. The perceived favouritism shown to the city in the distribution of arms was a persistent grievance. O'Duffy was satisfied with the performance of the city battalion since its unification in April: '5 or 6 bomb attacks were carried out, resulting in from 15 to 20 casualties to the enemy.' There had been a flurry of attacks, but O'Duffy exaggerated their impact. He disparaged the fighting record of O'Connell's battalion and questioned their courage. On the question of arms, the 'very unselfish' city also fulfilled his expectations. But while the old 2nd Battalion had transferred weapons to the brigade ASU, the dormant 1st Battalion had stored guns without making them available to their active colleagues.[91]

The result of the four years of 'jealousy and bitterness', according to O'Malley, was that the city 'did not seem to ruffle the surface of enemy occupation'. Jack MacCarthy also poured scorn on what he characterized as the city's inexcusable idleness.[92] The escalation in activity from April was spurred primarily by the killings of 7 March. The extra rifles were not used in the new wave of attacks (urban warfare required the use of revolvers at close quarters and hand-thrown bombs). Neither was city reunification the main impetus, because the old 2nd Battalion remained almost unilaterally front and centre. Outside the city, an attack by the Mid Limerick ASU under Forde on Black and Tans in Fedamore on 13 April killed one and wounded three. With good reason, Mulcahy was highly critical of the seemingly slovenly planning and queried 'why the whole patrol should not have been got'.[93]

Dromkeen was the last hurrah of the Limerick ASUs. In 1921 IRA tactics changed from extensive attacks to smaller, more frequent operations requiring fewer resources and less risk. The Crown forces limited their exposure. The trenching of roads and sabotage of bridges to interrupt the movement of the Crown forces, which had begun in Limerick in March, was endemic in the county in May and June. Access to transportation was vital for the IRA and bicycles, motorcycles and cars were regularly commandeered. A pattern of recurring destruction and reconstruction of bridges and roads was interrupted when the police introduced booby traps.[94] On 22 May West Limerick Volunteer Patrick O'Brien was killed by a booby trap when reopening a filled-in trench near Rathkeale and on 26 May East Limerick Volunteer Con Ryan was killed felling a tree for a roadblock near Cappamore. Ryan's hastily-buried body was 'raised' by Crown forces two weeks after his death. His sister had to view the corpse in Pallasgrean barracks but she 'denied' him to avoid reprisals. He was buried in the family plot after the truce.[95] IRA reports noted that British patrols travelled more slowly because of injuries sustained in crashes caused by trenching.[96] Yet CI Regan's claim that trenching did not stop his men from driving at high speed suggests that the threat of ambush preyed heavily on their minds.[97] Infrastructural damage was frustrating for civilians and created tensions between the IRA and prospective supporters. Local popula-tions were disrupted, especially farmers who had livestock and produce to move. Furthermore, these tactics often resulted in reprisals against civilians. People often preferred to pay a levy to the IRA rather than risk Crown forces burning their homes. One individual who informed the British about an obstruction and refused to pay the fine imposed had his pony and cart seized. Another man fell foul of the IRA for cutting down a large tree that he believed the IRA intended to use in an ambush. He was forced to pay a fine of £150.[98]

Ernie O'Malley's accounts of operational matters in East Limerick in June 1921 are uncomplimentary, although he was a notorious taskmaster. There were few maps, books or training manuals, and no schedule of organization. A memorandum admitted that 'it has been found difficult to obtain suitable officers for the Engineering Service and classes are not yet organised'.[99] There were no bombs or musketry, no signalling or scouting training. Communi-cations were haphazard and there was a lack of cooperation between some units, with fatal consequences: Caherconlish company did not forward cap-tured reports quickly enough with the result that a Volunteer was killed in Tipperary. O'Malley believed that some of the senior officers were sub-stan-dard. He was also concerned about 'people talking too much'. The situation was 'bad enough' in Mid Limerick where Volunteers 'did not clean their rifles, do guard duty or any wartime work and were generally undisciplined … roads are not trenched and there is no activity to make one realise there is a war on.' Nonetheless, O'Malley pressed the development of a piece of light artillery by Bob de Courcy for the purpose of firing missiles at barracks or lorries. Constructed around the time of the truce, it exploded during a test, injuring de Courcy.[100]

Lurking in the shadows of the confrontation between the IRA and Crown forces was the intelligence war. IRA GHQ demanded information not only on the military and police but on all who aided the 'machinery of oppression', including anyone who transacted business or 'fraternized' with Crown forces, such as 'girls going with peelers or enemy military'.[101] Hunted, mindful of historical examples and wary of British know-how, the IRA saw spies and informers everywhere. Forde warned O'Malley that 'there were many spies, touts and secret-service agents' in Limerick.[102] The Mid Limerick Brigade sought counsel from GHQ on how to deal with individuals who associated with the enemy, 'a pretty common practice', but against whom there was no explicit proof of spying. GHQ advised that such suspects should be warned to desist or face punishment.[103] There were so many potential spies, 'every Tom, Dick and Harry', that a sliding scale of intervention was devised:

> 1st offence a warning, 2nd offence a fine + if repeated that death will be the penalty, and if the association continues, this penalty should be inflicted without further evidence i.e. after the usual formalities have been gone through.[104]

Republican fears were not just paranoia. A number of Volunteers were killed on foot of 'specific information' provided to British intelligence services.[105] The 6th Division's 'Blacklists' illustrate the efficiency of Lieutenant Harold Browne in Kilmallock, among others. The Limerick Blacklist profiled, in comprehensive detail, sixty-nine members of the East Limerick Brigade.[106] Several IRA attempts to assassinate Browne failed but his RIC liaison, James Maguire, was killed. Lieutenant John Basil Jarvis was the intelligence officer for the Oxford and Buckinghamshire Light Infantry deployed in Limerick city from 1920. He was based in the Strand Barracks. His dossier is remarkable for its candid portrayals, including of himself: 'a great ruffian capable of doing anybody or anything, rides an antiquated Douglas motor cycle.' Volunteer Daniel Moloney was 'S.F. Stormtroops. ... 5' 10". Dark complexion, black curly hair, dark moustache, rather prominent chin, brown eyes, farmer.' 'Account closed' meant that a subject had been killed.[107]

Michael O'Meara, an ex-soldier, was shot as a spy in late 1920 and his corpse labelled accordingly. This was a typically grim ending for those found guilty by IRA court-martial of an offence 'against the life of the Nation', usually involving 'the communication to the enemy of information concerning the work of personnel of the Army or of the Civil Administration of the Republic'. Described in republican testimony as 'a constant drunkard' who would 'sell his soul for drink', O'Meara socialized with Crown forces and accompanied them on raids. A member of Kilmallock UDC was outraged when the White Cross forwarded £13 to O'Meara's family, his wife and eight children being deemed guilty by association: 'it was an awful thing that if after all the fine blood that had been spilled they were going to support spies' dependents'.[108] The intelligence war was brutal, especially in Munster. The Cork IRA was particularly unforgiving. At a minimum, it put 65 civilians to death for allegedly colluding with Crown forces. Sixteen people died in this manner in Tipperary, eight in Kerry, seven in Limerick, three in Clare and one in Waterford. Fewer people suffered this fate in the other twenty-six counties combined. There were twenty-one Protestants among those executed in Cork, five in Tipperary and two in Kerry. All of those executed in Limerick, Clare and Waterford were Catholics.[109]

A basic profile of the seven men executed by the Limerick IRA for alleged informing – Denis Crowley, Patrick Daly, James Dalton, Michael O'Meara, John O'Grady, James Boland and John Moloney – allows us to contextualize their deaths and to characterize the intelligence war.[110] A significant volume of IRA testimony indicates that Patrick Daly was providing important information to the Crown forces and was in their pay.[111] James Dalton was a Volunteer of the 1st Battalion, Mid Limerick Brigade. IRA members suspected of informing were usually granted a reprieve and of nearly 200 civilians executed as spies by the IRA during these years, as few as four came from within its own ranks.[112] Dalton's demise is illustrative of the kind of local intrigue and spite in which many cases of putative spying were shrouded but it was also exceptional. Dalton was never court-martialled and was not formally executed. Instead, he was ambushed by members of the city's rival 2nd Battalion despite the fact that he had already been acquitted of the charge of spying by a Dáil inquiry. He was exonerated again posthumously by a GHQ investigation. Undone by his weakness for alcohol and his naiveté, in the febrile atmosphere of 1919–20 Dalton's socializing with an RIC detective aroused intense suspicion and the simmering rancour between the 1st and 2nd Battalions proved deadly for him. On 15 May 1920 he was shot six times by multiple assassins. Though his name was officially cleared, in 1966 Dan Breen took up Dalton's cause and suggested that a conspiracy designed to conceal wrongdoing by 'high up' republicans surrounded his killing. Dalton's family held the Dalys responsible. Mired in half-truths and hidden agendas, his case encapsulates the murkiness of the intelligence war.[113]

Probably the most contentious charge laid against the IRA is that accusations of spying frequently served as a mere pretext for the persecution and murder of Protestants and former British soldiers, the real motivation being sectarian or social or antagonism. The charge of sectarianism is not relevant to Limerick but five of the seven victims were ex-soldiers, namely Crowley, O'Meara, O'Grady, Boland and Moloney. Such a disproportionate figure gives rise to a number of questions. Why were ex-soldiers targeted to such a degree? Were denunciations genuine? Commenting on Boland's case, CI

Regan reported that 'The campaign against loyal ex-soldiers has been notice-able here':

> I regret that I cannot afford these gallant fellows the protection which they deserve at my hands for their continuous loyalty after participat-ing in the Great War. It would seem that the ex-soldier must be with the IRA or else be regarded as an enemy ... The murder of this class of person has a bad effect on the population as they are all intimidated by an act of this kind from expressing their opinion and from any open display of loyalty.[114]

The IRA accumulated incontrovertible evidence that Crowley was a spy.[115] O'Meara, O'Grady and Boland were in obvious contravention of IRA rules governing interaction with Crown forces.[116] The Moloney case seems highly dubious, however. Moloney was a civil bill processer in the British justice system. Anecdotal evidence suggests that a grudge pertaining to this work, which involved serving writs, may have been the decisive factor in his death. The East Limerick Brigade, however, was considering charges of spying against him in June. IRA sources assert that he was shot when he tried to escape from custody: 'The man who shot him only wanted to wound him. It was a pity he did not stand trial. Even if he were guilty, which was not certain, the Truce ... would have saved him.' This claim about preventing an escape eerily echoes numerous British statements and is contradicted by medical evidence that Moloney was shot from above while stooping or kneeling.[117] The Cork IRA executed two ex-soldiers from Cork near Kilmallock.[118]

The social status of victims is another relevant factor. Jane Leonard describes ex-servicemen as 'the softest of targets' and Peter Hart concurs that the likelihood of a suspect being executed 'depended upon one's position within the community'. John Borgonovo does not subscribe to the notion of ex-soldiers as 'soft targets' but concluded that 'Faced with numerous cases of local complicity with the Crown forces, the [Cork] city's IRA leadership prob-ably found it easiest to assassinate isolated men of low social standing'.[119] O'Meara was an isolated and financially insecure figure who perhaps sought companionship from soldiers and policemen as well as monetary reward. Moloney's professional life may have made him something of a social pariah. Boland had lost an arm fighting in France. Like O'Grady, he was living in straitened circumstances and closely resembles the archetypal down-and-out ex-soldier. There are allusions to each of the seven men as having a depend-ence on alcohol. This had a variety of implications and affected them in dif-ferent ways: in their private lives, in their professional lives and finances, in their social lives and, crucially, in their decision-making.

IRA intelligence capabilities should not be underestimated. There was concern for fair judicial process and weight of evidence. The threshold of guilt and the criteria for punishment could be capricious, however, and in some exceptional instances, 'spy' or 'informer' was a label of convenience. IRA justice was not blind and not everyone was equal before IRA law. Their standing as ex-soldiers seems to have made some suspects more rather than less guilty in IRA eyes, and the low social station of victims probably contributed to the public acceptability of certain killings. In the region of 4,000 Limerick men enlisted in the British army between 1914 and 1918. More than 1,000 Limerick men died in the war. It is possible that 3,000 ex-British soldiers were living in Limerick in 1920–1. Many were unemployed, perhaps struggling to recover from their experiences in the trenches and to reintegrate into society. Unwanted and vulnerable, some were ripe for manipulation by intelligence services. But Crown forces also killed seven ex-British soldiers and one ex-Canadian soldier in Limerick. None were members of the IRA. One was accidentally killed by police fire during an IRA attack on Auxiliaries but the other seven deaths occurred in more contentious circumstances. Did Crown forces associate ex-soldiers generally with the IRA if they did not actively demonstrate their continuing loyalty, and target them on the basis of that perceived failing? Ex-soldiers found themselves in the impossible position of having to prove their allegiance or their innocence to two belligerent factions.

Another ex-soldier who fell foul of the IRA was Thomas Hanley of Newcastle West. He was in his mid-teens when he joined the Royal Munster Fusiliers in 1915. He joined the Auxiliaries in late 1920 and served with them until February 1921. He survived an IRA attempt on his life in Newcastle West in June 1921. Several other ex-soldiers left Newcastle West after this shooting. On 10 October Hanley appeared before a court in Limerick and was awarded £550 in respect of his injuries. He disappeared on 17 October and was never seen again. His passport, ticket to New York and £550 remained untouched. Garret McAuliffe, speaking to Ernie O'Malley some decades later, referred to Hanley in rather cryptic terms: 'we kept an eye on him, but after the Truce he went missing'. In 1929 Michael Hanley was granted legal liberty to presume the death of his son. Michael believed the rumours he heard in late 1921 that Thomas had been killed by the IRA in Cork and buried there.[120] There had been some history of ill-will between the IRA and ex-soldiers in Newcastle West. In January 1920, in the aftermath of the inauguration of the new town council, there were violent clashes between republicans and ex-soldiers. 'A mob of British soldiers were robbing and looting', according to McAuliffe, and the RIC 'did not do any duty'. The town commissioners established a 'vigilance committee'. When ex-soldiers confronted the vigilantes, one of their number was shot in the arm.[121] McAuliffe fired the shot after 'they tried to knife me'.[122] Hanley had initially given evidence against men charged for their role in these events but rescinded his testimony in court.[123] In April 1920 the Limerick Ex-Servicemen's Association, representing discharged and demobilized soldiers, repudiated and distanced themselves from a series of robberies that had occurred around the county.[124] Ex-soldiers suffered not only at the hands of republicans of course; in September 1920, for instance, a deputation of ex-servicemen in the city found it necessary to call on the military to demand protection from Black and Tans.[125]

Extraordinary chance twice saved civilian Patrick Gorman from execution. Gorman betrayed Volunteer William Slattery, who was killed in police custody. Gorman's court-martial was concerned too with offences against the moral 'life of the Nation' and Gorman was also found guilty of living 'with a woman to whom he was not married', an offence for which he was liable to be flogged. He was sentenced to death.[126] On 23 March a military patrol intercepted the Volunteer party escorting Gorman to the execution site. A faulty revolver scuppered an attempt to shoot him. Volunteer Ned Crawford, who was due to be a defence witness in an upcoming trial concerning the killing of policemen during the Knocklong rescue in 1919, was fatally wounded. His family subsequently claimed that he was recognized and deliberately targeted to prevent him testifying.[127] Gorman, meanwhile, escaped in the confusion. After recapture Gorman was shot, labelled as a spy and assumed dead. But the ammunition used was defective. He crawled to his sister's home nearby and she deposited him with the Crown forces, who took him into protective custody. Gorman was awarded £1,100 in damages at the Tipperary assizes in October 1921 and subsequently emigrated.[128]

Michael Connery from Kilfinane was another spy who got away. He told his own tale of life as an informer to the IGC:

> I was arrested [by the IRA in late 1920] on the charge of being in communication with British forces in Ireland. I was court-martialled and sentenced to be shot which was commuted to deportation for 3 years and went to Liverpool but I returned in about 15 months and was fired at and had to return to England with a larger number of pellets in my body – where I remained until July 1924 ... having my premises searched by the Irish Volunteers I wrote the military at Kilfinane giving the names of the parties – one of the letters fell into their hands and Volunteers dressed in British military uniforms called at my house and represented themselves as British soldiers and being thus deceived I gave them further information.

Connery's narrative is remarkably similar in detail to many IRA accounts of dealings with suspected informers. Furthermore, he was 'looked after' by the

RIC depot at Liverpool and cared for in the city's Royal Infirmary. He received aid from both the Southern Irish Loyalists Relief Association and the IGC, during which time, 'and in accordance with the usual practice', 'periodical reports were obtained from the local Constabulary'.[129] Comparable support structures were probably put in place for Patrick Gorman and others in similar positions.

Women found guilty of spying were ordered to leave the country within seven days, although it was hoped that the fear of being publicly shamed would discourage prospective female spies. 'Only consideration of her sex prevent[ed] the infliction of the statutory punishment of death' on convicted women.[130] They were more likely to have their hair cut off than to be shot. The execution of women by the IRA was a rarity and did not occur in Limerick, although there were numerous female suspects. Some were exiled while others were burned out of their homes. The IRA took measures to discourage 'fraternization':

> Some young girls created a problem. The British uniform was an attraction for them, as indeed would any uniform. They could be a real danger to the movement and gave bad example by consorting with the enemy. They were warned repeatedly and stronger measures had to be resorted to. No Volunteer liked the job, but on occasion these girls' hair had to be cut.[131]

CI Regan described one such woman as 'a pitiable sight'.[132] Crown forces also employed this tactic against women: a Black and Tan cut off Agnes Daly's hair.[133] The commanding officers of the 6th Division believed that that their men were especially attractive to Irish women and that anti-fraternization measures were inspired by jealousy because republicans 'had to fall back on sour-faced, and disaffected Old Maids, whom no decent person would be seen near.'[134] When Charles Barrington's daughter, Winifred, was accidentally killed in an ambush in Tipperary involving members of the Mid Limerick Brigade in May 1921, the *Irish Bulletin* declared that 'British officers engaged in this war have no right to go about accompanied by ladies' and were 'directly responsible for any harm that may unhappily befall [women] in the event of an attack. This is the rule in all wars.'[135] In the intelligence war, however, each side set its own arbitrary standards.

In the first week of July three policemen were killed in two IRA attacks in East Limerick. On 8 July Mid Limerick made a long-planned attack on the military near Killonan. An ambitious, large-scale ambush on a military convoy, scheduled weeks in advance by a combined West Limerick and North Cork force, was set to take place at Barnagh, between Newcastle West and Abbeyfeale, on 8 July. When the patrol passed earlier than expected, the return journey became the target. On 9 July a notice appeared in the local press announcing that a truce had been agreed, to begin at noon on 11 July. This was the first that the Limerick IRA had heard of the matter. Clearly, their fighting potential had not been exhausted. On that very night, in fact, an RIC man came under fire in Kilmallock. On 10 July the 2nd West Limerick Battalion, perhaps seeking to settle old scores, attempted in vain to engage the police in Abbeyfeale. At Barnagh, meanwhile, the attackers lay in wait until close to noon on 11 July before dismantling their ambush preparations. The Crown patrol returned shortly after the truce had officially come into effect. The rival forces encountered each other but no violence ensued.[136]

Whole tracts of rural Limerick had been rendered ungovernable for the British authorities. But Crown forces maintained heavily fortified strongholds in all population centres and would not be dislodged. The IRA were under severe pressure, but this was a constant condition. They had lived from hand to mouth, from ambush to ambush, and would continue to do so unless the British resorted to a level of warfare that was not a realistic option in the circumstances. The prospect of prolonging a costly war and further domestic and international embarrassment was not an enticing one for the British government. The mobilization of colonial resources contributed to Britain's success in the 1914–18 war, but fissures in the imperial structure were revealed. Britain was no longer on an active war footing in 1921 and was distracted from events on its doorstep by its involvement in a range of conflicts from Silesia to Siberia and from Asia Minor to the Middle East. It was more concerned with its unprecedented international military commitments, combined with the mess of insurgencies elsewhere in the Empire, than with what it regarded as the malcontents of the illegitimate Dáil Éireann and the murderers of the IRA. These weaknesses made it amenable to compromise. The truce represented an acknowledgment by both sides that they had reached a stalemate, a military impasse. Political compromise was a natural end to a war that was neither won nor lost by fighting alone. But the truce was a clear propaganda victory for the rebels because it amounted to a formal agreement between equals and bestowed legitimacy on the IRA as a belligerent army. None of this necessarily amounted to a republic, however, and here lay the germ of the Irish Civil War.

7 'The people of Limerick want food, wages and work – not war': Civil War, 1922–3

During the second half of 1921, between the announcement of the truce on 11 July and the publication of the Articles of Agreement for the Treaty between Great Britain and Ireland on 7 December, the republican movement consolidated control over Limerick city and county. The functioning of the counter-state's courts improved steadily and its local authorities began to reduce their financial deficits. Despite internal fissures and military frustrations, Limerick's IRA had remained intact and fought a successful War of Independence. Its strength was enhanced in the wake of the truce and training camps were conducted. Morale was high but some Limerick Volunteers seemed determined to flaunt an image of victory as brashly as possible. Behind the public arrogance lay uncertainty about the outcome of ongoing peace negotiations in London, however, and a deterioration in IRA discipline occurred nationally. Con Cregan, editor of the *Limerick Leader*, the first secretary of the Limerick City Volunteers and a loyal Redmondite, lost the run of himself somewhat in heralding the truce. He was buoyant to be leaving behind 'the dead and disastrous past': 'God grant that it is the prelude to a long period of song and dance and brotherly love, and that the reign of bloodshed is ended'. After republicans took 'decided objection' to his tone, he rowed back from his 'unintentional indiscretion' and emphasized that 'the history of this Journal is well known as a staunchly Nationalist one'.[1] Cregan had unwittingly revealed his real attitude to the War of Independence but the truce was greeted with almost universal enthusiasm. Disunity quickly followed news of the terms of the Treaty, however. Pro-Treatyites contended that it granted Ireland a degree of liberty that could be used as a stepping-stone towards full freedom. Anti-Treatyites objected primarily to the fact that the ideal of an Irish republic had been compromised. Limerick's newspapers employed their substantial local influence in support of the Treaty, as did both the Catholic Church and the Church of Ireland but there was no consensus among politicians. Dáil Éireann began to debate the Treaty on 14 December. Limerick County Council's last act of 1921 was to call on the Dáil to do everything possible to arrive at a unanimous decision.[2] The gesture proved futile.

The Dáil endorsed the Treaty on 7 January 1922, but only by 64 votes to 57. Anti-Treatyite Liam Manahan asserted that Liam Hayes, his local Dáil TD for Limerick City–Limerick East and a member of the East Limerick Brigade staff, had opposed the Treaty until his parish priest convinced him otherwise.[3] The fact that the debate extended over the Dáil Christmas break, however, was perhaps even more important. The encounter that Limerick TDs had with local public opinion at this stage probably influenced some to ratify the Treaty when they might otherwise have opposed it.[4] No polling took place in the general election for Southern Ireland's House of Commons under the 1920 Government of Ireland Act on 24 May 1921. All 128 SF candidates were unopposed and formed the 2nd Dáil. The four seats in the new Limerick City–Limerick East constituency were filled by Liam Hayes and Richard Hayes, who subsequently voted for the Treaty, and Michael Colivet and Kate O'Callaghan, who voted against it. The same four deputies were returned in the 1922 general election, again all unopposed. In the eight-seat Kerry–Limerick West constituency, most of the representatives also had impeccable pre-1921 republican credentials. Five of the eight rejected the Treaty, namely Con Collins, Austin Stack, Patrick Cahill of the 1st Kerry Brigade, and Thomas O'Donoghue and Edmund Roche, both of whom were first elected in 1921. The three pro-Treatyites were Rising veteran Piaras Béaslaí, War of Independence veteran James Crowley and Fionán Lynch of the National army (NA). All eight retained their seats without challenge in 1922. Of the eight, only Collins's primary affiliation would have been with the Limerick section of the constituency.

It was not the split in the Dáil that caused the Civil War, of course, but the rift within the IRA. Even if the Dáil had unanimously accepted the Treaty, there would probably have been some resistance to civil authority by sections of the IRA. Previous attempts by the Dáil during the War of Independence to bring the army fully under its control had not been completely successful. There was no tradition of political control of militant republicanism, and, ultimately, the IRA was beholden to itself alone. The majority of the Mid Limerick Brigade went anti-Treaty, but there was a significant pro-Treaty minority in and around the city. East Limerick was almost exclusively pro-Treaty while West Limerick was predominantly anti-Treaty. Opposing protagonists retrospectively acknowledged that control of Limerick was fundamental to the outcome of the Civil War. From the NA perspective, the city was strategically important to ensure that commands in Clare and Athlone did not become isolated from one another; the River Shannon served as a barrier as well as a means of access between the south and west. The NA in Limerick and Clare severed the so-called 'Munster republic' in Cork and Kerry from other strong anti-Treaty areas to the north and west. These were crucial factors in the NA winning the war. Civil war was not on the horizon when, just days into the truce, 'enemy troops invited Galbally IRA to a football match'.[5] This apparent bonhomie was short-lived. RIC violence against civilians resumed within days and IRA–RIC shooting started again in early September, although there would be no lethal incident in the county until mid-December. Both sides recorded almost daily 'breaches' of the truce by the other.[6] In August the Limerick police remarked perceptively on a dilemma facing republicans:

> if the attitude of passive resistance is hereinafter adopted, they have an excellent groundwork for carrying on. If, however, arms are again resorted to, the practice of open show of arms etc., will lead only to the ruination of the IRA forces.[7]

The transition from secret, self-contained guerrilla warfare to peacetime activities posed disciplinary problems for the IRA. Volunteers who had been on the run donned uniforms and socialized ostentatiously. At a dance in Caherconlish on 13 August Volunteers 'were drunk and brandished revolvers and automatics'.[8] Richard Mulcahy was alarmed by an allegation that in 'nearly the whole of west Limerick there was universal drinking among Volunteers'.[9] In November armed men seized documents from post office officials that supposedly proved the falsification of betting telegraphs at Kilmallock. GHQ ordered an inquiry into whether Volunteers were involved. It did not seem to be the raid or related threatening letters that worried GHQ, for these were not unusual IRA activities, so much as the illegal gambling, which they took as a sign of disintegrating discipline.[10] On 26 September an off-duty policeman sustained bullet wounds in the city.[11]

The truce provided the IRA with an opportunity to take stock. In August 1921 only 59 per cent of Limerick city men were rated as 'reliable' by divisional command, although 85 per cent of former 2nd Battalion men were thought of as solid performers.[12] In November, out of a total roll of 1,458 Volunteers in Mid Limerick, only 977, or 67 per cent, were deemed dependable, while in the wake of Richard O'Connell's threatened mutiny, a phenomenal thirteen of thirty-eight officers had been suspended.[13] Eoin O'Duffy had recommended that O'Connell, Seán Clifford and Seán Carroll be 'expelled from the army with ignominy' for disobeying GHQ.[14] The effectiveness of O'Duffy's approach can be deduced from a follow-up report detailing the recruiting of a suspended company into a new unit organized by suspended men.[15] Typical of the twists of the time, O'Connell and Clifford later forgave GHQ for their suspensions and joined the NA. Carroll was part of Mid-Limerick's anti-Treaty majority. An important factor was that IRA officers who were imprisoned automatically lost their rank. This was the situation in which O'Connell and Carroll found themselves at the time of the 'revolt'. Positions on offer from the IFS were tempting.

The remains of a number of IRA Volunteers, buried in rushed circumstances, were reinterred in family plots from September. As a procession for

William O'Riordan and Thomas Howard, killed at Lackelly in May, passed Hospital RIC barracks on route to Ballylanders, police photographed Donnchadh O'Hannigan. Volunteers entered the barracks and destroyed the photographic plates.[16] Paddy Ryan Waller and John Frahill, the other men killed at Lackelly, were buried in Murroe on 4 October. Some 2,000 Volunteers marshalled a procession of 15,000. Liam Forde's prescient graveside oration warned that 'it would be unwise for us to let our hopes rise too high now.'[17] Mid Limerick reported that 'the main aim of the RIC seems to be to revert to civil life as far as possible ... some individuals in the force ... are still bullying. The military are pursuing their usual activities in peace time but are not excessively active.'[18] On 7 November a constable from John Street barracks was wounded by a member of the republican police. The RIC wrote to the Mid Limerick IRA liaison, Paddy Barry, seeking information. Although Barry promised to assist the police in tracing the culprit, nothing more came of the matter.[19]

General Sir Peter Strickland, general officer commanding the 6th Division, protested that in Munster 'The so called 'Truce' is not a Truce at all'. Attacks on Crown forces were ongoing and 'it is believed that arms have been landed in large quantities'. SF was establishing uncontested control over the province through the Dáil courts and republican police. Strickland was of the opinion that British inaction was 'playing into the hands of the rebels, and allowing them to establish a republican form of government under our noses', and urged the resumption of military action on an extended scale if the IRA did not immediately fall into line. He was concerned that 'The position of the Loyalists is almost desperate. They are already being bullied, and in some cases ordered to leave the country'.[20] CI Regan claimed that the RIC in Limerick never sought information from loyalists because they 'would not allow the IRA to say with any truth that they were spies'. His claim is substantiated by the official British report on army intelligence which noted that, with the exception of the Bandon area in Cork, 'in the south the Protestants and those who supported the government rarely gave much information because, except by chance, they had not got it to give.'[21] An important source of information for the East Limerick Volunteers was Knocklong post office official Stanley Harris, a member of the Church of Ireland, whom Séamus Malone termed a 'good Protestant'.[22] Strickland and Regan were not alone in fearing for Munster's loyalists. In relation to Clare and Limerick, the British army reported that:

> The loyalist views with horror the present terms [of the truce], and has decided, in the event of these being accepted, to clear out of the country. They realise that they will only live on the sufferance of the IRA and will be bled by collectors for various funds weekly. They will only be allowed to live in the country as long as it pays the local inhabitants to keep them.[23]

Amid negotiations on how to move from truce to treaty, increased significance could be attached to otherwise relatively innocuous episodes. In late
November Crown forces served notice of their intention to occupy the former
Rathkeale workhouse. It had been abolished under the Dáil's amalgamation
scheme and the 'inmates' transferred to the county hospital in Croom and the
county home in Newcastle West. The IRA had been in possession of the
building for two months. Believing that 'the enemy had every intention of ful-
filling their threat re occupation', they burned it down. The planned occupation by the Crown forces was apparently called off just before the flames took
hold. Emmet Dalton, military liaison to the Dáil's representatives in the ongoing Anglo-Irish talks in London, regarded the Rathkeale case as a dangerous
public relations stunt by the British:

> It appears to be a game to place us in the wrong and to give them
> every advantage regarding publicity. I consider it a case that should be
> shown up as we obviously have nothing to loose [*sic*].

Éamonn Duggan, one of the envoys, wrote to Dalton about Rathkeale: 'I
think we came very well out of this and can quite understand Macready's
anxiety to avoid the issue.'[24]
On 5 December Kathleen Clarke and de Valera received the Freedom of
the City of Limerick. They were greeted by thousands of people and the
streets were lined with Volunteers.[25] On 7 December the full text of the
Treaty was published in Irish newspapers. Ernie O'Malley was in east
Limerick when he read it the following day. He was enraged, then numb:
'The dead, what did they think?' He looked at a map marking fatalities suffered by the local brigade:

> There the brigadier [Seán Wall] had been shot dead outside that house
> … Here Martin Conway, the fearless, had fallen in action against
> police and soldiers … the wounded [David] Tobin had dragged him-
> self to die, there, outside his mother's house. Here we had been
> chased, there we had stood and fought.[26]

O'Malley felt that the Treaty betrayed the republican dead. It offered more
independence than the restricted measure of control over internal affairs
promised by home rule a decade earlier. The British effectively conceded
dominion status (equivalent to the constitutional status of ex-colonies such as
Canada) to the twenty-six counties of Southern Ireland, now to be known as
the Irish Free State. This entailed practically complete domestic sovereignty
but severely curtailed foreign policy powers. Arguments for and against the
Treaty were, for the most part, reasonably uncomplicated. The issue of par-

tition was not prominent because most republicans assumed that it was temporary and would be corrected by the Boundary Commission established by the Treaty. The prerequisite that TDs would be obliged to take an oath of allegiance to the Crown proved particularly objectionable to doctrinaires like Kate O'Callaghan. From her perspective, the nation's struggles and her personal sacrifices, seamlessly recalled as one and the same, would be rendered meaningless by such an oath. O'Callaghan stood by the republic but Richard Hayes felt that it had ceased to exist with the truce and negotiations. Emphasizing the practical over the ideal, he subscribed to the stepping-stone theory: the Treaty was a compromise but not an ignoble one and it would enable Ireland 'to achieve its full destiny'.[27] The oath was also one of the main reasons why anti-Treatyites were later willing to engage in civil war. Limerick Chamber of Commerce supported the Treaty but O'Callaghan rejected its authority to take a public stance on the issue, and Deputy Mayor Máire O'Donovan refused to put a motion supporting the Treaty to Limerick Corporation.[28] On 14 January 1922, a week after the Treaty passed the Dáil, the one and only meeting of the parliament of Southern Ireland, as established under the 1920 Government of Ireland Act, set up the 'Provisional government'. The political administration of the twenty-six counties became the responsibility of the Provisional government on 16 January, although the IFS did not officially come into being until 6 December.

On 14 December 1921, the day the Dáil opened deliberations on the Treaty, Thomas Enright of the RIC was killed in Kilmallock. A second constable was seriously wounded. Donnchadh O'Hannigan insisted that the East Limerick Brigade was not involved.[29] Stripped of specific context, the timing of the shooting might look like an offshoot of heightened tensions surrounding the Treaty. In reality, as Maurice Meade clarified, Enright was 'particularly active and bitter against our men, on one occasion bombing some of our captured men. For this we decided he should pay the death penalty.'[30] A RIC sergeant in Kilmallock was fired at twice on 10 February 1922 but escaped injury.[31] Black and Tan Lauchlin McEdward was killed at Garryowen on 17 February.[32] These were the same targets that the Volunteers had been pursuing the year before. If anything differentiated these attacks from the usual revenge or reprisal killings, it was that hostile British reaction might have helped to resuscitate IRA unity; that did not happen.

The RIC departed their barracks in Limerick on 22 February.[33] On 9 February the army laid out its schedule for departure from Limerick over the next two weeks. Things went awry, however, and withdrawals had to be staggered to account for Provisional government manpower deficits. On 4 March army GHQ had to request the pro-Treaty IRA (now known as the National army) to 'increase your staff at Limerick for taking over purposes'.[34] On the same day, an officer in the New Barracks wrote to General Strickland about the 'unsatisfactory' condition of Limerick: 'I cannot help feeling that this place is rapidly becoming chaotic, and unless the Provisional Government really grip the situation there will be really serious trouble after we have gone'. He also thought that 'the future of people living around here such as the Cleeve's and Goodbody's is not a happy prospect'.[35] Further deadlines passed. On 20 March the NA had a representative 'already in Limerick awaiting orders, but he does not know to whom the Barracks will be handed over.' The last British troops departed on 21 March, a section of them cheered off by a small group consisting mostly of young women, some of whom waved Union Jacks. On 1 April the NA wrote to British GHQ about 'the invasion by "Republican Forces"' of Limerick's New and Ordnance Barracks:

> I believe this could have been avoided if you had seen your way to facilitate us by holding up evacuation for 2 or 3 days. However, in view of the way things have turned out, I suppose the responsibility for any damage done must rest on us.[36]

After 700 years, the British had left Limerick too soon for the liking of the independent Irish army, who only reluctantly accepted any liability for the chaotic events of the previous weeks.

The first group to respond decisively to British withdrawal were not pro- or anti-Treatyites but locals in need of better living standards. On 13 March slum residents, led by William James Larkin of the Limerick City Workers' Housing Association, commandeered houses at Garryowen Villas that had previously housed families of the Royal Engineers Corps. Forty adults and eighty-seven children moved into twenty-seven houses.[37] This bold step, a challenge to the legal status quo, prompted a duel between the men of no property and the city's landlords. Limerick Corporation's social housing plans had been undermined by financial weakness and were abandoned altogether when ties were cut with the LGB, but the conflicting interests of property-owning councillors were also important.[38] The Housing Association, backed by the Trades Council, called for emergency measures to address housing shortages in the city. Minister for local government Cosgrave, more worried perhaps about radicalism and rates than workers' rights, was perturbed enough to demand a report from the mayor.[39] The corporation increased rates in a grudging effort to raise funds for housing.[40] Dr Michael McGrath, superintendent of public health, pointed out that 'in 1919 there were in the city 1,774 houses unfit for human habitation, and today that number was practically double.'[41] Only sixty-four new houses were built by the corporation between 1922 and 1925.[42] Most of the houses were soon back in landlord hands. The occupying families had been tolerated by the IRA, who intervened when workers occupied creameries, but who could hardly condemn poor people fleeing desperate conditions for taking shelter in old British army billets. Bishop Hallinan, as he had during the soviet, again proved himself the protector of the middle class.[43]

Pro- and anti-Treaty competition for control of newly vacated strong points quickly evolved into a crisis which very nearly precipitated civil war. Mid Limerick's internal quarrels had regularly been a source of irritation for GHQ. On 18 February 1922 Brigadier Liam Forde issued a proclamation denouncing the Treaty, repudiating the authority of GHQ, and declaring Mid Limerick's fealty to the republic.[44] GHQ responded by ordering one division into another's territory for the first time:[45] General Michael Brennan's 1st Western Division from east Clare and south Galway entered Limerick city, part of Ernie O'Malley's 2nd Southern Division territory. Heretofore, the Provisional government had not been disconcerted when anti-Treaty IRA (ATIRA) replaced British forces in local barracks, but Limerick's strategic significance stirred them. As the piecemeal withdrawal of the British army unfolded and the RIC evacuated its city barracks, the NA stepped in. Ernie O'Malley arrived on 2 March and ATIRA reinforcements followed. The majority of the Mid Limerick Brigade were anti-Treaty but the situation was complicated by the hundreds of outside fighters in the city. On 3 March Captain Bill Stapleton of the NA (and a former member of Michael Collins's counter-intelligence assassination 'Squad') was shot and wounded by ATIRA men.[46] Stapleton had brought the first armoured car that the IFS had received from the British government to John Street police barracks. His crew of four in the Rolls Royce included two NA troops and two Black and Tans seconded as trainers.[47] Brennan was worried at the inadequate training of his men and believed that some had 'too many old associations with the mutineers to be properly reliable'.[48]

Arthur Griffith, president of the Dáil, was intolerant of opposition to the Treaty. He favoured aggression in Limerick. Griffith's hardline approach prompted Mayor Stephen O'Mara, fearful that the city would become a battleground, to wonder if it would be better to burn the barracks.[49] Richard Mulcahy refused to countenance action, however, because his National army was as yet ill-prepared. O'Mara facilitated dialogue between the two camps and a compromise was patched together, preventing civil war in the short-term. Outsiders returned to whence they came and the city was left in local hands. O'Malley reckoned 'we had won without firing a shot. We had maintained our rights'.[50] No one, apart perhaps from O'Malley, really wanted to fight at this stage. The NA was content to shadow box until satisfied with its own level of preparation. The British were relieved at the tentative peace but sensed how precarious it was. Winston Churchill wrote to Collins on 14 March:

You seem to have liquidated the Limerick situation in one way or another. No doubt you know your own business best, and thank God you have got to manage it and not me. An adverse decision by the convention of the Irish Republican Army (so-called) would, however, be a very grave event at this juncture. I presume you are quite sure there is no danger of this.[51]

On 15 March the Provisional government banned an upcoming IRA convention, which went ahead anyway on 26 March. The proceedings made it clear that the majority of the IRA leadership opposed the Treaty. An executive was appointed that subsequently refused to accept the authority of any civilian body.

Limerick edged gradually closer to the precipice. In February Broadford police barracks had been taken over by Brennan's NA troops. The garrison switched allegiance in April, however, and one of its number was killed in a firefight with the NA.[52] As they stepped up preparations for war, five anti-Treatyites were killed in accidental circumstances in Limerick city between early April and late May (although one may have committed suicide).[53] At least seven members of the NA were killed by accidental discharges of weapons in Limerick during 1922–3. One soldier was deliberately killed by a colleague, one was killed in action by 'friendly fire' and one committed suicide. A certain level of self-inflicted attrition, inadvertent or intentional, is to be expected in war but questionable standards of training and professionalism were contributory factors in some cases. The competence and discipline of the NA were often called into question by senior officers in Limerick.

Before the general election of 16 June, women's suffrage briefly topped the Dáil agenda. All men over twenty-one had the vote and on 2 March Kate O'Callaghan introduced a bill to enfranchise Irish women 'on the same terms as Irish men', not just those over thirty with certain property qualifications. Women in their twenties had earned the right to a say on the Treaty because of their revolutionary efforts, she argued: 'Without their votes or their voice, nobody can say that the will of the whole people of Ireland will have been ascertained.' Arthur Griffith interpreted the motion as a cynical delaying tactic and an attempt to 'torpedo' the Treaty. Griffith believed in universal adult suffrage but it would have to wait. O'Callaghan's bill was defeated.[54] An electoral pact agreed on 20 May 1922 by Collins, chairman of the Provisional government, and de Valera, leader of anti-Treaty SF, aimed to preserve whatever fragile bonds remained between the two sides and prevent civil war. It was contingent on a constitution with a republican character and an electoral procedure (albeit a somewhat undemocratic one that prevented voters from directly expressing their opinion on the Treaty), which would guarantee coalition government and shared cabinet participation. The British government

objected and the pact fell apart shortly before the election. The proposed constitution of the IFS was redrafted to satisfy Prime Minister Lloyd George and
published on the morning of the vote. Of 620,283 ballots, pro-Treaty Sinn
Féiners won 239,193 and anti-Treaty Sinn Féiners 133,864, while other candidates secured 247,226 votes. The substantial pro-Treaty majority was discounted by anti-Treatyites because of the threat of British coercion.
Significantly, 40 per cent of the electorate supported non-Sinn Féiners. Fifty-
eight pro-Treaty candidates were returned, thirty-six anti-Treaty, seventeen
Labour, seven Farmers' Party, six independents and four Dublin University
representatives. The four sitting TDs in Limerick City–Limerick East and
the eight in Kerry–Limerick West were all returned without a ballot being
cast. Only five of these twelve had voted for the Treaty. Of the five
Limerick-based deputies, only Richard Hayes and Liam Hayes in Limerick
City–Limerick East were pro-Treaty, with their constituency colleagues
Michael Colivet and Kate O'Callaghan opposing it, along with Con Collins in
west Limerick. But plenipotentiaries had signed the Treaty and cabinet, Dáil
and popular majorities had subsequently accepted it. This played a significant
role in establishing the status and credibility of the IFS government and
undermining the anti-Treaty case. The ability of the IFS to get a functioning
administration in place was vital, and gave it authority and power. It provided
a concrete rallying point for civilian supporters. The Catholic Church and
national press had bestowed explicit moral licence on the Treaty and the IFS,
while denying it to the anti-Treatyites and effectively casting them in the role
of heretics. There was a widespread desire for stability and action on pressing social and economic issues, as well as a growing apathy towards ideological abstractions. A distinct advantage that the NA enjoyed over the ATIRA
when it came to dealing with civilians was the fact that they were funded by
the Provisional government, thanks to credit from the Bank of Ireland, and
could thus purchase supplies. Their record was not without blemish, however. When Michael Collins inspected accounts in Limerick in August 1922,
he discovered 752 outstanding bills, some going back to April. He emphasized
that this was damaging the interests of traders, especially smaller ones.[55] The
great drawback of such a concentration of ATIRA Volunteers as there was in
Limerick early in the Civil War was shortages. Food and shelter were most
readily available in towns, which explains why most of the preliminary clashes
took place in and around larger population centres. The NA was thus facilitated in bringing to bear its advantage in heavy equipment, particularly
artillery, which could be deployed against fortified positions. The ATIRA had
no artillery and no anti-artillery defences. Their expertise lay in conducting
guerrilla warfare. The level of civilian support that had allowed the IRA to
compensate for deficiencies in transport, supplies and communications during
the War of Independence was no longer forthcoming. ATIRA commandeer-

ing and forced levies caused friction with civilians, and there was often at least some truth in the claim, which regularly appeared in newspaper accounts of the arrival of IFS forces in areas where republicans had previously held sway, that there was great joy at the relief of the town, with the people coming out to welcome the troops. On Wednesday 27 July 1922, for instance, *Sgéal Chatha Luimnighe* (*Limerick War News*), a NA propaganda sheet, in an article headlined 'The Robbers', claimed that 'irregulars' had looted thousands of pounds worth of goods from shops in Rathkeale.

From mid-July to mid-August *Sgéal Chatha Luimnighe* was issued from the publicity department, field GHQ, South Western Command, which was based in Cruise's Hotel in the city. The *Leader* did not appear between 30 June and 13 October. Editions of the *Chronicle* were published on 8 and 22 July. The *Chronicle* then appeared regularly until 12 August but not again until 17 October. 'Irregular' demands for censorship rights, fighting, and shrinking advertising revenue in a stagnant trading environment had all acted as disincentives to publication. Much of the material reported in the *Chronicle* overlapped with that in *Sgéal Chatha Luimnighe*. Republicans had no real local equivalent and were heavily defeated in the propaganda war in Limerick.

The Civil War officially started on 28 June when, at the behest of Britain and using British field guns, the NA shelled the anti-Treatyites occupying the Four Courts. Militarily, the early engagements of the Civil War were on a much greater scale than those of the War of Independence. The NA had its most spectacular battleground successes during these months. From the autumn of 1922, intense fighting was only intermittent. ATIRA resistance gradually dissolved. The death in action of Liam Lynch on 10 April 1923 and his replacement as ATIRA chief of staff by Frank Aiken, who was perhaps more realistic in his assessment of the capability of his forces, prompted a ceasefire on 30 April 1923 and the dumping of arms from 24 May. The war was initially a much more finely balanced affair than its denouement might suggest. The shortcomings of republican political and military strategy and tactics were often matched by the incompetence of their pro-Treaty rivals and the outcome of the war was by no means a foregone conclusion. Mobility was one of the fundamental features of the opening phase as both sides needed to establish their physical control over the country quickly. The NA had the greater resources and displayed more gusto in this race for territory. Initially, the ATIRA had the upper hand in manpower and experience but the NA held key positions for moving against ATIRA strongholds. Mulcahy's reluctance to face down the ATIRA in Limerick in February–March betrayed his lack of confidence in the new NA. Its weaknesses were gradually compensated for by the recruitment of 30,000 paid men and a steady supply of British guns. The ATIRA's reactionary stance and failure to forestall the government offensive allowed the NA to dictate the pace and direction of the war. The so-called Munster republic was an almost exclusive bastion of anti-Treatyism. It lay south of Liam Lynch's notional defensive line from Limerick city in the west, bordered on the north by the River Shannon, to Waterford city in the east, flanked by the River Suir. As the war progressed, it shrank further back into Cork and Kerry. The ATIRA preoccupation with the Munster republic, combined with the contradictory abandonment of inland urban centres such as Kilmallock while the NA was landing along the coast, was its undoing.

On 29 June Liam Lynch established ATIRA HQ in the New Barracks, Limerick. At the start of July Lynch, Liam Deasy, O/C 1st Southern Division, and Seán Moylan, O/C North Cork Brigade, commanded 700 men in the city. They faced 400 NA troops, drawn from the 1st Western and 4th Southern Divisions under Michael Brennan and Donnchadh O'Hannigan respectively. Lynch and O'Hannigan came from the same parish: Anglesboro/Kilbehenny in south-east Limerick. Lynch may have hoped that, along with his old colleagues Brennan and O'Hannigan, he could present a unified southern front to the Provisional government and prevent the spread of the war from Dublin. The only possible way that civil conflict could have been restricted to Dublin, however, was if Lynch had marched the full array of his forces on the capital in a *coup d'état*. As Lynch dawdled, ATIRA from Cork and Kerry advanced largely unhindered towards Limerick city through the west of the county. In a major tactical miscalculation, Lynch agreed a series of peace deals. A formal truce was signed on 4 July. Lynch was fancifully optimistic that O'Hannigan and Brennan would opt for neutrality. Even when General Dermot McManus of NA GHQ told Lynch on 5 July that the pact was void, he remained in a kind of stupor.[56] McManus, nervous of Brennan's intentions and blind to his superb performance, warned GHQ that there was 'very grave danger of disaster'.[57] Brennan held fast and on 7 July convinced Lynch to stall further. The delay was to the distinct advantage of pro-Treaty forces. Brennan, outgunned as well as outmanned, was content to keep talking while additional NA troops, backed up by armoured cars, were deployed to Limerick. Moylan was not duped but he was outranked. He called on Deasy to act: 'There is no use in fooling around with this question any longer. Send on the men and let us get on with the war.'[58]

The local entente lapsed on 11 July when 18-year-old Private Thomas O'Brien of the NA was killed in a tussle with the ATIRA on Roche's Street, just two streets from his home on William Street. O'Brien's people were all anti-Treatyites and it was reputedly stated by them that 'Thomas had disgraced the family'. In reviewing a military service pension application from relatives of O'Brien in the mid-1920s, Michael Brennan raised the possibility that he had been deliberately targeted and killed because of his perceived treachery.[59] Most of the fighting during the next ten days was centred on ATIRA-occupied barracks. Thousands of civilians fled the city. Many of the remaining townspeople emptied their chamber pots into the street from their windows so they did not have to risk going outside. Commerce ground to a halt. Food was scarce. For a couple of weeks, there was no rail access to or from the city, no mail delivered and no newspapers available, apart from propaganda sheets.[60] Government forces were continually being reinforced, but their progress was slow and the fighting remained indecisive until an 18-pounder field gun arrived on 19 July. The Strand Barracks surrendered on 20 July, but only after it had been reduced to 'a palsied pile, a grim tribute to the accuracy of the national artillery'.[61] Lynch soon ordered the burning of posts. Connie Neenan was among the last to leave the New Barracks and described the retreat as a 'stampede': 'it was a scene of chaos ... We were so hungry that I went out and stole a loaf of bread. But then, we Republicans ... were hopeless at looking after the commissariat.'[62] The worst of the destruction to property was confined to military and police barracks, but the battle for Limerick claimed the lives of as many civilians as it did combatants – five ATIRA, six NA and eleven civilians – due to the high population density in the city and the concentrated nature of the fighting.[63]

By September 1922, £195,000 worth of claims emanating from the July fighting in the city had been prepared under the Malicious Injuries Act.[64] In November 1923 at the Limerick Quarter Sessions, the court heard malicious injuries claims relating to the period 11 July 1921 to 20 May 1923. There were more than 600 applications from the city and 1,000 from around the county. The vast majority ranged from 30s. to £250 and covered 'loss of profit, consequential losses, destruction of property, loss of house accommodation, loss of clothing etc'. Many claims related to goods allegedly looted by ATIRA forces, including tobacco and foodstuffs. The highest individual claim was submitted by the Community of the Convent of Mercy for £23,801 12s. 4d. in respect of the gutting of the Ordnance Barracks by retreating ATIRA. Anti-Treatyite Madge Daly claimed £2,250 for damage to the family bakery. A series of big businesses – Boyd's, Denny's, Masterson's, Shaw's, Spaight's, Bannatyne's, Cannock's and Cleeve's Condensed Milk Company – claimed over £1,000 each.[65]

Waterford, the easternmost point of the Munster republic, fell to the NA on the same day as Limerick. Lynch's illusory defensive line vanished. Many of the ATIRA retreating from Limerick fell back to the south of the county. This was followed by one of the largest and most protracted military engagements in Irish history. Between 21 July and 5 August the battle for Kilmallock was conducted in the Bruff–Bruree–Kilmallock triangle. It marked a juncture in the war, between the decisive fixed-position fare of June, July and early August (with which both sides were ill-at-ease), and the drawn-out, guerrilla phase. Although the NA was at a numerical disadvantage, news of army landings along the south-west coastline (which prompted the departure of many Cork and Kerry natives from Kilmallock's ATIRA garrison), better generalship and the use of artillery tilted the scales. The ATIRA made a stand at Kilmallock because it was the first large town between Limerick city and the Cork border. This zone was a buffer against a NA advance from Limerick city on the heartland of the Munster republic. It blocked the route to Cork and could threaten the flank of any move westwards to Kerry. The NA cleared a path for itself by 5 August, however. Thereafter, the ATIRA were effectively penned in Cork and Kerry.

Liam Deasy and Seán Moylan pitted their wits and resources against their fellow ex-guerrilla, General Eoin O'Duffy. O'Duffy's second-in-command was Major-General W.R.E. Murphy, a highly-decorated former British officer. In the only line fighting of the Civil War, the opponents squared off in a type of cross-country warfare with a well-defined front line, each side maintaining a string of outposts at crossroads and on hilltops, with a 'No-Man's Land' varying in width between 100 yards and a mile. The fighting temporarily took on more than a semblance of the orthodoxies of the 1914–18 war. This played into the hands of the better-equipped NA. Murphy had 1,000 men at his disposal by early August. Many were raw recruits, inexperienced and unreliable.[66] The ATIRA could muster 500 well-armed men around Kilmallock and another 1,000 just south of the Cork border. But their morale was low after the loss of Limerick, and there were also inter-county rivalries. Supplies were scarce all round. Deasy admitted that he had to demobilize some men who could not be fed; O'Duffy complained that the NA had to 'scrounge on the countryside. This leads towards undiscipline [*sic*] and is unfair to the people.'[67] Desertion and transfer of allegiance were not uncommon. At times, coordinated action on any large scale proved beyond the capabilities of either side, particularly the ATIRA. Deasy, like O'Duffy, had grave concerns about 'laxity'.[68] NA recruits were considered 'semi-disciplined' at best and unease about their quality was constant. Many were 'undesirables'.[69]

There was a growing mutual antipathy manifest in Limerick during these weeks. Two incidents give the lie to the myth that Irish men were reluctant to kill their fellow countrymen and former comrades. The ATIRA were the guilty party on both occasions but it was not long before the NA displayed equivalent spite, much of it extrajudicial. Four members of the NA were killed on 24 July at Ballingaddy, near Kilmallock. It appeared that they were shot after surrendering.[70] Four days later there was a similar episode at Ballygibba near Bruree when another four soldiers were killed. A war correspondent left a disturbing account of the bodies:

> Capt[ain] Power's brains had been blown out and his arms were tied in front about the wrists with what appeared to be a cycle strap. Murphy was shot through the heart, and his boots and leggings are

missing. Carey had a terrible wound in the mouth and an injury to his hands, which were coated with dried blood, and O'Mahony was killed by a bullet in the head.[71]

The ATIRA-controlled *Cork Examiner* of 4 August strongly refuted any suggestion of wrongdoing. William O'Brien, a NA soldier who had been 'ill-treated' while a prisoner of the ATIRA in the area during the previous weeks, died on 17 July 1923. The beating he received in ATIRA custody was a significant contributory factor.[72] The killings at Ballingaddy and Ballygibba suggest that atrocities may well have reared their ugly head earlier in the conflict than is widely thought and that they were a feature of the conventional as well as the guerrilla phase of the war. The NA in Limerick city soon became involved: Harry Brazier was shot dead on 22 August while 'resisting' arrest; veteran Volunteer Michael Danford was taken into custody on 28 August, then riddled with bullets before his body was dumped.[73]

Bruff and Bruree repeatedly changed hands until the NA finally secured the villages in the last days of July. Once again, artillery was crucial at Bruree. There was no ultimate battle for Kilmallock. The NA opened up a second front to the rear of the Munster republic when troops landed north of Tralee on 2 August. This played on local loyalties and the Kerry ATIRA prioritized the defence of the 'kingdom' over the Munster republic. The Cork contingent defending Kilmallock anticipated the coastal attack on Cork that would come the following week and also slipped away. The additional seaborne element aside, retreat seemed inevitable in the short-term anyway, as nearly 2,000 NA troops were converging for the final push, backed by artillery. The NA marched into Kilmallock on 5 August. There was a simultaneous thrust westwards and Adare, Rathkeale and Newcastle West were taken in the following days. By mid-October Garret McAuliffe stated that his ATIRA force was severely curtailed 'owing to enemy activity in his brigade and the arrest of practically all his staff'.[74] By the end of 1922 west Limerick, which was predominantly anti-Treaty, was in NA hands.

Around Limerick, the lead-up to the snap general election of 27 August 1923 was subdued. When a fund-raising event for a War of Independence memorial attracted 4,000 people to Ballylanders on 15 August, for example, there was clear potential for significant unrest but candidates agreed not to electioneer.[75] Contestants were still reeling from the Civil War, including Cumann na nGaedheal, as pro-Treaty SF had been rebranded by the government, and local media coverage was scant. The seven-seat Limerick constituency replaced Limerick City–Limerick East and Kerry–Limerick West. Cumann na nGaedheal won three seats, anti-Treaty republicans two, Labour one and the Farmers' Party one. Of the three incumbents who ran, only Richard Hayes, for Cumann na nGaedheal, was successful. Michael Colivet and Kate O'Callaghan were defeated. From an electorate of 79,340, 50,807 or 64% voted (the average national turnout was about 70%) and 10,498 gave Hayes their first preference and a resounding win. Next came his party colleague James Ledden, a founding member of the Limerick City Volunteers, with more than 6,000 votes. Still, republican sentiment remained strong in Limerick at a trying time for anti-Treatyites: thousands of their number were imprisoned around the country and state pressure did not relent post-cease-fire. Mid and West Limerick ATIRA leaders Seán Carroll and James Colbert (brother of 1916 martyr Con) had just under 6,000 and 5,000 votes respectively. Carroll was something of a bogeyman for the NA and he had been playing 'the game of "Blindman's Buff" with our [NA] troops' until the end of the war.[76] A supporter of Carroll's had a lucky escape in Castleconnell when celebratory shots were fired and a bullet went through his hat.[77] The remaining seats were filled by John Nolan (Cumann na nGaedheal), Patrick Clancy (Labour), and Patrick K. Hogan (Farmers' Party). In simple pro-Treaty versus anti-Treaty terms, this was a five to two majority. Pro-Treaty did not mean pro-government of course and citizens had a variety of other concerns. Fifth-placed Nolan's 1,476 first preferences were less than half of sixth-placed Clancy's 3,305, but he attracted more transfers. Five unsuccessful candidates had more first preferences than Hogan's 1,537 and it was not until the seventeenth count that he was elected. Matthew Murphy of Labour, for instance, received 3,382 first preferences. Hayes was a doctor but Laffan, Nolan and Hogan, as well as Colbert, were farmers. Carroll, like Murphy, was a labourer; Clancy was a carpenter. At a point of frequent industrial relations disputes in Limerick's agricultural sector and rising unemployment in the city, the pattern suggests that support for Labour candidates was strictly confined to urban working-class or rural labouring-class voters. Pettiness was still a feature that had to be reckoned with also: in east Limerick, a decisive factor in candidate selection, and possibly even voting preferences, was the influence of a large farmer who had recently developed a grievance against the government over a public appointment by Limerick County Council.[78]

The battle for Kilmallock was the last large-scale, deliberately planned conventional field action of the entire war. Within two weeks of the fall of Kilmallock, the NA held every significant population centre in north Munster. The ATIRA reverted to guerrilla tactics and the Civil War became marked by tit-for-tat outrages. The Public Safety bill of 27 September, which came a month after the death from illness of Arthur Griffith and the death-in-action of Michael Collins, signified that the IFS was about to institute martial law. The government, relying heavily on its capacity for violence to assert its authority, embarked on a concerted policy of executing ATIRA prisoners. There were eighty-one executions under a variety of emergency powers legislation and many more unofficial executions. On 20 January 1923 Patrick

Hennessy and Cornelius McMahon were executed in Limerick prison for carrying arms illegally and damaging railway line in Clare.[79] Nationally, fourteen men were executed for such offences during the first few weeks of January. Hennessy and McMahon were the only official executions in Limerick. Donnchadh O'Hannigan's opposition to the policy was a redeeming feature when there was so little glory to be found anywhere in the Civil War. He had displayed a ruthless streak in 1920–1 but his attitude during the Civil War contrasted sharply with that of Michael Brennan, who oversaw the execution of five Mid Clare Brigade men in his divisional area, including Hennessy and McMahon. The relationship between Brennan's East Clare Brigade and Mid Clare had been vindictive and its legacy was bitter.[80] In February 1923 a dozen ATIRA leaders in Limerick jail, fearing a 'war of extermination', signed a prescient but futile statement purporting to represent 600 prisoners warning that 'an era of vendetta and insane hate will surely follow' the executions and 'for generations to come Ireland will be rent with feuds and factions'.[81] One of the signatories, Bob de Courcy, later endured forty-one days on hunger strike in Kilmainham, during which he was elected mayor of Limerick in October 1923. This was 'a stroke of genius on the part of the diehard elements' on the corporation according to the NA:

> it was hoped that some useful advantage might be reaped from having an imprisoned mayor starving to death for the Republic, but the game did not work and it is questionable if 15% of the population of the City know or care who the Mayor is or what political creed he professes.[82]

The new order was far from universally welcome and there was 'wholesale evasion of ordinary civil obligations', people sidestepping the financial machinery of the state – its process servers and bailiffs – to avoid paying rates, taxes or debts during the Civil War.[83] Tensions remained high after the conflict. NA intelligence reports were gloomy, archly conservative, and particularly nervous about the likely influence of demobilized soldiers and released ATIRA prisoners: 'it is greatly to be feared that many having learned the use of firearms and having had their civic and moral consciences dulled during the recent past, will not be slow to adopt drastic means in order to replete their finances.'[84] In the run-up to Christmas, a crime wave featuring armed robberies was predicted. Economic circumstances were held largely responsible but 'latent criminal inclinations' were not dismissed. These dire prophesies apparently fulfilled themselves; robberies were 'numerous' but mostly perpetrated by ex-NA men.[85] Members of the nascent unarmed Civic Guard (later An Garda Síochána) were shot on at least two occasions in Limerick between October 1923 and March 1924 but escaped with their lives.[86] The victors continued to look at the vanquished as enemies whose politics or past deeds meant that they deserved whatever treatment was meted out to them. When Thomas Portley, on leave and awaiting demobilization from the NA, shot and wounded William Guerin, who was unarmed, on 22 December 1923 in Boher, he was not found guilty of any offence. The two had clashed before. Guerin was 'a bully and a rogue' and had provoked Portley to shoot him. Worst of all, Guerin was 'of Irregular tendencies'. The implication was not subtle: he got what was coming to him.[87] Reconciliation was not a priority for some of those who had lost loved ones in Limerick. On 17 October 1922 Lieutenant Joseph Hanrahan, a Limerick city native, was fatally wounded in an ATIRA attack. Gerald Fitzgibbon was sentenced to death for the killing. Joseph O'Connor got fourteen years.[88] They escaped from Frederick Street barracks on Christmas Eve. A 17-year-old girl was shot dead during the ensuing pursuit.[89] In 1925 Hanrahan's father complained bitterly that the family were awarded only £75 by the IFS instead of a maximum of £150. He was indignant about the general pardon afforded men like Fitzgibbon and O'Connor:

> I gave my son willingly and he gave his life in assisting to establish law and order, while today walking the streets of Limerick, the men that were tried and convicted for his death are as free as the air, well clothed and well fed and not interfered with by the established forces of Saorstát Éireann.

Hanrahan's mother regarded the situation as a 'disgrace to the government' and a 'travesty of justice'.[90]

The 1923 general election was the most normal since 1910. The military crisis had been ongoing in Limerick since the spring of 1919, with the only interlude the false promise of the summer of 1921. Violence and the threat of violence were only now at last easing, and political stability was being restored. Whereas the War of Independence had at least given some Limerick people some cause for celebration, the Civil War only heaped trauma upon loss. It was wholly divisive and degenerated into considerable vindictiveness, reflecting little credit on either side. The settling of old scores would continue in the years ahead. Furthermore, the political and military turmoil of 1922–3 was paralleled by social strife and class conflict. The lengthy agricultural boom that had been so beneficial for Limerick city and county ended in the summer of 1921. Demand for labour collapsed and employers wanted fewer workers to do longer hours for lesser pay. More than 1.2 million work days were lost to strikes or lock-outs in 1923. In Waterford city and county, for instance, there were thirteen strikes involving 3,000 workers.[91] There was extensive and persistent labour agitation in Limerick city and county in 1922–3 also. A printers' strike in the city was followed by a dockers' strike, which affected coal and general merchants. A pork butchers' strike in turn influenced the dockers because it impacted the bacon export trade. In rural Limerick, at least eleven incidents of arson in 1922–3 were connected to employee–employer disputes.[92] Unemployment was rife and a postal workers' strike did not help trade. Farmers faced not only a poor harvest but the termination of production at Cleeve's Condensed Milk Company. This was a major setback for both county and city. Dairying was severely affected by the closure of creameries. Hundreds of jobs were lost at the central Lansdowne plant. The ending of government contracts for the manufacture of uniforms led to a drastic reduction in the workforce at the Limerick Clothing Company. The next chapter provides an assessment of the deteriorating economic conditions and the treatment of vulnerable and exposed members of society in a vacuum of law and order. This will allow us to define more clearly the nature of the revolution in Limerick.

8 'We were obliged to leave our beautiful home': social strife, 1922–3

Limerick witnessed significant social change during the revolution as well as being a centre of political and military drama. There was pervasive communal upheaval in the city and county. The luckiest individuals and the most powerful groups came through the revolution with their position or reputation enhanced, while more vulnerable parties suffered humiliation or were transformed into figures of suspicion and hate. Problems of land and politics, and questions about allegiance, identity, religion and status co-existed so closely in Limerick that it can be difficult to distinguish between them. Institutions fundamental to the functioning of the state, such as the RIC, were pressurized to breaking point. Neither truce nor Treaty offered respite to policemen and others perceived as being cogs in the British system of rule. Amid the agrarian and labour disputes that followed the truce as recession set in from 1921, landlords and men of no property, farmers and farmhands, and employers and workers all clashed.

Peter Switzer's sorry story begins with a land 'grab' at the end of the nineteenth century and touches on many of the vexatious issues that troubled revolutionary Ireland. When Patrick Mulqueen was evicted from his farm at Moig East, Castletown, Pallaskenry for failing to pay his mortgage, local woman Susan Switzer purchased the property from the bank. Mulqueen then resorted to a campaign of boycott and intimidation against the Switzer family, two of the methods traditionally used against 'grabbers' who took over farms after evictions. On 20 January 1898, at Pallaskenry Petty Sessions, Mulqueen was convicted of harassing a servant of Peter Switzer (Susan's brother) and attempting to prevent the sale of Switzer's sheep.[1] Peter Switzer was nearly fifty years old at the time, Susan was a few years younger, and another sister was two years younger again. The siblings lived together on the farm. Their house scored eleven in the census classification system in 1911. Twelve would have made it '1st class'. The Switzers were Palatines, mainly a farming community of German origin which settled in Limerick in the eighteenth century. Most Palatines were Methodists but some, like the Switzers, had become members of the Church of Ireland. How the family were regarded by their neighbours was likely to have been coloured by the circumstances in which they acquired their farm. The UIL publicly vilified so-called 'grabbers'.

More than twenty years after Mulqueen targeted them, the Switzers were again subjected to unsolicited, hostile attention. By 1920 Peter Switzer was in his early seventies. Known to possess firearms, the Pallaskenry IRA were wary of him. But without consulting the local unit, the Ballysteen company conducted an arms raid on the Switzer home on 18 April 1920. Switzer opened fire on the raiding party, mortally wounding Lieutenant Dan Neville. The raiders retreated. Seán Finn reported the incident to Richard Mulcahy, who ordered that no reprisals be taken. Thereafter, Switzer habitually carried arms when in public. The RIC put on additional patrols around Castletown throughout that summer but this was a heavy drain on resources and an additional risk, particularly since the Pallaskenry and Kildimo barracks had been closed and the police had to travel from Adare or Patrickswell. Despite the additional security presence, the Pallaskenry IRA seized two revolvers from Switzer as he was going to church on 19 September. They then took him to his home: 'his womenfolk, thinking he would be shot, brought us out a shotgun and ammunition' before he was released 'unharmed'.[2] The Volunteers heeded Mulcahy's orders and resisted the temptation to avenge their fallen comrade at this point, but Switzer's reprieve was only temporary. On 10 January 1922 Switzer was fatally wounded in a gun attack while attending the funeral of his sister, Susan. As the cortège was nearing the burial ground at Castletown two shots were fired from Castletown Wood. Switzer, who was a passenger in a motorcar, was hit in the head. He died in Barrington's Hospital on 13 January. An inquest was opened at Barrington's on 15 January under the auspices of the republican police, but in the absence of evidence of identification of the deceased, it was adjourned. Officials, anxious perhaps to avoid participating in a controversial case, cited jurisdictional reasons for their refusal to participate, and no inquest was held. Switzer was buried in the cemetery of St Mary's Cathedral on 16 January.[3] The Switzers transgressed social codes regarding land ownership. Peter Switzer defended his convictions and his property by force. He was targeted in the first place for his guns, and also perhaps for his politics, his loyalism. Richard Mulcahy was acutely aware of the sensitivities involved and anxious that he not be targeted as a Protestant.[4] A local Volunteer later described Switzer as 'a loyalist' and as 'an elderly man and a fighting Protestant'. These were fine lines to tread. In the vacuum of early 1922, whoever killed Switzer no longer cared about such distinctions or felt that they were irrelevant. Switzer was an old enemy and the primary motivation for his killing was revenge.

Another category of individual who often faced a difficult post-revolutionary fate was the ex-policeman. The RIC was the agent of British power that Irish people had encountered most directly and former members worried about how their old communities would receive them after the dissolution of the force in 1922. A majority, as it turned out, settled quietly around Ireland but some were *personae non gratae*. The Treaty recommended that the RIC sub-divide into north and south but the rank-and-file preferred to disband. John Regan made the telling observation that most Black and Tans and Auxiliaries 'could return to their native land after the conflict ended, but many former members of the RIC could not remain in theirs.'⁵ The British administration recognized the uniquely perilous position of ex-policemen among former state employees. It administered the cost of assisted passage overseas, pensions and compensation. Pensions were adjusted to provide a living wage during what was anticipated to be an 'unemployable period' and could be commuted into lump sums for those who wanted to start a new life by emigrating and purchasing property or a business. Initially, there was free rail travel to any destination in Ireland or England and a special grant available to Irish policemen to move their families to England. A resettlement branch helped ex-members and their families to relocate elsewhere in the Empire.⁶ By early April 1922 the RIC had effectively ceased to exist. The *Irish Times* regretted that a body of men who had given 'magnificent service to the Empire was not only being disbanded, but being sent virtually into exile.'⁷

Some former police outlined the anxieties and traumas they experienced after disbandment in compensation claims to the IGC. When men who had been serving elsewhere returned to Limerick, they could be met by an ultimatum from the local IRA: exile or death. Property and employment prospects were lost to displaced or isolated families. They encountered violence and intimidation. Their mental health suffered and this included that of wives and children. Maurice Reidy counted himself lucky to secure a house in Glin, even though it was 'entirely unfit for our proper accommodation ... These were times when ex-members ... were thankful for small mercies'.⁸ Patrick Sullivan of Limerick city was reduced to 'running from place to place like a wild animal for 9 m[on]ths and expecting to be hourly assassinated. You could imagine the state of mind of a man in such circumstances ... my wife's health broke down with absolute terror'.⁹ Isaac Langrill served for nearly thirty-eight years in the RIC and lived in Ballybrown, Clarina, about six miles from Limerick city. His three sons 'fought for England' with the Irish Guards. In fear of his life 'on account of extreme terrorism', he fled to England with his wife and daughter in February 1923.¹⁰ Margaret Murphy, a maternity nurse from Broadford, was boycotted from 1918 because her husband was a policeman in Dublin. She left Limerick in May 1922 and suffered a nervous breakdown. She was pregnant at the time and a doctor who treated her attributed the loss of her baby in September 'directly' to 'the distress of mind due to her expulsion from and loss of her home.'¹¹ Rachel Walker's late husband, William, had served for thirty-two years in the RIC. She was too poor to leave Adare, even after armed raiders damaged her crops, gates and water supply in 1922. No shop would give her a line of credit – this was probably a financial and social decision. She claimed £50 but the IGC granted her £150, indicating its sympathetic disposition to poorer claimants.¹²

The O'Briens of Ashroe, Murroe, were a twelve-strong Catholic family. For thirty-five years, Michael O'Brien worked for J.B. Barrington, brother of Sir Charles, and a county councillor from 1902–17. The family lived on Barrington land. Two of Michael's sons were policemen for which reason from 1920 the family were 'avoided and shunned by everyone with the exception of a few loyalist families living in the district'. The creamery apparently only took their milk because Crown forces threatened to burn it down otherwise. Similar threats of severe reprisals prevented direct action against the O'Brien home until May 1922 when their house was surrounded by armed men and shots fired. They left Limerick under threat of death and emigrated to England in 1923.[13] Maurice O'Brien had been a successful cattle, horse and pig trader in Limerick. He received £75 compensation.[14] He worked as a labourer in Kent and felt he had paid a high price for his loyalty. John O'Brien (no relation), from Mary Street in the city, was a member of Limerick Corporation's Night Watch (a municipal police force that had been in existence in Limerick since the early nineteenth century). When he joined the army in 1915, it was on agreement that he would be reinstated in his permanent position on demobilization. He was not restored to the role, however, and in October 1919 Limerick Assizes awarded him damages for breach of contract. The LGB then re-employed him, but in October 1921 O'Brien was 'summarily dismissed solely on account of his loyalty': 'As a result of the vendetta against him he was unable to find other employment ... his health became affected ... he is now without any means of subsistence and living on charity.' The IGC regarded his claim for £1,000 as 'too high' and did not see a direct link between his anxiety over local hostility against him and his medical troubles. On what seem to have been largely compassionate grounds in view of his genuine hardship, he was awarded £400.[15]

In Limerick and around the country, the position of landowners was destabilized during the revolution. Land problems beset Irish politics and society for much of the nineteenth century. Despite the success of legislation in transferring ownership from landlords to tenants, there remained a pressing need for redistribution of land, especially that held by large graziers, to alleviate the plight of smallholders. A significant number of farms – up to 65 per cent in many counties – were economically unviable and unlikely to have been able to sustain an average-sized family. In rural areas, small farmers, labourers and the landless were most likely to join the IRA, while large farmers remained aloof. Many IRA veterans were rewarded with land grants from the Land Commission in the 1920s and 1930s. Agrarian crime escalated across much of rural Ireland from spring 1920, including County Limerick, and the majority of it was attributable to demands for land division. A campaign by tenants at Glenduff Castle, near Monagea, for instance, compelled the sale of the estate: 'the Old Bitch [Frances Ievers] ... had the place long enough ...

it was about time to get it divided up'.[16] The traditional forms of agrarianism continued: boycotting, cattle driving, threatening letters, intimidation, and destruction of property. Agitation involved individuals, gangs and associations representing landless labourers and evicted tenants. This led to ideological or class-based violence but opportunities were also taken to settle festering personal scores, as in the Switzer case. SF arbitration courts stifled such violence before the truce but it flared again in the vacuum of transition from British to Irish rule. Religion was not a factor in campaigns for land redistribution; Protestant landlords had mostly been bought out already anyway.

There was a spate of cattle driving around Croom in early 1922. Between January and March fifty-nine of Denis Hickey's cattle were driven from his land, followed by another twenty-three in May. Hickey interpreted the actions in terms of land hunger:

> Local small holders and landless people were anxious to have the lands of Croom ... divided up and sold to them, and with that object in view, sought to strip the lands, so as to render same useless to the owner.[17]

The motive for a drive in March was 'to focus attention on the need for land by uneconomic holders and labourers in the district'.[18] In April Michael Brennan warned agitators to desist but pledged to support land redistribution once political stability was secured. Brennan's intervention made little difference.[19] When Edward Westropp's land in Pallaskenry was seized by local smallholders, he was doubly aggrieved because the IFS afforded him 'no protection'.[20] Colonel William Yielding's family held nearly 700 acres near Athea for seventy years before it was taken over. He stated that 'the Irish Free State Government was repeatedly asked to restore order but were apparently unable to do so and the situation is now hopeless'.[21] The IGC questioned the legitimacy of this claim because Yielding apparently 'took no active steps to cooperate with the Irish Free State Government when the latter offered assistance in the protection of his property.'[22] Yielding's assessment that the government was 'unable' to intervene might well have been accurate, however. It was more than willing to stamp out radicalism but did not have the capacity to do so until near the end of the Civil War. In early 1923 Kevin O'Higgins, minister for home affairs, established a special infantry corps to suppress agrarian crime in the most disaffected areas. It made a limited number of arrests in Limerick. Its impact was most keenly felt in areas like east Waterford, where it broke a prolonged farm labourers strike in 1923.[23] In addition to the NA's pro-farmer intervention, Patrick Hogan, minister for agriculture, designed the 1923 Land Act to further land distribution and calm disquiet in rural Ireland.[24] It proved highly effective.

Digby Hussey de Burgh owned 230 acres in Dromkeen in east Limerick. There were two residences on the land, one containing twenty rooms and the other fifteen rooms. He was a magistrate and had resisted efforts to force his resignation. On 4 September 1920 armed men called to the family home in search of Digby's son, Ulick, but he had departed on his return journey to Sandhurst, where he was a cadet. Before the end of September, 'under threats of murder', the family left Limerick but were unable to find buyers for their property. De Burgh returned to Dromkeen in early 1922, but the boycott remained in place. While he barricaded the house, it was the surrounding land that was at the heart of the matter. He acknowledged that there was 'great trouble with the labouring class who were plotting to divide the property of their employers', and local notices proclaimed 'land for the landless', but de Burgh alleged that, in addition to these agrarian motivations, there were class-envy and sectarian dimensions to disputes in east Limerick:

> A conspiracy was formed to plough out the lands of certain Protestants ... The larger Catholic farmers sympathised with us privately ... The conspirators were told that the Irish Government would pass a new land Act that would enable the small farmers and labourers to take the property of the Loyalists.[25]

In April 1924 Labour TD Patrick Clancy addressed a public meeting in Dromkeen that coincided with de Burgh striking a deal to sell. Led by a long-time employee of de Burgh, locals intimidated the potential buyer into backing out and one of the houses was largely destroyed by fire. On 5 September de Burgh sustained serious gunshot wounds in 'a regular pitched battle'.[26] He claimed that the Land Commission did him 'a lot of mischief' during his time in London in 1925 and 1926 by interfering in a sale. He published *Western thugs: or, Ireland and the English speaking world*, in which he expressed an array of bigoted attitudes. De Burgh attributed the uncertain state of Ireland to a nefarious combination of Catholicism and communism.[27] Making a compensation claim from his new Canadian property in 1927, he outlined his plight as he saw it.[28] De Burgh understood his former great privilege as his natural right. Revolution, for de Burgh, meant more than nearly being killed. It meant a terrible transformation in his place in the world. He was driven from the luxury of the Limerick mansion that was his home and belittled, stripped of the status and even the staff which he regarded as properly his. His reduced position, in his eyes, was as a frontiersman. A degree of self-pity (deliberately exhibited perhaps with the IGC in mind) was offset by a remarkable strain of resilience (though not tolerance) as he struggled to come to terms with the reality of the new life which had been forced upon him.

De Burgh's 'Catholic Conspiracy' rant brings into focus again the question of sectarianism in Limerick. There was no religious significance ascribed to the destruction of the windows, organ and furniture in Glin Protestant church in April 1920 or the burning of Kilbehenny rectory, near Anglesboro, two months later.[29] The police acknowledged that the burning of Doon Glebe House in June 1921 was to prevent its occupation by the military.[30] On 5 August 1920 Councillor Patrick O'Flynn protested against what he saw as the failure of the unionists of Limerick city to condemn the persecution of northern Catholics and nationalists. He claimed that out of fifty-six businesses on O'Connell Street, Protestants, all doing a good trade and enjoying toleration, operated forty. He would be sorry if any reprisals took place but expected that the treatment meted out to nationalists in the north be meted out to loyalists in the south.[31] There were no reprisals and O'Flynn did not have to be sorry for his invective. By this point, many Limerick unionists were reconciled to the idea of political change in the nature of the Union and supported the campaign led by aristocrats such as Lord Monteagle for dominion status for Ireland. The interests of the middle classes of both denominations were gradually converging and there was no southern support for the exclusion of a six-county Ulster from home rule. On 21 August a large gathering of prominent local Protestants, including Sir Charles Barrington, James Goodbody, president of Limerick Chamber of Commerce, Frederick Cleeve and Monteagle called for the withdrawal of the Government of Ireland bill then before parliament and its replacement with a 'full measure of self-government on Dominion lines within the Empire and with complete control of finance'. They once again registered their stance 'against any form of religious intolerance which has happened in other parts of Ireland, which, happily, does not exist in the South.'[32] Some of these individuals were cocooned by privilege, however, and anxious perhaps to ensure that their economic interests remained as insulated as possible against the chaos whirling around them. Not all of their co-religionists were so lucky. Barrington suffered his own terrible loss when his daughter, Winifred, was killed in an IRA ambush of her Auxiliary companion in May 1921.

At a Limerick Corporation meeting on 28 March 1922, as the IRA was preparing to re-initiate the Belfast boycott, Patrick O'Flynn again singled out the Protestants of Limerick city and said it was remarkable that not one had condemned the anti-Catholic violence occurring in Belfast.[33] Prior to O'Flynn's outburst, a collection of Limerick's Protestant merchants had used the *Chronicle* to condemn sectarian police actions in Northern Ireland. Five Protestants who worked for Limerick County Council publicly declared their equitable treatment by their employer.[34] The Limerick Protestant Young Men's Association pavilion at Farranshone was burned down on 29 March; its premises at 97 O'Connell Street was damaged by gunfire on 30 March and a bomb on 2 April. The IRA reportedly combed the surrounding streets after the bombing but failed to apprehend the culprit. Liam Forde condemned the attacks and claimed that the Mid Limerick Brigade had nothing to do with them. The corporation registered its disgust and Michael Colivet denounced the actions as 'immoral'. A raid on Limerick's Masonic hall compelled Charles Barrington to defend what he regarded as a 'purely philanthropic' body that had no political or sectarian leanings. Masonic paraphernalia were damaged and the Union Jack burned during incursions into the Havergal hall on Glentworth Street in the city, a charitable school for poor Protestant boys which had close ties to the military.[35]

On 1 April Barrington, as vice-lieutenant of the county, called for an assembly of Limerick Protestants 'to condemn the outrages which have been perpetrated in Belfast'. They met in the Chamber of Commerce on 4 April and paid tribute to the good relations between Catholics and Protestants in Limerick and the south generally. The minority had 'thrived', said Barrington, thanks to a tolerant environment. Barrington's sentiments hint at the increasingly proximate interests of middle- and upper-class Protestants and Catholics. Attendees unanimously resolved that they had 'never suffered intolerance of any kind and that they lived in perfect harmony with their Catholic neighbours'. Among those present was Archibald Murray, president of the Protestant Young Men's Association, just days after his club had been attacked.[36] Murray, a Presbyterian, was chief executive of Todd's department store and presided over the Association for more than half a century. He either believed that there was no hint of sectarianism involved in the campaign against the Association or he felt coerced through circumstances and the fear of further repercussions into keeping his head below the parapet. Murray led the Association in pledging allegiance to the IFS during the Civil War.[37] Brian Murphy is absolute in his conviction that there was no sectarian conflict between Catholics and Protestants in Limerick. Life for unionists did, however, 'become more difficult during the Civil War owing to their support for the Free State' according to Murphy.[38] The distinction between political and religious intolerance was a fine one and it would have meant little to those who were targeted. There was another malicious fire inside the Farranshone pavilion on 17 December 1922. The Association had played the Catholic Institute in the North Munster Hockey League at Farranshone in late November and, displaying remarkable spirit, they managed to host another home game in January 1923.[39] Lieutenant H.A.D. Pierson, a member of the Limerick Young Men's Protestant Association, was fatally wounded in Kerry in 1923 fighting for the NA.[40]

A number of Protestant communities in Limerick made a point during the spring and summer of 1922 of highlighting the friendly relations they enjoyed with Catholics.[41] On 18 April, for instance, Reverend Neill of the

Limerick Presbyterian Church announced that 'there have been abnormal cases, but the great body of people have not suffered ... no one has suffered as a Presbyterian. There is no religious animus.'[42] In west Cork in late April 1922 thirteen Protestant civilians were killed. This prompted Liam Forde to issue a statement in the press on 2 May from the Mid Limerick Brigade, IRA. It warned that 'drastic action' would be taken against anyone guilty of threatening Protestants and called on 'every citizen to help in putting down conduct of this nature'. In a city recently vacated by the RIC and Crown forces, where the Workers' Housing Association had only weeks before staged a putsch at Garryowen Villas, and where the IRA were apparent powerless to prevent renegades from destroying Protestant property, the business class acted decisively to defend their interests. Mayor O'Mara called a supposedly public meeting in the Chamber of Commerce at 4.30 p.m. on Friday 5 May for the 'purpose of taking immediate steps to form a police force in the city'.[43] The identity of the gathering's convenor, its venue and its timing meant that it was for employers rather than workers and during the event O'Mara unambiguously described it as a 'meeting of the merchants and traders of Limerick' prompted by 'the insecurity of property'.[44] Of fifty attendees, fourteen had also graced the conference of the Protestant business community the month before.[45] The Limerick City Police Force was recruited exclusively from the ranks of the republican police.[46] In October 1921 Limerick Corporation had adopted the recommendations of a retrenchment committee to abolish the Night Watch and pension off its members. The raising of a new local civil police force in a country on the brink of civil war was no mean feat, even if its ultimate role was to protect bourgeoisie Limerick. Thirty-eight men were soon on the job, funded by subscriptions from business owners, and answerable to the civic authorities. Most of them were armed with revolvers, even though the corporation's legal adviser believed 'they had no power to shoot'. The force petered out as civil war wracked Limerick but its daily reports from 9 May to 29 June provide a valuable historical insight into the types of crime encountered: drunkenness, domestic abuse, petty theft. Water wasters, street hurlers and public swimmers were vigorously discouraged. After the battle for Limerick, it was left to the NA to police the city.[47]

When an attempt was made in March 1923 to burn Kilpeacon rectory, the home of ex-army chaplain Canon Charles Atkinson, he assumed it was because he was 'loyal to the British Connection'.[48] There does not seem to have been any possible military impetus, however, for the destruction by fire of the Methodist chapel at Ballylocknane, near Adare, on 28 December 1922.[49] There were only 273 Methodists in County Limerick in 1911. More than a dozen Methodists from west Limerick claimed compensation for various hardships endured between the truce and the end of the Civil War. The community of small farmers around Ballingrane, Askeaton, seemed to organize their claims to the Grants Committee as a collective, perhaps hoping that this would emphasize the shared nature of their experience. The Doupe brothers, Edward and John, both had their bicycles commandeered by the IRA. Edward's ten cows 'were driven into the turnips', causing £5 of damage. He lost one cow through 'over-eating'. At another point, his hay was burned, and because he was boycotted, he could not buy fodder for his animals and had to sell them below cost.[50] Henry Gilliard's bicycle was taken and he was prevented from working his two-acre quarry. His cabbage patch was continually trampled on.[51] Michael Ruttle had his bicycle and food seized and his wife 'became ill from fright'.[52] Henry Ernest Shier, from Barrigone, had a £10 bicycle and then its £12 replacement appropriated. The £2 model he bought next was untouched. He was stopped from tilling land and from moving livestock to market. The temporary removal of a horse delayed his harvest.[53] Enforced billets were common. John Sparling, Rathkeale, was boycotted. The refusal of labourers to work for him had dire financial consequences. Land was untilled and livestock unattended. Milk production on his farm fell because calves were over-reliant on cows. The animals had to be sold at a loss. His trees were cut. His motor bicycle and sidecar were taken, as well as his gun. Shots were fired at his wife. He was 'in a bad state of health, owing to persecution and worry'.[54] Two of the Sparling brothers were apparently court-martialled and condemned to death by the IRA but their sentences were not implemented. Their watchmaking and bicycle businesses were affected and their sister became unfit for work: 'She became a nervous wreck from shock occasioned by these outrages ... We are unable to afford to pay anyone to look after her.'[55] In 1928 Reverend W.A. Manning wrote of Kilfinane that the 'IRA were able to do what they liked ... owing to the absence of British military forces or RIC. Anyone who did not actively join the IRA and all Protestants were regarded as loyalists and fair game for looting and damage.' Manning's sexton, John Clancy, a Catholic, was boycotted 'for being a loyalist'. Clancy's village store was regularly raided and he was warned not to stock or sell British goods while another shopkeeper escaped such attention. Because he ran the local post office, Clancy was 'regarded by the ignorant folk as a minion of an enemy government and an object accordingly for their disfavour'. According to Manning, this was 'the unhappy position of any opposed to the IRA'.[56]

While the petit bourgeoisie sometimes lived on the sufferance of the IRA, big business was vulnerable to the revolution also. The *Church of Ireland Gazette* declared the 'Southern minority' to be 'one of the finest assets of the infant state'; 'it would be a serious matter if their energy and character were eliminated'. They paid the 'greater share' of taxes and their 'education and upbringing' meant it was natural for them to take a leading economic role.[57]

The Condensed Milk Company of Ireland, founded in 1889, controlled a large portion of the dairy industry in Limerick, with further units in Cork, Tipperary and Waterford. It was a Cleeve family enterprise. The Cleeves were members of the Church of Ireland and described themselves as 'supporters of the Government of the United Kingdom.'[58] At its most profitable from 1914 to 1918, when it provided condensed milk to the army, the business employed 3,000 people in Munster, with up to 700 employed at the flagship Landsdowne site in Limerick city (see map 2). There were 5,000 farmers in its supply chain.[59]

After the war, as British demand fell sharply, production and wages followed suit. In April 1919 output was affected by a two-week strike at Lansdowne. The Cleeve empire included a string of creameries around Knocklong. On 16 May 1920, frustrated by low wages, workers declared a soviet. Several dozen such 'soviets' sprung up around Ireland between 1919 and 1922. The majority, like Knocklong, were short-lived industrial actions. The Knocklong soviet made butter rather than profits, according to its own rhetoric, but it made sure to fly the tricolour alongside the red flag. ITGWU organizers Jack Hedley and John Dowling, who had been involved in the Limerick soviet, had pre-arranged continuing milk supplies and butter orders. On 22 May, when wages and demands about conditions were met, the Knocklong soviet disbanded. The local IRA had kept a close watching brief. Ironically, Frank Ryan of nearby Elton, who later founded the Republican Congress and served in the International Brigade during the Spanish Civil War, was the Volunteer who lowered the red flag. In August 1921 bakery and mill workers in Bruree replicated the example of their Knocklong comrades. They hoisted the customary tricolour and red flag, and a banner reading 'Bruree Workers Soviet Mills – We make bread not profits'. The ITGWU claimed that a wage increase and price decrease doubled sales. Minister for labour Countess Markievicz intervened on behalf of the Cleeves and seemed set to use the IRA against the soviet.[60] It relinquished control on 3 September. In December there was a similar outcome to a long-running stand-off in Castleconnell between fisheries workers and their employer, SF councillor Anthony Mackey. Markievicz again threatened to turn the IRA on the soviet, and this was enough to dislodge it.[61]

At the beginning of 1922 creamery workers in the Kilmallock area allied themselves to labourers claiming a harvest bonus. Donnchadh O'Hannigan reportedly declared IRA martial law in response, drafting in 200 Volunteers to protect farm produce and property. Four union officials were arrested. A farmer was kidnapped by strikers.[62] In February 1922 more than seventy cattle belonging to John Halpin, an 'extensive farmer' and chairman of the Kilmallock branch of the Farmers' Party – which may have provided a motivation for the attack – were left without fodder following the burning of his hay shed.[63] Arson of this nature attacked the heart of farming life, compromised feeding and caused real hardship to farmers big and small. Similar attacks in the area a few weeks later were condemned from the pulpit but they continued sporadically over the next couple of years.

The ministry for labour, meanwhile, was arbitrating between unions and Cleeves, who were pressing for swingeing cuts. Cleeves felt defeated in the propaganda stakes: the *Cork Examiner*, for instance, claimed that they cleared £1,000,000 profit between 1914 and 1918.[64] Multiple plants around the province, including those at Knocklong and Kilmallock, were occupied by striking workers in April and May 1922.[65] Creameries were sabotaged. The NA stationed troops at the Landsdowne factory. Production ceased from 15 April to 28 June, when the industrial action was called off. Cleeves, backed by the state, church and farmers, had faced down the workers on this occasion, but the battle for Limerick city prevented an immediate resumption of production.[66] English writer V.S. Pritchett was assigned to Ireland as a journalist during this period:

> Limerick was in an edgy state. It had just been relieved of a siege and there was still a crack or two of sniping at night. There was a strike on at the bacon factories and there was an attempt to start a Soviet. I went to see the committee and politely took my hat off and made a small French bow. The leader told me to put my hat back on. They had finished, he said, with bourgeois manners.[67]

In March 1923 the Cleeve creamery at Pallasgrean was destroyed by fire.[68] According to NA intelligence reports, 'at a meeting of Farmers held after 2nd Mass in Pallasgreen ... it was decided that Cleeves should be burned out of the country.'[69] They received compensation from the IFS for buildings, machinery and goods, but it was not enough to sustain the business. Coupled with a bad harvest, the collapse of the Condensed Milk Company acutely affected farmers and contributed to rampant unemployment in the city.[70]

The cost of the destruction of bricks and mortar, and even the scale of wounds inflicted on bodies, was more easily quantifiable than psychological trauma. The Church of Ireland rectory in Kilmallock was the scene of fierce fighting in late July 1922, after which Reverend Canon Sackville Taylor's wife suffered shock, neurasthenia and 'an element of brain fever'.[71] Cara Griffin, wife of Major P.J. Griffin, left Riddlestown for England with her children as early as December 1919. Major Griffin was serving abroad and Cara and the children were 'constantly threatened and persecuted on account of our loyalty'. She feared they would be burned out and that their lives were in danger: 'we were obliged to leave our beautiful home & that caused my nervous breakdown ... & my boy's breakdown.'[72]

Just days before the truce, Dean Hackett, whose worshippers in St Mary's Cathedral regularly sang 'God Save the King' under the Union Jack, and included a strong contingent of Royal Welsh Fusiliers, among other members of the Crown forces, told the diocesan synod that religious relations in Limerick remained harmonious, that his clergy were treated courteously in all circumstances and that there was no intolerance in Limerick.[73] Harry de Vere White succeeded the reserved Raymond d'Audemar Orpen as Church of Ireland bishop of Limerick in 1921. Addressing the diocesan synod in November 1921, de Vere White was outspoken about the wrongs inflicted on his congregation. He deplored any implication that Protestants should be indebted for sharing in the rights and liberties of all citizens and 'refuse[d] to be grateful to anyone other than the Almighty for permission to breathe the air of my native land'. They did not yearn for their old ascendancy, he stressed, but wished to move on in peace with their fellow Irish, despite being subjected to severe provocation. That Protestants were fleeing Ireland would be to the great detriment of the country, he warned.[74] By the summer of 1923, the amalgamation of parishes in de Vere White's diocese had been made necessary owing to the loss of numbers through, he claimed, burnings and intimidation. He suggested that Protestants were leaving because they felt they were not welcome and could not secure satisfactory careers.[75] The most forensic review of this movement of people concluded that 'revolutionary terror accounted for a relatively small share of Protestant departures.'[76] The change was most pronounced in the western seaboard counties of Galway, Mayo and Roscommon, none of them revolutionary hotbeds, suggesting that factors other than violence were key in the exodus.[77] Nonetheless, involuntary migrants – those pressured out by boycott, intimidation or violence – probably numbered well into the thousands, possibly into the teens of thousands.[78]

Just over 327,000 non-Catholics (almost all of them Protestants) lived in the twenty-six counties in 1911. Only 220,723 lived there in 1926. The cause and precise course of this collapse (33 per cent as against a 2 per cent decrease in the Catholic population) are complex issues.[79] British withdrawal was central but emigration, land reform, negative natural change (a higher death rate than birth rate) and the disproportionate commitment of Protestant Ireland to the First World War were all relevant. There was also anxiety among some Protestants about their place under the new dispensation post–1921. Between 1911 and 1926, the population of Limerick as a whole fell by 2 per cent. But its Protestant population dropped by 42 per cent, from 3,653 to 1,808 in the city and from 3,049 to 2,102 in the county.

When British-born Protestants serving in the armed forces (1,010 people) are removed, the decline of the Protestant population in Limerick is still a striking 27 per cent. Limerick city's Protestant population halved while the minority population of the county fell by a third. The decrease in urban areas

Table: Population of Limerick, 1911 and 1926[80]

Year	*Area*	*Total persons*	*Roman Catholic*	*Other Religions % Total persons*	*Actual numbers*
1911	City	38,518	34,865	9.5	3,653
1926		39,448	37,640	4.6	1,808
1911	County	104,551	101,502	2.9	3,049
1926		100,895	98,793	2.1	2,102

Year	*Area*	*Sects Episcopalian (C of I)*	*Presbyterian*	*Methodist*	*Jew*	*Baptist*	*Other*
1911	City	2,316	847	213	119	79	79
1926		1,285	147	104	30	38	204
1911	County	2,550	136	273	3	17	70
1926		1,691	65	206	3	10	127

was proportionately greater because the military were stationed in towns and cities, along with their families.[81] The longer-term view is even starker: the Protestant proportion of the population of the city went from 11.5 per cent in 1871 to just 3.1 per cent in 1936.[82] Thomas Keane's case-study of Limerick Boat Club reflects the fortunes of elite Protestant Limerick society. Founded in 1870, members of the club were predominantly Protestant unionists. Its ethos was distinctly imperial. Before the end of the century, however, as the Catholic bourgeoisie increasingly adopted the mores of the fading Protestant upper and middle classes, its denominational profile was diluted. The overall membership of the club declined by 56 per cent from 1922 to 1938, while the Presbyterian membership declined by 65 per cent from 1871 to 1936. From 1927 the majority of junior members were Catholic.[83]

9 Limerick in 1923

In 1912 Limerick's nationalists and separatists, and even its suffragists, all sensed opportunities for transformation. But Limerick unionists were wary and Limerick socialists were on the sidelines. They all had different ideals for Ireland. In 1923 they were all disappointed or marginalized to some degree. The unionist community was not in a position to resort to the extra-parliamentary tactics adopted by their Ulster brethren, nor did they show any desire to do so. Traditionally in the vanguard of Irish revolutionary movements, Limerick was simultaneously a major recruiting ground for the British army. Both nationalists and unionists paid a heavy toll while attempting to prove their loyalty in the trenches from 1914 to 1918. Joint sacrifice did not unite orange and green. Sectarian rather than civic markers continued as the most reliable symbols of identity. Leading unionists resigned themselves quickly to the fact that their form of political dissent was not widely welcome in Limerick. They adapted and improvised, promoting dominion status for Ireland before accepting the IFS. Those who could not embrace the new dispensation chose to leave Limerick; a number were not given the choice to stay and were forced out. The Protestant population plummeted. The IPP dominated local politics for four decades but did not achieve home rule for Ireland. Republicans did not realize a republic, much less a thirty-two county version. Self-imposed restrictions stymied the forward march of the left. Suffragists and feminists became increasingly peripheral as the martial characteristics of separatist republicanism took centre-stage. None of these competing philosophies had wanted partition, but none of them could avert it. In 1923 the majority were content that a mounting sense of anarchy was contained, and the middle classes were especially relieved that the social status quo was preserved largely intact. But bitter land and labour disputes persisted in Limerick, as elsewhere. The revolution was divisive in all of these ways and all sections of Limerick society were discommoded at some point during the decade.

The twin *raisons d'être* of the IPP were land reform and home rule. When these dual pillars were removed, the IPP edifice crumbled. Land war helped the IPP to establish its power before land purchase helped to undermine it. As redistribution afforded small farmers with prospects for a better livelihood, they disengaged from party politics. In Limerick city, the IPP was subverted by John Daly at the turn of the century and temporarily displaced by the AOH in the early 1910s. From 1914 the IPP was a prisoner of the war. As the value of land and the cost of farm products soared between 1917 and 1920, republicans viewed renewed agrarian agitation as a potentially dangerous distraction from their cause. SF, nonetheless, was happy to exploit the land question in the service of the national question and to benefit from this association in the same way that the IPP had in the late nineteenth century. In 1918 the voters' abandonment of the IPP for SF did not require a great leap of faith into the unknown. It was part evolution, part revolution. Some Limerick MPs had not been shy of flirting with potentially violent disorder when they felt such a combination would benefit their political agendas. The constitutional and physical-force traditions were never mutually exclusive, and their means and ends often closely coincided. They regularly intersected around agrarian agitation in Limerick. Significant slumbering sympathy for separatism was roused after 1916. So, while SF represented a new form of Irish nationalism, the influence of established local leaders helps to explain how it became a mass movement as quickly as it did: rather than creating a totally new organization, SF initially formed around the skeleton and built on the bones of an old one.

Republicanism was not Limerick's only source of revolutionary vigour between 1912 and 1923. Economic deprivation and the conditions created by the First World War fuelled an upsurge in union militancy in the city. Farm labourers demanded their share of agricultural spoils. Workers made substantial gains in terms of wages and representation rights. The Trades Council, backed by thousands of strikers, launched the Limerick soviet of early 1919. But Limerick was not a mini-Moscow and the soviet was not a local interpretation of Bolshevism. Crown militarism had incited the anti-imperial instincts of socialists, and separatists capitalized. At first glance, the soviet seemed to form one of the decade's most compelling and potentially fundamental challenges to the old regime. It was fleeting, however, and conservative in its ambitions. This was precisely because Limerick's reactionary Catholic and wider bourgeois interests were represented in the soviet alongside its radical elements. Working-class Limerick was in thrall to the hegemonic, thousands-strong, Redemptorist-led Confraternity. Radicals would harbour a lingering sense of disillusionment about the prosaic product of insurrection and hanker after lost revolutionary opportunities, the Limerick soviet among them. The economic model of 1912 was still in vogue in Limerick city and county in 1923. Farming and the land remained the priority. Slow improvements were being made in living and working conditions for the urban poor but in 1926 about 15,000 people or 40 per cent of Limerick's population of 40,000 still lived in slum conditions.[1]

On a practical level, the conversion of local government to republican purposes and the creation of a republican justice system was one of the most innovative and influential developments of the revolution. SF's operation of councils and courts was a regionally, rather than centrally, driven initiative. It was the staff of local authorities and parish justices rather than the officials of Dáil Éireann who provided leadership on key issues. Events in Limerick illustrate how moderate nationalists, including bureaucrats, rate collectors and bank managers, who were otherwise passive, acted as agents of revolution. Anyone who looked to the Dáil courts to settle a personal problem or legal wrangle lent authenticity to the republic. The campaign for independence was not simply a series of violent clashes between the IRA and Crown forces. The IRA's military struggle was ably supported by the Dáil's democratic work. In addition to facilitating the IRA, the republican counter-state simultaneously removed an essential function from British jurisdiction, grievously undermining British rule and assisting the Dáil in becoming the de facto government of the country. The perception of certain areas as having been 'inactive' is often based on considerations restricted to purely military matters and does not make adequate provision for other forms of protest and resistance. The success of the counter-state also fulfilled a fundamental propaganda function by expressing Irish ability to self-govern.

These attainments smoothed the path to an independent state. While not directly dependent on the IRA, these crucial advances would probably not have occurred without the simultaneous threat and actual use of force. Republicans had to sustain a delicate balance between the military and the political. It is possible that, had the truce not intervened, nothing short of a military victory by the IRA would have guaranteed the survival of local services. Without the protection afforded them by the Volunteers, the Dáil courts could have been undermined. The collapse of local government and justice under SF would not automatically have meant the end of the revolution but it would have been a severe psychological blow to republicans. Had the counter-state failed and SF been reduced to a solely disruptive role, more questions would have been asked about the tactics employed and the heavy attendant costs. But the continued survival of the IRA would not in itself provide a home for the elderly, nor solutions to those with legal problems. The revolution was a civil as well as a military struggle. Assessing the constitutional settlement of the Treaty from the republican perspective means considering the condition of the movement as a whole, not only the capacity of the IRA to prolong its war.

The IRA in Limerick was plagued by personal and organizational rivalries, class tensions, regional and rural–urban divides and, occasionally, mediocre leadership. This hampered the fighting record of the three Limerick brigades during the War of Independence. There were significant variations in performance levels, however. East Limerick, the only unit to seek confrontation with the British army, was by far the most active and effective. Mid Limerick, in turn, outperformed West Limerick. This is counterintuitive given that the East and Mid Limerick Brigades suffered debilitating internal splits. There is no correlation with the influence of the IRB, which was erratic. Neither can the inconsistencies be attributed to the role of IRA GHQ, which was limited up to the end of 1920. There was no discernible continuation of traditions of agrarianism. Principles of socio-economics or geography were not applicable. The fertile land of the Golden Vale provided for a stronger economy in east Limerick than elsewhere in the county, which theoretically should have reduced popular support for revolution. The territory of the West Limerick Brigade was more rugged and mountainous than that of East Limerick, which theoretically should have made it more amenable to the demands of guerrilla warfare. East Limerick was criss-crossed by a series of roads and its flat terrain was ideal territory for a highly mobile, mechanized military but not for rebels employing hit and run tactics and travelling on foot. Only the mountainous Galtee Battalion area around Ballylanders and Galbally was classic guerrilla country. The greater strength of the Crown forces in Mid Limerick, including the city, was a double-edged sword; there were more targets for the IRA, but more concurrent dangers. Furthermore, whereas there should have been two functioning IRA battalions in Limerick city, one carried all the burden. The units that saw most action were those that forged opportunities to fight. East Limerick had more guns than West Limerick because it seized more from the police and other sources. Mid Limerick had guns but they lay idle. The mixed fortunes of the Limerick IRA underscore the capacity of the popular and democratic roots of republicanism, and the importance of its political and civil wings. The complementary nature of these two dynamics was personified by Seán Wall in his dual role as brigadier of the East Limerick IRA and chair of the county council. Wall was an administrator and organizer rather than a fighting man and he delegated martial matters to soldiers. He regularly attended council meetings but was rarely involved in combat. Wall's detachment from military affairs is illustrated by, and was a contributory factor to, the circumstances in which he met his death at Annacarty, County Tipperary, on 6 May 1921. During an engagement with Crown forces, the unarmed Wall was proffered a weapon but refused. He blundered into the enemy patrol and was taken prisoner before being killed.[2] A memorial to Wall, which stands prominently in the village of Bruff, depicts him as a military leader and reflects the centrality of the IRA in how the revolution is remembered.

At least Wall is remembered. Some of Limerick's revolutionaries thrived in their role as heroes and benefitted materially but others were forgotten very quickly, and cast aside by the new Ireland. Joseph Treacy, 2nd Battalion, Mid Limerick, 'lost his mind' and spent six months in the mental asylum after illtreatment by Crown forces in March 1921. He fought with the ATIRA before being hospitalized again in late 1922 due to another 'nervous breakdown'. In 1924, when his claim for a wound pension was denied, he was homeless and destitute. Ex-servicemen suffering from 'shell shock' were commonly diagnosed with neurasthenia and the Army Medical Board diagnosed Treacy with

'traumatic neurasthenia'. In 1934 a Pensions Branch official, who had perhaps
seen many of these cases and succumbed to despair or callousness, judged
Treacy as 'naked & good for nothing but for the scrap heap like every other
Human machine.' From 1939 he lived in a billiards room at Bank Place. In
1940 Treacy appealed to the minister for defence, Oscar Traynor:

> I am a most unfortunate case ... I have not a copper to my name or no
> one to give it to me because I cannot approach my friends who have
> being so good to me in the past. I live in an old sellar and for long
> periods without food or clothes until charitable people come to my aid.

In 1951 he was certified as suffering from 'General Debility & Chronic
Bronchitis & Emphysema'. He complained of continuous noise in his ears and
suffered dizziness and falls. He was malnourished. His ongoing mental health
problems were diagnosed as 'Inadequate psycopathic Personality' and he was
provided with a special allowance but he had to move from his building at
Bank Place in 1951 as it was due to be demolished. From then until 1967, he
made his home in rent-free accommodation at Cornmarket Row. Listed as
'unfit for human occupation' in 1957, it was not condemned for another
decade. At the time of his death in 1968, Treacy was living in a hostel in St
John's Square.[3]
    Of all the changes wrought by the revolution, its obliteration of the RIC
was probably the most complete. The bloody battle between the IRA and the
police was one for moral authority as much as military supremacy. The IRA
won this war by reducing its adversary to expedient and gratuitous killing. As
the Black and Tans and Auxiliaries augmented the RIC from spring 1920, fear
and loathing increasingly dictated police behaviour. Membership of a besieged
faction encouraged the dilution of personal responsibility. The British cabinet,
rather than restoring order, created a 'climate of lawlessness' and exacerbated
an already chaotic situation. The Tans and Auxiliaries were recruited, trained
and deployed with indecent haste.[4] The Tans were integrated into the structures of the RIC and served alongside regular policemen, while the Auxiliaries,
a force apart, were designed explicitly for raiding purposes. The confusion of
the roles of policeman and soldier had predictably messy results. Increasing
militarization culminated in martial law. Thrust into extreme circumstances, the
Tans and Auxiliaries committed heinous actions. Many veteran constables
proved themselves just as capable in the art of reprisal. CI John Regan accepted
that while his charges could 'deal with a few armed moonlighters ... dealing
with organized bodies of violent men was completely out of the class of most
of them.'[5] Middle-aged policemen with families were unprepared for the challenge presented by a young and dedicated guerrilla army. The IRA clinically
exposed their deficiencies and weaknesses.

In Limerick, the war between the IRA and Crown forces partly descended into a self-perpetuating cycle of violence, often highly localized or even personalized, that could acquire its own logic independent of wider strategic concerns. Perhaps one half of IRA and two-thirds of Crown casualties died in what might be called combat engagements. Crown forces were responsible for the vast majority of civilian deaths in Limerick in 1920–1, employing lethal violence more readily and less discriminately than the IRA.[6] If there was any ethnically motivated killing in Limerick in 1920–1, it was committed by Crown forces. Most of the 'tit-for-tat' violence in Limerick was perpetrated by Crown forces, either in the course of reprisals or in the targeting of Volunteers. The majority of Crown forces targeted by the IRA were selected on the basis of tactical military deliberations, although this changed in the post-truce period. Crown force violence was stimulated by the frustration and rage engendered by guerrilla warfare. An implicit aim of some IRA actions was to provoke reprisals, which horrified public opinion and made an extension of martial law and troop numbers unpalatable. The political damage caused to the government by coercion and reprisals was irreparable. In this context, an assessment in terms of a purely military framework has limited value. The armed campaign of the IRA, however, in conjunction with the political manoeuvres of the Dáil, did play an invaluable part in bringing the British to the negotiating table. Not only did the use of force represent the most direct manifestation of resistance to British rule, it created propaganda opportunities to highlight British misrule.

Two hundred or so people were killed in revolutionary violence in Limerick, the vast majority of them between 1920 and 1923. The history of the revolution as a military confrontation between rebel freedom fighters and an oppressive imperial regime needs telling, but it is not a simple story. It was by turns gallant and hateful. Amid the collapse of state authority and the conditions of war, violence was more than just a military phenomenon. It was also a rational, versatile social tool, used to influence, intimidate and isolate. Occasionally, its application was purely punitive. The anti-imperial campaign for self-determination and national liberation should be central to any narrative of the War of Independence, as must the Treaty debate to the Civil War. But a military paradigm is inadequate in explaining some of the callous, intimate violence of the revolution, including that inflicted on civilians, whether in intra-community or state-citizen contexts. The character of much of the violence of the post-truce period became increasingly ambiguous, often lacking a definite military purpose. Provocateurs, perpetrators and victims often swapped roles or were one and the same. Both the ATIRA and NA killed prisoners in Limerick.

What it meant to be a unionist or loyalist is less easily definable than what it meant to be a Protestant but loyalists and Protestants in Limerick and elsewhere in the south lacked the strength in numbers, social networks and political power of their counterparts in more northern counties like Sligo and border counties like Monaghan.[7] Their former privileges had been dismantled and they were vulnerable. In some instances, a minority group in Limerick, whose Protestantism seemed inseparable from their culture, politics, social position, land ownership and connection with the old regime, suffered boycott, intimidation and physical harm because of that status. There is no evidence that it was common or coordinated enough to have constituted a systemic effort. Avarice and local opportunism appears to have been a big factor, vengeance and control featured less so. Concerns about IRA secrecy did not feature to any appreciable extent. Protestant emigration was a long-term demographic trend but it intensified in the crucible years of 1920–3. Emigration, of course, could be a personal preference, an economic choice, or a reaction to harassment or anxiety. On 6 October 1922 the *Church of Ireland Gazette* declared that a 'campaign of persecution is in progress' but absolved the government and the majority of the 'Irish people' of blame. At no stage was there state-sanction or popular support for the expulsion of Protestants. IFS rhetoric on religion carried a tone of goodwill and always emphasized inclusion. High profile Protestant figureheads were given a representative voice in the Senate. The interests of all landowners were generally zealously guarded and Protestants occupied senior positions in state land agencies and the Department of Agriculture. Sectarian attrition was not republican policy, and the state made all the right gestures of support for minority religious rights, but there was a disparity between this public policy and the lived experience of some Protestants. What it felt like to be caught up in the revolution cannot be communicated through statistics. Numbers do not tell people's stories. The honestly perceived experience of some victims was that sectarian impulses were at play. This impression was most pronounced after the truce of mid-1921 but there were precursors in the earlier phase. John Holmes, a court clerk from Galbally, felt that he was victimized because of his religion and his politics simultaneously, as if the two were one and the same: 'I am a member of the Church of Ireland and it was because of my being a member of this church and being loyal to the British government that I was boycotted'.[8]

Amidst the fog of war, it becomes increasingly difficult to differentiate between acts of violence, whatever form they took, and moral arguments are side-tracked. From gossip to rumour to suspicion, to decisions on innocence or guilt, life or death, is a slippery slope. Violence, whether minor or major, has the power to produce disproportionate emotional responses and levels of anxiety. There were often a range of motives or conditions determining a particular action rather than a single defining feature. Incidents of wanton cruelty, however, and the occasional presumption that life could be easily cast aside, sit uneasily with images of the heroic, selfless revolutionary or the disciplined, stoic policeman. Sometimes, there is no reconciliation. Most of the events of the period were non-violent, of course, and important only to the individuals and communities immediately concerned. People's primary concerns were for their personal safety and the well-being of their families, and they were happy to encounter the revolution only in small, indirect ways and to emerge unscathed from those encounters. Not everyone trusted the NA, but there is little to disagree with in its verdict at the close of 1923 that the 'feelings of the people' of Limerick were those of a 'normal community': 'One revolution and a civil war seems to satisfy most people for a life time'.[9] Some had benefitted and some had not, but everybody was weary and nearly all wanted to move on.

Notes

CHAPTER ONE *Limerick in 1912*

1 *Limerick Leader (LL)*, 29 May 1923.
2 *Census of Ireland 1911*, Table II: Comparative view of houses and population of the city and county of Limerick, as constituted at each of the ten censuses, from 1821 to 1911.
3 *Census of Ireland 1911*, Table VI: Area in 1911, and houses and population in 1891, 1901 and 1911, in the city of Limerick, and in each county district and District Electoral Division comprised thereof in the county of Limerick; W.E. Vaughan & A.J. Fitzpatrick (eds), *Irish historical statistics: population, 1821–1971* (Dublin, 1978), pp 28–41.
4 Vaughan & Fitzpatrick (eds), *Irish historical statistics*, pp 28–41.
5 *Census of Ireland 1911*, Table V: Area in 1911, and houses and population in 1891, 1901 and 1911, of the municipal boroughs and towns under local government or of 2,000 inhabitants and upwards, in the county of Limerick.
6 David Fitzpatrick, 'The geography of Irish nationalism, 1910–21', *Past & Present*, 78 (1978), statistical appendix, 138–9.
7 Department of Industry and Commerce, *Saorstát Éireann: Census of Population 1926*. Vol. 1, Population, area and valuation of each DED and each larger unit of area, Table 2: Population of each province and county in Saorstát Éireann as constituted at each of the eleven censuses from 1821 to 1926 (10 vols, Dublin, 1928).
8 *Census of Ireland 1911*, Table XXIX: Religious professions of the people; Vaughan & Fitzpatrick (eds), *Irish historical statistics*, p. 67.
9 Phil Lovett, 'Quakers in Limerick', *Old Limerick Journal*, 37 (Summer 2001), 3–9.
10 My position on the question of sectarianism in Limerick has evolved slightly since publication of John O'Callaghan, *Revolutionary Limerick: the republican campaign for independence in Limerick, 1913–21* (Dublin, 2010).
11 Patrick Maume, *The long gestation: Irish nationalist life, 1891–1918* (Dublin, 1999), p. 50.
12 J.J. Long, *History of the Limerick medical mission* (London, 1911).
13 *Hansard (Commons)*, 14 Apr. 1904, vol. 133, cols. 202–3.
14 *Census of Ireland 1911: area, houses and population; also the ages, civil or conjugal condition, occupations, birthplaces, religion and education of the people. Province of Munster, county and city of Limerick*. Table I: Area, houses and population of the city and county of Limerick in 1911, House of Commons, 1912–13 (Command Paper (Cd.) 6050).
15 Erhard Rumpf & Anthony C. Hepburn, *Nationalism and socialism in twentieth-century Ireland* (New York, 1977), p. 54.
16 P.J. Meghen, 'Social history' in Jeremiah Newman (ed.), *Limerick rural survey, 1958–64* (Tipperary, 1964), p. 157.
17 Gloria Maguire, 'The political and military division in the Irish nationalist movement, January 1921–August 1923' (DPhil, Oxford University, 1986), pp 68–9.
18 Fitzpatrick, 'The geography of Irish nationalism', statistical appendix, 138–9.
19 *LL*, 5 June 1914; Pat McCarthy, *Waterford: the Irish Revolution, 1912–23* (Dublin, 2015), p. 4.
20 Ruth Guiry, *Pigtown: a history of Limerick's bacon industry* (Limerick, 2016).
21 *Limerick Chronicle (LC)*, 23 Jan. 1915.
22 Jacqui Hayes, Brian Hodkinson, William O'Neill & Matthew Potter, *They dreamed and are dead: Limerick 1916* (Limerick, 2016), p. 11.
23 John Logan, 'Frugal comfort: housing Limerick's labourers and artisans, 1841–1946' in Liam Irwin, Gearóid Ó Tuathaigh & Matthew Potter (eds), *Limerick: history and society: interdisciplinary essays on the history of an Irish county* (Dublin, 2009), pp 571–2.

24 Thirteenth Annual Report on the Health and Sanitary Condition of the City of Limerick, 1915 (Limerick Archives (LA)).
25 *LL*, 2 Feb. 1910.
26 Ibid., 21 July 1913.   27 Ibid., 25 July 1913.
28 Jonathan Cherry, 'Landlords, estates, demesnes and mansion houses in County Limerick *c.*1870–*c.*1920' in Irwin et al. (eds), *Limerick*, pp 533–56.
29 Fergus Campbell, *Land and revolution: nationalist politics in the west of Ireland, 1891–1921* (Oxford, 2005), pp 90–1; Meghen, 'Social history', p. 157.
30 Rumpf & Hepburn, *Nationalism & socialism*, pp 47–8.
31 Donal J. O'Sullivan, *The Irish constabularies, 1822–1922: a century of policing in Ireland* (Dingle, 1999), pp 185–6.
32 Figures based on 1911 census returns from individual RIC bases.
33 UIL returns (The National Archives, London (TNA), Colonial Office (CO) 904/20).
34 O'Callaghan, *Revolutionary Limerick*, p. 17.   35 *LL*, 9 Aug. 1899.
36 Ibid., 29 Apr. 1907.   37 Ibid., 15, 22, 29 Dec. 1909.
38 David Fitzpatrick, *Politics and Irish life, 1913–21: provincial experiences of war and revolution* (2nd ed., Cork, 1998 [1977]), Table 4.1, p. 133.
39 McCarthy, *Waterford*, pp 12–13.   40 *LL*, 14 Feb. 1910.
41 RIC Inspector General's monthly report (IG), Jan., Dec. 1910 (TNA, CO 904/80, 82).
42 O'Callaghan, *Revolutionary Limerick*, p. 23.
43 IG, Apr., May 1912 (TNA, CO 904/86–7).
44 RIC County Inspector's monthly report (CI) Limerick, June 1909, Nov. 1910 (TNA, CO 904/78, 82).
45 CI Limerick, Jan. 1911 (TNA, CO 904/83); *LC*, 5 Jan. 1911.
46 CI Limerick, June 1911 (TNA, CO 904/84).
47 CI Limerick, Jan.–Feb., July 1912 (TNA, CO 904/86–7).
48 *LL*, 12 May 1913; UIL returns (TNA, CO 904/20).
49 Des Ryan, 'Women's suffrage associations in Limerick, 1912–14', *Old Limerick Journal* (Winter 1993), 41–6.
50 O'Dwyer's pastoral comments on suffrage prompted a flurry of responses, see *Irish Times* (*IT*), 19, 21, 24 Feb. 1912.
51 *LL*, 31 Jan. 1913.   52 *LC*, 2 May 1913.   53 Ibid., 13 Oct. 1913.
54 *LL*, 29 Dec. 1905, 19 Aug., 2 Dec. 1907, 12 Feb. 1908; *Sinn Féin* (weekly), 1 Feb., 14 Nov. 1908; *Sinn Féin* (daily), 8 Sept. 1909.
55 IG, Mar. 1900 (TNA, CO 904/70).
56 Quoted in Fergal McCluskey, 'The development of republican politics in East Tyrone, 1898–1918' (PhD, Queen's University Belfast, 2007), p. 54.
57 Michael V. Spillane, 'The fourth earl of Dunraven (1841–1926): local realities and "conciliation" politics' in Irwin et al. (eds), *Limerick*, pp 499–514.
58 Revd R.W. Jackson, 'Notes on the history of St Michael's (Limerick) Company No. 653 of the Church Lads for use on the occasion of the laying up of the Company colour in St Michael's Church at Evening Service on Sunday, 28 June 1942' (unpublished). Courtesy Johnny Conn.
59 My thanks to Johnny Conn for sharing his knowledge of the history of the Church Lads in Limerick.
60 Bulmer Hobson (BMH WS 31, p. 4).
61 Tom Clarke to John Daly, 26 Dec. 1912 (University of Limerick Glucksman Library Special Collections (ULGLSC), Daly papers, Box 2, Folder 47).
62 IG, May 1912 (TNA, CO 904/87).
63 Madge Daly, 'Con Colbert of Athea: hero and martyr' in Brian Ó Conchubhair (ed.),

Limerick's fighting story, 1916–21: told by the men who made it (Cork, 2009), p. 72. There are three versions of *Limerick's fighting story*, all of which are referenced in this book at various points.

64 Marnie Hay, 'The foundation and development of Na Fianna Éireann, 1909–16', *Irish Historical Studies*, 36:141 (2008), 54; Marnie Hay, 'Moulding the future: Na Fianna Éireann and its members, 1909–23', *Studies*, 100:400 (2011), 444.

65 Ibrahim Rashad, *An Egyptian in Ireland* (private print, 1920), pp 88–90.

66 National Archives of Ireland (NAI), Department of Finance (DF), 392 series. These claims are uncatalogued.

67 Compensation Claims to the IGC (TNA, CO762).

68 The release of MSPC files for public consultation remains ongoing at the time of writing.

69 Brian Hughes, *Defying the IRA?: intimidation, coercion and communities during the Irish Revolution* (Liverpool, 2016), pp 3, 208.

CHAPTER TWO *'The unionists went back into their shell': the home rule crisis, 1912–14*

1 *FJ*, 17 Dec. 1920.   2 *Cork Examiner (CE)*, 26 Dec. 1912.

3 *Irish Independent (II)*, 1 Dec. 1913; *CE*, 1 Dec. 1913.

4 *Sinn Féin* (weekly), 5 Mar., 14 May 1910.   5 *II*, 27 Feb. 1912.

6 *Freeman's Journal (FJ)*, 24 Feb. 1912.

7 CI Limerick, May 1912 (TNA, CO 904/87).

8 *CE*, 12 July 1912.   9 *LL*, 7 Aug. 1912.   10 *CE*, 11 Sept. 1912.

11 *LL*, 9, 11 Oct. 1912; *LC*, 12 Oct. 1912.

12 *LL*, 11 Oct. 1912; *LC*, 12, 15 Oct. 1912; *FJ*, 14, 18 Oct. 1912; IG and CI Limerick, Oct. 1912 (TNA, CO 904/88).

13 *II*, 18 Oct. 1912; *CE*, 18 Oct. 1912.

14 *Hansard (Commons)*, 14 Oct. 1912, vol. 42, cols. 784–5; 17 Oct. 1912, vol. 42, cols. 1401–3.

15 *LL*, 29 Jan. 1913.

16 *LC*, 22 Oct. 1912; *FJ*, 23 Oct. 1912; IG, Oct. 1912, (TNA CO 904/88).

17 *Evening Herald (EH)*, 8 Nov. 1912; *FJ*, 9 Nov. 1912.

18 *FJ*, 23 Oct. 1912.   19 *II*, 12 Oct. 1912.   20 *FJ*, 14 Oct. 1912.

21 CI Limerick and IG, Nov. 1912 (TNA, CO 904/88).

22 Jeremiah Cronin (BMH WS 1,423, p. 3).   23 *FJ*, 19 Jan. 1914.

24 Quoted in Peter Hart, *The IRA at war, 1916–23* (Oxford, 2003), pp 232–3.

25 *FJ*, 10 Feb. 1914; *CE*, 10 Feb. 1914.   26 *LC*, 3 Mar. 1914.

27 *FJ*, 3 Mar. 1914.   28 *LC*, 3 Mar. 1914.

29 Ibid., 14 Mar. 1914; *CE*, 16 Mar. 1914; *Southern Star*, 21 Mar. 1914.

30 *CE*, 7 Mar. 1914.   31 *II*, 20 Mar. 1914.

32 Ibid., 2 Mar. 1914; *CE*, 2 Mar. 1914; *Anglo-Celt*, 7 Mar. 1914; *Ulster Herald*, 7 Mar. 1914; *EH*, 28 Feb. 1914.   33 *FJ*, 28 May 1919.

34 *LL*, 3 Nov. 1916; *II*, 18 Jan. 1917; *CE*, 18 Jan., 11 July 1917; *Anglo-Celt*, 27 Jan. 1917.

35 *LL*, 5 Feb. 1913.   36 CI Limerick, Nov., Dec. 1913 (TNA, CO 904/91).

37 *LC*, 14 Dec. 1913.

38 Ibid., 27 Jan. 1914; Michael Brennan, *The war in Clare, 1911–21* (Dublin, 1980), p. 8; Liam Forde (BMH WS 1,710, pp 2–3); Tom Clarke to John Daly, 26 Jan. 1914 (ULGLSC, Daly papers, Box 2, Folder 47); Alphonsus J. O'Halloran (BMH WS 1,700, pp 1–4).

39 Pearse to Daly, 29 Jan. 1914 in Louis le Roux's unpublished biography of Daly, 'The life and letters of John Daly', ch. 13, p. 4 (ULGLSC, Daly papers, Box 3, Folder 73).

40 CI Limerick, Jan. 1914 (TNA, CO 904/92).

41 'Prosecution of civilians' (TNA, War Office (WO) 35/96).
42 Madge Daly memoir, p. 47 (ULGLSC, Daly papers, Box 3, Folder 77); Le Roux, 'John Daly', ch. 15, p. 9 (ULGLSC, Daly papers, Box 3, Folder 73).
43 *LC*, 16 May 1914.   44 Ibid., 30 July 1914.
45 Ibid., 9 June 1914; Madge Daly, 'Gallant Cumann na mBan of Limerick' in *Limerick's fighting story, 1916–21* (Tralee, 1947), pp 201–2; Madge Daly memoir, p. 51 (ULGLSC, Daly papers, Box 3, Folder 77); *Irish Volunteer*, 1 May 1915.
46 Robert Monteith, *Casement's last adventure* (Dublin, 1953), pp 51–2.
47 Casement to Daly, 24 Mar. 1914 (ULGLSC, Daly papers, Box 2, Folder 46); Casement to Daly, 28 Mar. 1914 in Madge Daly memoir, p. 32 (ULGLSC, Daly papers, Box 3, Folder 77).
48 Casement to Daly, 28 Mar. 1914 (ULGLSC, Daly papers, Box 2, Folder 46).

CHAPTER THREE *'It is England's war, not Ireland's': Limerick, 1914–16*

1 *LC*, 15 Aug. 1914.   2 *LL*, 2 Aug. 2014.   3 Ibid., 12 Aug. 1914.
4 Patrick J. McNamara, *The widow's penny: the memorial record of the Limerick men and women who gave their lives in the Great War* (Limerick, 2000); Tadhg Moloney, *The impact of World War One on Limerick* (Newcastle-on-Tyne, 2013).
5 *Limerick Post*, 21 Aug. 2014.   6 IG, Sept. 1914 (TNA, CO 904/94).
7 Fitzpatrick, *Politics*, Table 4.1, p. 133.
8 Alphonsus J. O'Halloran (BMH WS 1,700, p. 8); Madge Daly memoir, p. 50 (ULGLSC, Daly papers, Box 3, Folder 77); Mannix Joyce, 'The story of Limerick and Kerry in 1916' in *Capuchin Annual* (1966), 330.
9 O'Callaghan, *Revolutionary Limerick*, p. 38.
10 Madge Daly memoir, p. 51 (ULGLSC, Daly papers, Box 3, Folder 77).
11 Minutes, 1 Oct. 1914 (Limerick Archives (LA), Limerick Corporation minute book).
12 Minutes, 5 Sept. 1914 (LA, Limerick County Council (LCC) minute book).
13 McNamara, *The widow's penny*, p. 54.
14 CI Limerick, Aug., Dec. 1914 (TNA, CO 904/95); IG, Oct. 1914 (TNA, CO 904/95).
15 Parsons to Maurice Moore, 29 Oct. 1914 (NLI, Maurice Moore papers, MS 10,561).
16 Tadhg Moloney, 'The impact of World War One on Limerick' (MA thesis, Mary Immaculate College, Limerick, 2003), p. 36.
17 *LL*, 28 Aug., 2 Sept. 1914; Mac Diarmada to John Daly n.d. (ULGLSC, Daly papers, Box 2, Folder 52).
18 Le Roux, 'John Daly', ch. 15, pp 10–11 (ULGLSC, Daly papers, Box 3, Folder 73); Madge Daly memoir, p. 58 (ULGLSC, Daly papers, Box 3, Folder 77).
19 *LL*, 28 Aug., 2 Sept. 1914.
20 *LC*, 2 Feb. 1915; *FJ*, 12 Mar. 1915.
21 Breandán Mac Giolla Choille (ed.), *Intelligence notes, 1913–16* (Dublin, 1966), pp 149, 181–2.
22 *Statement giving particulars of men of military age in Ireland*, House of Commons, 1916 (Cd. 8390), p. 3.
23 *LL*, 16 May 1916.
24 *Report on recruiting in Ireland*, House of Commons, 1914–16 (Cd. 8168), p. xxxix.
25 *LL*, 2 Aug. 2014.
26 CI Limerick, Dec. 1914 (TNA, CO 904/95); Mac Giolla Choille (ed.), *Intelligence notes*, pp 80, 110.
27 *Irish Volunteer*, 15 May 1915.
28 Précis of information received by the Crime Branch Special (CBS), June 1915 (TNA, CO 904/97); Michael Hartney (BMH WS 1,415, p. 1); James Gubbins (BMH WS 765, p. 5).

29 Mick Quirke memoir, 'My life and times, 1896–1973', p. 6 (Des Long private collection (DLPC)).

30 Dan Breen, *My fight for Irish freedom* (Dublin, 1989 [1924]), p. 14.

31 *LC*, 25 May 1915; Liam Manahan (BMH, WS 456, pp 3–4); Ernest Blythe (BMH, WS 939, p. 45).

32 Pearse to Madge Daly, 28 May 1915 (ULGLSC, Daly papers, Box 1, Folder 29).

33 Mossie Harnett, *Victory and woe: the West Limerick Brigade in the War of Independence*, ed. James Joy (Dublin, 2002), pp 15–16.

34 CI Limerick, Apr., July 1915 (TNA, CO 904/97); *LL*, 28 May 2015.

35 *LC*, 7 Aug. 1915.

36 Monteith, *Casement's last adventure*, pp 39, 50–3, 198; Madge Daly memoir, pp 53–5 (ULGLSC, Daly papers, Box 3, Folder 77).

37 IG, July 1915 (TNA, CO 904/97).

38 Madge Daly memoir, pp 76–8 (ULGLSC, Daly papers, Box 3, Folder 77); CBS 'Personality file' on Ernest Blythe (TNA, CO 904/193/14A); Army records: 'Prosecution of civilians' (TNA, WO 35/96).

39 *Sinn Féin* (daily), 4 July 1914.

40 Quoted in James Gubbins (BMH WS 765, pp 8–9).

41 *Irish Volunteer*, 13 Feb. 1915, 16 Jan. 1916.

42 IG, Oct. 1915 and CI Limerick, Nov. 1915, Feb.–June 1916 (TNA, CO 904/98–100); Mac Giolla Choille (ed.), *Intelligence notes*, pp 149, 215, 222.

43 CI Limerick, Mar. 1916 (TNA, CO 904/99).

44 Ernest Blythe (BMH WS 939, pp 52–3).   45 *LL*, 4 Jan. 1915.

46 Ibid., 20 Jan. 1915.   47 Ibid., 25 Jan. 1915.   48 Ibid., 16 July 1915.

49 CI, Limerick, Jan. 1915, (TNA, CO 904/96).

50 IG, May 1915 (TNA, CO 904/97). See also CI, Limerick, June 1915 (TNA, CO 904/97) for more on anti-conscription speeches at UIL reorganization meetings.

51 See *LL* editorial, 2 June 1915. See also *Leader* reports on branch meetings of the Young Ireland, Cappamore and Croom UIL (4 June), Murroe UIL (16 June) and Abbeyfeale UIL (23 June).

52 CI, Limerick, June 1915 (TNA, CO 904/97).

53 *LC*, 7 Jan., 17 Apr. 1915; CI Limerick, Sept.–Oct. 1914, June, Nov.–Dec. 1915 (TNA, CO 904/95, 97–8).

54 CBS 'Personality file' on James Dalton (TNA, CO 904/1908/192).

55 Mac Giolla Choille (ed.), *Intelligence notes*, pp 170–4, 179.

56 *LC*, 9, 11 Nov. 1915; Précis of information received by the CBS, Nov.–Dec. 1915 (TNA, CO 904/120/2); CBS 'Personality file' on Bishop O'Dwyer (TNA, CO 904/207/246); *Nationality*, 27 Nov. 1915; *Report of the Royal Commission on the rebellion in Ireland. Minutes of evidence and appendix of documents* (1916) Cd. 8311, p. 3; O'Callaghan, *Revolutionary Limerick*, p. 40.

57 *LC*, 15, 19 June, 14, 21 Oct. 1915.   58 *LL*, 11 Feb. 1916.

59 Quoted in R.B. McDowell, *Crisis and decline: the fate of the southern Unionists* (Dublin, 1997), p. 63.

60 *LC*, 25 Jan. 1916.   61 CI Limerick, July 1914 (TNA, CO 904/94).

62 Tom Crean, 'The labour movement in Kerry and Limerick, 1914–21' (PhD, Trinity College Dublin, 1996), pp 98–9.

63 *LC*, 7 May 1918; *LL*, 8 May 1918.   64 *LL*, 22 Mar. 1916.

65 *LL*, 14 June 1915, 1 Mar. 1916.   66 Ibid., 16 June 1916.

67 Ibid., 27 Nov. 1918.   68 *Irish Examiner (IE)*, 18 Jan. 2016.

69 *LL*, 20 Nov. 1916, 18 May, 1 Aug. 1917.   70 *LL*, 15 Sept. 1916.

71 Ibid., 8 Feb. 1918.   72 *IE*, 18 Jan. 2016.

73 CI Limerick, Mar. 1915 (TNA, CO 904/96); McNamara, *The widow's penny*; Moloney, *The impact of World War One*.

74 *IE*, 18 Jan. 2016; Moloney, *The impact of World War One*, pp 19, 135.

75 *LL*, 10 Sept. 1915.

76 IG, Dec. 1915 (TNA, CO 904/98). Reports on the mail monitoring and the Limerick informant were all marked 'Secret' and presented to the CBS, Dublin Castle, between Nov. 1914 and Feb. 1915 (TNA, CO 904/164).

77 John O'Callaghan, *Con Colbert* (Dublin, 2015).

78 *Report of the Royal Commission on the Rebellion*, p. 1.

79 Compensation claim of John Wright's family (IMA, MSPC, DP8576).

80 Mac Giolla Choille (ed.), *Intelligence notes*, p. 215.

81 CI Limerick, May 1916 (TNA, CO 904/100).

82 Michael Colivet (BMH Contemporary Document (CD) 145).

83 Mac Giolla Choille (ed.), *Intelligence notes*, pp 240–1; CI Limerick, May 1916 (TNA, CO 904/100); *LC*, 11 May 1916.

84 Quoted in James Gubbins & Alphonsus O'Halloran, 'Limerick's projected role in Easter Week 1916' in Jack MacCarthy (ed.), *Limerick's fighting story from 1916 to the truce with Britain* (Tralee, 1965), p. 39.

85 Kathleen Clarke, *Revolutionary woman*, ed. Helen Litton (Dublin, 1991), pp 71–3; Madge Daly memoir, pp 113, 145–6 (ULGLSC, Daly papers, Box 3, Folder 77).

86 Transcript of interview of Peadar McMahon and Richard Mulcahy, 15 May 1963 (UCDA, Richard Mulcahy papers, P7b/181, p. 10).

87 *LL*, 28 Apr., 1, 10, 12 May, 19 July 1916.

88 *Hansard (Commons)*, 22 May 1916, vol. 82, cols. 1805–8.

89 CI Limerick, Apr. 1916 (TNA, CO 904/99); IG, July 1916 (TNA, CO 904/100).

90 Minutes, 6 May, 8 July 1916 (LA, LCC minute book).

91 O'Callaghan, *Colbert*.

92 *LL*, 29 May 1916; *LC*, 3 June 1916.

93 Thomas J. Morrissey, *Bishop Edward Thomas O'Dwyer of Limerick, 1842–1917* (Dublin, 2003), pp 378–9; Jérôme aan de Wiel, 'From "castle" bishop to "moral leader"? Edward O'Dwyer and Irish nationalism, 1914–17', *History Studies*, 2 (2000), 63.

94 Leon Ó Broin, *The chief secretary: Augustine Birrell in Ireland* (London, 1969), p. 189.

95 Mac Giolla Choille (ed.), *Intelligence notes*, p. 215.

96 Fitzpatrick, *Politics*, pp 96–9; Marie Coleman, *County Longford and the Irish Revolution, 1910–1923* (Dublin, 2003), pp 40–2.

97 Brian Murphy, *The life and tragic death of Winnie Barrington: the story of the Barrington family of Glenstal Castle, County Limerick, c.1800–1925* (Limerick, 2018), p. 109.

98 CI Limerick, June–July 1916 (TNA, CO 904/100); *LL*, 26 July 1916.

99 *LL*, 26 July 1916.

CHAPTER FOUR *'A centre of turbulence and rioting': from Rising to soviet, 1916–19*

1 Douglas Goldring, *A stranger in Ireland* (Dublin, 1918), p. 103. Éamon de Valera, leader of Sinn Féin, was unopposed in Clare East and won a contest in Mayo East.

2 *FJ*, 5 Oct. 1914.   3 IG, July 1915 (TNA, CO 904/97).

4 *LC*, 23 Jan. 1917.

5 Minutes, 5 July 1917 (LA, Limerick Corporation minute book).

6 R.B. McDowell, *The Irish Convention, 1917–18* (London, 1970), p. 175.

7 *LL*, 23 Jan. 1918.   8 *LC*, 16 Apr. 1918.

9 IG, Aug. 1916; CI Limerick, May–Aug. 1916 (TNA, CO 904/100).

10 CI Limerick, Aug., Sept., Oct.; IG, Oct. 1916 (TNA, CO 904/100–101); Coleman, *County Longford*, p. 78; Mobilization order to Limerick City Battalion, 3 Sept. 1916 (NLI, Florence O'Donoghue papers, MS 31,179).

11 IG, Nov. 1916 (TNA, CO 904/101).

12 Patrick Whelan (BMH WS 1,420, p. 13).

13 Brennan, *The war in Clare*, p. 21.

14 *LC*, 23 Jan. 1917; *LL*, 29 Jan. 1917; 'Confidential Print' (TNA, CO 903/19, pp 9–10).

15 *LL*, 3 Feb. 1917.

16 Reports by Weldon and Grandage, 18 and 19 Jan. 1917 respectively, to Headquarters, Southern District, Cork (TNA, WO 35/94).

17 CI Limerick and IG, Feb. 1917 (TNA, CO 904/102); *LL*, 23 Feb. 1917; *LC*, 24 Feb. 1917.

18 Bill Fraher (UCDA, Ernie O'Malley notebooks, P17b/129, p. 17).

19 Michael Hartney (BMH WS 1,415, pp 4–5); Peadar McMahon and Richard Mulcahy interview transcript, 15 May 1963 (UCDA, Mulcahy papers, P7b/181, pp 7–8, 10); George Embush (UCDA, O'Malley notebooks, P17b/130, p. 18); Michael 'Batty' Stack (BMH WS 525, p. 1); Brennan, *The war in Clare*, pp 21, 37.

20 Patrick Whelan (BMH WS 1,420, p. 14); James Gubbins (UCDA, O'Malley notebooks, P17b/129, pp 56–7, 60); Clarke, *Revolutionary woman*, pp 71–3; Madge Daly memoir, pp 113, 145–6 (ULGLSC, Daly papers, Box 3, Folder 77).

21 John J. Quilty (BMH WS 516, pp 16–7).

22 McMahon and Mulcahy interview transcript, 15 May 1963 (UCDA, Mulcahy papers, P7b/181, pp 2–3, 7–8); James Gubbins (UCDA, O'Malley notebooks, P17b/129, pp 56–7, 60); Dave Hennessy (UCDA, O'Malley notebooks, P17b/129, p. 63).

23 Peter Hart, 'The social structure of the Irish Republican Army, 1916–23', *The Historical Journal*, 42:1 (1999), 216.

24 James Gubbins (UCDA, O'Malley notebooks, P17b/129, p. 58).

25 McMahon and Mulcahy interview transcript, 15 May 1963 (UCDA, Mulcahy papers, P7b/181, pp 7–8).

26 Ernest Blythe (BMH WS 939, p. 75).

27 IG, June 1916, Jan. 1917 and CI Limerick, Jan., Mar. 1917 (TNA, CO 904/100, 102).

28 *LL*, 20 Oct. 1916, 8, 10, 12, 16 Jan. 1917; *LC*, 9, 11, 16, 18, 20 Jan., 3 Feb. 1917.

29 Tom Toomey, 'The rise of militant nationalism in Limerick city, 1912–17' (MA thesis, University of Limerick, 2006), pp 29–35, 38.

30 James Gubbins (UCDA, O'Malley notebooks, P17b/129, p. 56).

31 CI Limerick and IG, Mar. 1917 (TNA, CO 904/102); 'Confidential Print' (TNA, CO 903/19, p. 10).

32 Blythe to Madge Daly, 27 Mar. 1917 (ULGLSC, Daly papers, Box 1, Folder 4).

33 Staniforth to his parents, 14 Mar., 30 Apr. 1917 (Imperial War Museum, London (IWM), 'J.H.M. Staniforth papers: Kitchener's soldier, 1914–18. The letters of J.H.M. Staniforth', 67/41/1, pp 195, 198).

34 *LC*, 21, 23, 24 Apr. 1917; *LL*, 25 Apr. 1917; CI Limerick; IG, Apr. 1917 (TNA, CO 904/102).

35 CI Limerick and IG, Apr., May 1917 (TNA, CO 904/102–3); 'Confidential Print' (TNA, CO 903/19, p. 10); *LL*, 11 May 1917; *LC*, 12 May 1917.

36 *LL*, 8 June 1917; Liam Manahan (BMH WS 456, p. 25); Quirke, 'My life and times', p. 11; CI Limerick, June 1917, CO 904/103.

37 *LL*, 27 Feb., 20 Mar. 1918; CI Limerick, Mar. 1918 (TNA, CO 904/105).

38 Michael Laffan, *The resurrection of Ireland: the Sinn Féin party, 1916–23* (Cambridge, 1999), pp 185–7.

39 CI Limerick, Nov. 1918 (TNA, CO 904/107).
40 'Confidential Print' (TNA, CO 903/19, p. 22).
41 *LL*, 1 Oct. 1917.   42 Laffan, *Resurrection*, pp 62–4.
43 James Dore (BMH WS 1,302, pp 1–2).
44 'Sinn Féin Movement' (TNA, CO 904/23); CI Limerick and IG, June 1917 (TNA, CO 904/103); *Factionist*, 28 June 1917; *LC*, 26 June 1917.
45 James Dalton speech, Ballyvaughan, Co. Clare, June 1917 (NAI, microfilm MFA 54A–136).
46 Alphonsus J. O'Halloran (BMH WS 1,700, p. 25).   47 *LC*, 17 July 1917.
48 CI Limerick, June 1917 (TNA, CO 904/103); *LL*, 25 July 1917.
49 *LL*, 20, 22 Aug. 1917.
50 *Nationality*, 23 Mar. 1918; *LL*, 20 Mar. 1918.
51 IG, Sept. 1917 (TNA, CO 904/104); CBS 'Personality file' on Edward Punch (TNA, CO 904/213/363); *Times*, 6 Oct. 1917.
52 CI Limerick, Sept. 1917 (TNA, CO 904/104).
53 *LC*, 3 Nov. 1917.   54 *LL*, 7 Dec. 1917.
55 CI Limerick, Dec. 1917 (TNA, CO 904/104).
56 'Report on organisation of Sinn Féin', 19 Dec. 1917 (NLI, Count Plunkett papers, MS 11,405).
57 Fitzpatrick, *Politics*, p. 167.
58 Michael Conway (BMH WS 1,419, p. 3).   59 *Factionist*, 26 Apr. 1917.
60 'Confidential Print' (TNA, CO 903/19, p. 22).
61 *Factionist*, 17, 24 May, 14 June 1917.
62 *LL*, 20 July 1917; *Factionist*, 9 Aug. 1917.
63 *Nationality*, 13 Apr. 1918; *LL*, 22 Apr. 1918.
64 Liam Cahill, *Forgotten revolution. Limerick soviet 1919: a threat to British rule in Ireland* (Dublin, 1990), p. 38.
65 *Bottom Dog*, 20 Oct. 1917.
66 'Confidential Print' (TNA, CO 903/19, p. 22).
67 *Bottom Dog*, 18 June 1918.   68 *LL*, 6 Mar. 1918.
69 Michael Conway (BMH WS 1,419, pp 4–5).
70 Minutes, 13 Apr. 1918 (LA, LCC minute book).
71 *LL*, 15 Apr., 31 May, 10 June 1918. The presence of the defendants at the making of the resolutions was not proved. A number stated that they did not support the resolutions.
72 *LL*, 15, 17, 22, 24 Apr. 1918; *LC*, 16, 25 Apr. 1918; *Nationality*, 20 Apr. 1918; CI Limerick, Apr. 1918 (TNA, CO 904/105).
73 *LC*, 20 Apr. 1918; *LL*, 22 Apr. 1918.
74 *LC*, 4, 9 May 1918; *LL*, 3 May 1918.
75 O'Callaghan, *Revolutionary Limerick*, pp 74–5.
76 Laffan, *Resurrection*, p. 155.   77 *Nationality*, 19 Oct. 1918.
78 *Limerick Leader*, 20, 30 Sept., 4, 8 Nov. 1918.
79 Harnett, *Victory and woe*, pp 25–7; Volunteer, 'West Limerick activities' in MacCarthy (ed.), *Limerick's fighting story*, pp 228–9.
80 *LL*, 12 Sept., 18 Oct. 1918.   81 Ibid., 14, 18, 30 Oct. 1918.
82 Ibid., 14 Oct. 1918.   83 Ibid., 15, 24 Oct. 1917; *LC*, 23, 27 Oct. 1917.
84 CI Limerick, Nov. 1918 (TNA, CO 904/107); Fr Tomás Wall to Madge Daly, 6 Nov. 1918 (ULGLSC, Daly papers, Box 1, Folder 39); *LL*, 6 Nov. 1918.
85 *LL*, 8, 25, 29 Nov., 2 Dec. 1918; *LC*, 3 Dec. 1918.
86 CI Limerick, Dec. 1918 (TNA, CO 904/107).
87 *LC*, 14, 17 Dec. 1918.

88 *LL*, 30 Dec. 1918; Jack MacCarthy (BMH WS 883, p. 34); Daniel O'Shaughnessy (BMH WS 1,435, p. 3); 'Confidential Print' (TNA, CO 903/19, p. 22).
89 CI Limerick, Jan.–Mar. and IG, Mar. 1919 (TNA, CO 904/108).
90 *LL*, 12 Mar. 1919.
91 CI Limerick, Dec. 1918, Jan. 1919 (TNA, CO 904/107–8).
92 CI Limerick and IG, Apr. 1919 (TNA, CO 904/108); *An tÓglach*, 15 May 1919; Michael Hartney (BMH WS 1,415, p. 5); Michael 'Batty' Stack (BMH WS 525, pp 1–3); David Dundon (UCDA, O'Malley notebooks, P17b/114, p. 140); *LC*, 8 Apr. 1919.
93 *LL*, 7, 11 Apr. 1919.
94 Ruth Russell, *What's the matter with Ireland?* (New York, 1920), p. 129.
95 Conor Kostick, *Revolution in Ireland: popular militancy, 1917–23* (London, 1996), p. 70.
96 Quoted in Crean, 'The labour movement', p. 245.
97 Russell, *What's the matter with Ireland?*, p. 130.
98 *Munster News*, 26 Apr. 1919; Thomas Keane, 'Class, religion and society in Limerick city, 1922–39' (PhD, Mary Immaculate College, 2015), pp 29–30; Cahill, *Forgotten revolution*; D.R. O'Connor Lysaght, *The story of the Limerick soviet: the 1919 strike against British militarism* (Limerick, 2003).
99 *Worker's Bulletin*, 21 Apr. 1919.
100 CI Limerick and IG, Apr. 1919 (TNA, CO 904/108).
101 *II*, 21 Apr. 1919.   102   Michael 'Batty' Stack (BMH WS 525, p. 3).
103 *The Republic*, 3 May 1919.
104 Tom Crean, 'Crowds and the labour movement in the southwest, 1914–23' in Peter Jupp & Eoin Magennis (eds), *Crowds in Ireland, c.1720–1920* (London, 2000), p. 252.
105 CI Limerick, Mar., June, Dec. 1919, June 1920 (TNA, CO 904/108–10, 112).
106 *LL*, 14 June 1916.   107   Crean, 'The labour movement', pp 125, 141–3.
108 Russell, *What's the matter with Ireland?*, pp 126–42.
109 *LL*, 6 Dec. 1918.

CHAPTER FIVE *'We are the government of the country': the republican counter-state, 1919–21*

1 Ernie O'Malley, *On another man's wound* (Dublin, 2002 [1936]), p. 353.
2 Dorothy Macardle, *The Irish Republic* (4th ed., Tralee, 1968 [1937]), Appendix 33.
3 Ministry of Home Affairs report, Aug. 1920 (NAI, Dáil Éireann Courts (Winding Up) Commission papers (DÉCC) 2/51).
4 *II*, 5 July 1920.
5 *Dáil Éireann debates*, 19 June 1919, vol. F, no. 11, col. 130; 19 Aug. 1919, vol. F, no. 12, col. 143.
6 Arthur Mitchell, 'Making the case for Irish independence' in John Crowley, Donal Ó Drisceoil, Mike Murphy & John Borgonovo (eds), *Atlas of the Irish Revolution* (Cork, 2017), pp 474, 476.
7 O'Callaghan, *Revolutionary Limerick*, p. 84.
8 *LL*, 13 Aug. 1919.   9   Ibid., 16 July 1920.
10 Weekly summaries of outrages against the police and returns of recruitment, retirement and dismissal (Weekly summaries), 16 May 1920 (TNA, CO 904/148).
11 Daily summaries of reports on outrages, 19 June 1920 (TNA, CO 904/139).
12 Weekly summaries, 16 May 1920 (TNA, CO 904/148).
13 Compensation claim of Mountiford Westropp (TNA, CO 762/98/21).
14 Daily summaries, 10 July 1920 (TNA, CO 904/141).
15 East Limerick Brigade to Bottomstown tenants, undated (UCDA, Con Moloney papers, P9/248–6).

16 Daily summaries, 20 June 1921 (TNA, CO 904/146).
17 Compensation claims: various (TNA CO 762/40/2–3, 31/8, 43/8, 49/12, 53/2, 79/6).
18 *LL*, 8 Mar. 1920.
19 East Limerick Brigade report (UCDA, Moloney papers, P9/248–13).
20 6th Division Weekly Intelligence Summary, 12 July 1920 (IWM, General Sir Peter Strickland papers).
21 *FJ*, 4 June 1920.   22 Harnett, *Victory and woe*, pp 91–2.
23 Denis McDonnell (BMH WS 1,273, pp 2–3); Weekly summaries, 16 May 1920 (TNA, CO 904/148).
24 Jack MacCarthy (BMH CD 29/5/7); *LL*, 7 July 1920.
25 *LL*, 2 July 1920.   26 Ibid., 23 June, 5, 7, 9, 16 July, 2, 4, Aug. 1920.
27 Michael Sheehy (BMH WS 1,095, p. 7); James Collins (BMH WS 1,272, pp 20–1).
28 Casey to Stack, 15 Oct. 1921, and Stack to Casey, 18 Oct. 1921 (NAI, DÉCC 10/39).
29 *LL*, 21 July 1920; Jeremiah Cronin (BMH WS 1,423, p. 15).
30 Unnamed Limerick unionist to Sir Walter Hume Long, 30 June 1920 (TNA, Cabinet papers, 27/108, SIC 1693).
31 Quoted in Francis Costello, 'The republican courts and the decline of British rule in Ireland, 1919–1921', *Éire–Ireland*, 25:2 (1990), 46.
32 Thomas Moynihan (BMH WS 1,452, p. 4); Joost Augusteijn (ed.), *The memoirs of John M. Regan: a Catholic officer in the RIC and RUC, 1909–48* (Dublin, 2007), pp 160–1; Diary of Joseph Graham (Limerick Museum (LM), LM 1995.0138); Seán Carroll (UCDA, O'Malley notebooks, P17b/114, p. 126; P17b/130, p. 10); Seán Hynes (UCDA, O'Malley notebooks, P17b/129, p. 51); *LC*, 4 Dec. 1920; Daily summaries, 3 Dec. 1920 (TNA, CO/904/143).
33 *LL*, 30 July, 11, 16 Aug. 1920; *LC*, 10 Aug. 1920.
34 Daily summaries, 14 July 1920 (TNA, CO 904/141).
35 McDowell, *Crisis and decline*, p. 86.
36 David Foxton, *Revolutionary lawyers: Sinn Féin and Crown courts in Ireland and Britain, 1916–23* (Dublin, 2008), p. 181.
37 IG, Aug. 1920 (TNA, CO 904/112).
38 Irish Situation Committee meeting, 6 Aug. 1920 (TNA, British Cabinet papers 27/107).
39 CI Limerick July 1920; IG, July 1920 (TNA, CO 904/112).
40 Fr Punch to Stack, 8 Oct. 1921 (NAI, DÉCC 10/14).
41 West Limeric district court records (NAI, DÉCC 10/40).
42 Bridget Kennedy, West Limerick court registrar, to Ministry of Home Affairs, 9 Nov. 1921 (NAI, DÉCC 10/40).
43 CI Limerick, Oct.–Nov. 1920 (TNA, CO 904/113).
44 John MacNeice, Limerick City court registrar, to Stack, 18 July 1921 (NAI, DÉCC 10/38).
45 Stack to John Fogarty, East Limerick court registrar, 17 and 22 Aug.; Fogarty to Stack, 29 Aug. 1921 (NAI, DÉCC 10/39).
46 CI Limerick, Oct. 1921 (TNA, CO 904/116).
47 Fitzgerald to Stack, 4 Dec.; Stack to Fitzgerald, 5 Dec. 1921 (NAI, DÉCC 10/40); *CE*, 30 Nov. 1921.
48 *LL*, 16 Jan. 1920; *LC*, 17 Jan. 1920.   49 *LL*, 19 Jan. 1920.
50 Minutes, 30 Jan. 1920 (LA, Limerick Corporation minute book).
51 Crean, 'The labour movement', p. 253.   52 *LL*, 19 Jan. 1920.
53 CI Limerick, July 1921 (TNA, CO 904/116).
54 Minutes, 30 Jan. 1920 (LA, Limerick Corporation minute book).
55 *LL*, 2 Feb., 4 June 1920.
56 Tom Garvin, *1922: the birth of Irish democracy* (Dublin, 1996), p. 66.

57 *LL*, 12, 14, 31 May, 9, 11 June 1920.
58 CI Limerick, May 1921 (TNA, CO 904/115).
59 Minutes, 22 May 1920 (LA, LCC minute book).
60 Fitzpatrick, *Politics*, p. 155.
61 Minutes, 30 Jan. 1920 (LA, Limerick Corporation minute book); Minutes, 25 June 1920 (LA, LCC minute book).
62 *Dáil Éireann debates*, vol. F, no. 15, 29 June 1920, pp 169, 185; Local Government report no. 1, May 1920 and DÉLG to Public Bodies, 1 June 1920 (NAI, Dáil Éireann Secretariat Files 1919–22 (DÉ) 2/243).
63 Minutes, 3 July 1919, 20 June 1920 (LA, Limerick Corporation minute book); Minutes, 5 July 1919, 25 June 1920 (LA, LCC minute book).
64 Minutes, 17 July 1920 (LA, LCC minute book).
65 'Claims arising out of official reprisals in Ireland', 9 Apr. 1921 (TNA, WO 35/169).
66 DÉLG to Public Bodies, 'Severance of local authorities from the Local Government Board: instructions regarding the safeguarding of funds', 10 Aug. 1920 (NAI, DÉ 2/62).
67 *LL*, 15 Jan. 1927.
68 Minutes, 20 Oct., 3, 8, 18 Dec. 1920 (LA, LCC minute book).
69 Circular No. 21, DÉLG to Public Bodies, 19 Nov. 1920; DÉLG to Public Bodies, 7 Dec. 1920; Circular No. 25, DÉLG to Public Bodies, 13 Dec. 1920 (LM, Limerick Corporation: miscellaneous, LM 1987.5487, 5488, 5490).
70 Minutes, 9, 18 Oct., 6 Nov., 8 Dec. 1920, 22 Apr. 1921 (LA, LCC minute book); *LL*, 15 Jan. 1927.
71 Minutes, 30 Jan., 5 Feb., 15 Apr., 6 May, 21 June 1920, 6, 31 Jan., 17 Feb., 7 Apr. 1921 (LA, Limerick Corporation minute book).
72 Robert Graves, *Good-bye to all that* (London, 1929).
73 Minutes, 25 June, 17 July, 18, 24 Aug. 1920 (LA, LCC minute book).
74 Markievicz to LCC, 8 Sept. 1920 (NAI, DÉLG 17/15).
75 LCC, 6 Nov. 1920 (NAI, DÉLG 17/15); Minutes, 6 Nov. 1920 (LA, LCC minute book).
76 Minutes, 9 Nov., 8 Dec. 1920, 7 Jan. 1921 (LA, LCC minute book); LCC, Jan. 1921 (NAI, DÉLG 17/15).
77 Minutes, 24 Apr., 22 May, 18 Aug., 18 Oct. 1920, 1 Apr., 25 June, 13 Aug., 1 Oct., 3, 17 Dec. 1921 (LA, LCC minute book); Meany to DÉLG, 5 Sept. 1921 (NAI, DÉLG 17/15).
78 Minutes, 18 Oct. 1920 (LA, LCC minute book).
79 LCC (NAI, DÉLG 17/15).
80 Kildare County Council, 28 Oct. 1921 (NAI, DÉLG 13/11).
81 Limerick Union, June 1921 (NAI, DÉLG 17/6); *LL*, 17 Mar., 15 June 1921.
82 Kildare County Council, 28 Oct. 1921 (NAI, DÉLG 13/11); LCC, 10 Nov. 1920 (NAI, DÉLG 17/15).
83 LCC, Sept.–Nov. 1921 (NAI, DÉLG 17/15).
84 Forde to Mulcahy, 7 Oct.; Mulcahy to Forde, 18 Oct.; Mulcahy to Brugha, 18 Oct. 1921 (UCDA, Mulcahy papers, P7A/27). In an exchange of letters with Mulcahy on 21 Sept., Michael Brennan denied signing a reference for his brother.
85 LCC, Sept.–Nov. 1921 (NAI, DÉLG 17/15).
86 Minutes, 14 Oct., 18 Nov. 1920 (LA, Limerick Corporation minute book); Minutes, 20 Oct., 8 Dec. 1920 (LA, LCC minute book). The documents were returned after the truce.
87 Minutes, 24 May, 10, 24 June, 26 July, 6 Sept., 20 Dec. 1919, 28 Feb., 24 Apr., 15 May 1920 (LA, LCC minute book).
88 Minutes, 25 June, 3, 17, 31 July, 14, 24, 28 Aug., 11, 25 Sept., 9, 18, 23 Oct., 6, 9, 20 Nov., 3, 8, 18 Dec. 1920; 7, 15 Jan., 4, 24 Feb., 12 Mar., 1, 22 Apr., 25 May, 25 June, 13 Aug., 1, 22 Oct., 5, 19 Nov., 3, 17, 31 Dec. 1921 (LA, LCC minute book).

89 Minutes, 30 Jan., 5, 12 Feb., 4 Mar., 1, 15 Apr., 6 May, 3, 17 June, 1 July, 5, 16 Aug., 2 Sept., 14, 27 Oct., 3 Nov. 1920 (LA, Limerick Corporation minute book).

90 Compensation claim of Annie Dalton, James's widow (IMA, MSPC, ID467).

91 Foxton, *Revolutionary lawyers*, pp 225–6; Colm Campbell, *Emergency law in Ireland, 1918–25* (Oxford, 1994), pp 27–9.

92 Cosgrave to the Secretary of each County Council and Borough Council, 10 Sept. 1920 (LM, Limerick Corporation: miscellaneous, LM 1987.5486); Minutes, 9 Oct. 1920 (LA, LCC minute book); LCC, Sept.–Nov. 1921 (NAI, DÉLG 17/15).

93 Minutes, 4 Feb. 1921 (LA, LCC minute book); Mary Daly, *The buffer state: the historical roots of the Department of the Environment* (Dublin, 1997), pp 71–2.

94 Minutes, 2 Sept. 1920 (LA, Limerick Corporation minute book); Minutes, 9 Oct. 1920 (LA, LCC minute book).

95 *Dáil Éireann debates*, 18. Aug. 1921, vol. S, no. 3, col. 18–19.

96 O'Callaghan, *Revolutionary Limerick*, pp 107–8.

CHAPTER SIX *'Prepare for death': IRA versus Crown forces, 1919–21*

1   Richard Mulcahy, Staff memorandum, 24 Mar. 1921 (UCDA, Mulcahy papers P7/A/17). The 'War Zone' comprised the eight counties where martial law had been declared and which were garrisoned by the British army's 6th Division, specifically the six Munster counties along with Kilkenny and Wexford.

2   For a succinct typology, see Charles Townshend, *Political violence in Ireland: government and resistance since 1848* (Oxford, 1983), pp 334–6.

3   John O'Callaghan, 'Munster' in Crowley et al. (eds), *Atlas of the Irish Revolution*, p. 544.

4   Diary of Joseph Graham (LM, LM 1995.0138).

5   IRA public notice, undated (TNA, WO 35/96).

6   CI Limerick and IG, May 1919 (TNA, CO 904/109).

7   Compensation claim of Jane Gallagher (TNA, CO 762/106/13).

8   CI Limerick, June 1919 (TNA, CO 904/109).

9   Charles Townshend, *The British campaign in Ireland, 1919–21: the development of political and military policies* (Oxford, 1975), p. 138.

10 Tom Toomey, 'RIC consolidation in Limerick, 1919–21', *Old Limerick Journal*, 42 (Winter, 2006), 33–5.

11 Diary of Brigadier General Netterville Guy Barron, RIC Divisional Commissioner (UCDA, O'Malley papers, P17a/9).

12 *LL*, 19 Mar. 1920; *LC*, 20 Mar. 1920.

13 Toomey, 'RIC consolidation in Limerick'.

14 Diary of Barron (UCDA, O'Malley papers, P17a/9). Operation Strength Return 6th Division (TNA, WO 35/179) gives figures for May 1920 and Aug. 1921.

15 O'Callaghan, 'Munster', p. 549.

16 Weekly summaries, 11, 17 Apr. 1920 (TNA, CO 904/148).

17 Jeremiah Kiely (BMH WS 851, p. 9).

18 IG, Aug. 1920 (TNA, CO 904/112).

19 Daily summaries, 8 May 1920 (TNA, CO 904/139); Weekly summaries, 2 May 1920 (TNA, CO 904/148).

20 Military court of inquiry on Constable Patrick McCann, RIC (TNA, WO 35/154).

21 Military court of inquiry on Constable IG Moscrop, RIC (TNA, WO 35/155B).

22 Jeremiah Kiely (BMH WS 851, p. 10); James Collins (BMH WS 1,272, pp 14–15).

23 Seán Carroll (UCDA, O'Malley notebooks, P17b/114, p. 127; P17b/130, p. 9).

24 Tomás Malone (UCDA, O'Malley notebooks, P17b/106, pp 87–9); Tomás Malone (BMH

WS 845, pp 34–6); Daniel O'Shaughnessy (BMH WS 929, p. 27); Weekly summaries, 2 May 1920 (TNA, CO 904/148).

25 Seán Meade (BMH WS 737, pp 4–5).
26 Dave Hennessy (UCDA, O'Malley notebooks, P17b/129, p. 61).
27 Report of DI W.A. Egan, 28 May, in Daily summaries, 30 May 1920 (TNA, CO 904/139); Cornelius Kearney (BMH WS 1,460, pp 4–7); James Maloney (BMH WS 1,525, p. 19).
28 James Maloney (BMH WS 1,525, p. 19).
29 Tomás Malone (UCDA, O'Malley notebooks, P17b/106, p. 91); Garret McAuliffe (UCDA, O'Malley notebooks, P17b/124, p. 55); Ned Cregan (UCDA, O'Malley notebooks, P17/b124, p. 67); James Roche (BMH WS 1,286, p. 5).
30 *IT*, 29 May 1920; 'The Irish Rebellion in the 6th Divisional Area. From after the 1916 Rebellion to December 1921. Compiled by the General Staff, 6th Division' (History of the 6th Division), p. 25 (IWM, Strickland papers).
31 CI Limerick and IG, June 1920 (TNA, CO 904/112); Diary of Joseph Graham (LM, LM 1995.0138); Thomas Moynihan (BMH WS 1,452, p. 5); *LC*, 6 July 1920; Daily summaries, 18, 19 June, 10, 23 July, 22 Oct. 1920, 22 June 1921 (TNA, CO 904/140–1, 143, 146).
32 *LL*, 28 Apr. 1920.   33 *FJ*, 23 Oct., 27 Dec. 1920.
34 Daniel O'Shaughnessy (BMH WS 1,435, pp 61–2).
35 Jack MacCarthy (BMH WS 883, Appendix F).
36 Prescott-Decie to Assistant Under-Secretary Taylor, 1 June 1920 (NAI, Chief Secretary's Office (CSO), CBS Other papers, Carton 24).
37 *LL*, 30 June 1920.
38 CI Limerick and IG, July 1920 (TNA, CO 904/112).
39 Augusteijn (ed.), *John M. Regan*, p. 166.
40 CI Limerick, July–Aug. 1920 (TNA, CO 904/112–13); Weekly summaries, 8 Aug. 1920 (TNA, CO 904/149); Augusteijn (ed.), *John M. Regan*, pp 132–3.
41 CI Limerick, July 1920 (TNA, CO 904/112).
42 *LL*, 2 June 1920.
43 ULGLSC, Daly papers, Box 5, Folder 88; *LL*, 16, 20 Aug. 1920.
44 CI Limerick, Aug. 1920 (TNA, CO 904/113).   45 *LC*, 24 Aug. 1920.
46 CI Limerick and IG, Dec. 1920, Jan. 1921 (TNA, CO 904/113–14).
47 John Anthony Gaughan (ed.), *Memoirs of Constable Jeremiah Mee* (Dublin, 1975), pp 353–5.
48 Compensation claim of William Hall (TNA, CO 762/122/7); Compensation claim of Bridget Meade (TNA, CO 762/126/4).
49 Augusteijn (ed.), *John M. Regan*, pp 136, 145–6, 150, 154, 156, 162–3; Lord Monteagle to Joint Under-Secretary Sir John Anderson, 10 Sept. 1920 (NLI, Lord Monteagle papers, MS 13,416/1); Denis McDonnell (BMH WS 1,273, p. 3); Weekly summaries, 29 Aug. 1920 (TNA, CO 904/149); *LL*, 27 Aug. 1920; *FJ*, 28 Aug. 1920; *LC*, 28 Aug., 4 Sept. 1920; Daily summaries, 8 Sept. 1920 (TNA, CO 904/142).
50 *LC*, 14 Apr. 1921.
51 *LL*, 20, 22, 24 Sept. 1920, 24 Jan. 1921; *LC*, 21, 25 Sept. 1920; Harnett, *Victory and woe*, pp 65–6; Patrick Lynch, 'Terror in west Limerick' in MacCarthy (ed.), *Limerick's fighting story*, pp 244–51; James Collins (BMH WS 1,272, pp 14–5, 17–9); James Roche (BMH WS 1,286, pp 7–9).
52 Peter Hart, 'Definition: defining the Irish Revolution' in Joost Augusteijn (ed.), *The Irish Revolution, 1913–23* (London, 2002), p. 25.
53 Compensation claim of Pat Hartnett's family (TNA, CO 762/60/1).
54 Tom Toomey, *The War of Independence in Limerick, 1912–21* (Limerick, 2010), pp 317–18, 436.
55 Augusteijn (ed.), *John M. Regan*, pp 132, 162–3.

56 *LL*, 18 Oct. 1920.
57 Military court of inquiry on James O'Neill and Michael Blake (TNA, WO 35/151B).
58 Toomey, *War of Independence*, pp 318, 420, 438.
59 Augusteijn (ed.), *John M. Regan*, p. 162.
60 Military court of inquiry on Tim Madigan (TNA, WO 35/155A); Statement of Willie Madigan (NLI, Lord Monteagle papers, MS 13,416/2); Denis McDonnell (BMH WS 1,273, p. 4); Madge Daly memoir (ULGLSC, Daly papers, Box 3, Folder 77, p. 267); *LL*, 31 Jan. 1921; West Limerick Old IRA Memorial pamphlet (DLPC).
61 Compensation claim of William Hall (TNA, CO 762/122/7).
62 John Borgonovo, *Spies, informers and the 'Anti-Sinn Féin Society': the intelligence war in Cork city, 1920–21* (Dublin, 2007).
63 *LL*, 23, 26, 28 July, 2, 4, 6 Aug. 1920; *LC*, 22, 27 July 1920; Michael Hartney (BMH WS 1,415, p. 8).
64 'Brothers of the Faithful Circle' to O'Callaghan, 31 May 1920 (National Museum, HE EW 332).   65 *LL*, 18 Oct. 1920.
66 Kate O'Callaghan (BMH WS 688, pp 1–47); Kate O'Callaghan (UCDA, O'Malley note-books, P17b–116, p. 28A); Kate O'Callaghan, *The Limerick curfew murders of March 7th 1921. The case of Michael O'Callaghan (councillor and ex-mayor). Presented by his widow* (Dublin, 1921).
67 Frank Percy Crozier, *Ireland for ever* (London, 1932), p. 288.
68 Mid Limerick Brigade Intelligence Report to GHQ for July 1921, 25 July 1921 (UCDA, Mulcahy papers, P7a/8).
69 See Prescott-Decie to Assistant Under-Secretary Taylor, 1 June 1920 (NAI, CSO, CBS Other papers, Carton 24); O'Callaghan, 'Munster', p. 548.
70 Quoted in Gaughan (ed.), *Memoirs of Constable Jeremiah Mee*, p. 100.
71 Morgan Portley (BMH WS 1,559, p. 25); Paddy McCormack (UCDA, O'Malley note-books, P17b/130, p. 2); Military court of inquiry on Richard Leonard. Including a copy of General Cameron's report to Headquarters, 6th Division, Cork, 8 Jan. 1921 (WO 35/153B); *LL*, 31 Dec. 1920, 3, 5, 12 Jan. 1921.
72 Military court of inquiry on Denis O'Donovan, Sergeant William Hughes, RIC, and Temporary Cadet Donald Pringle, Auxiliary Division RIC. Including report by Macready, 1 May 1921, and report by Deputy Adjutant General, 3 May 1921 (TNA, WO 35/157A); Townshend, *British campaign*, pp 166–8; *LL*, 22, 25, 27 Apr. 1921; *LC*, 21, 23, 26 Apr. 1921; Bill Kelly, 'Cold blooded murders in hotel yard in Castleconnell' in MacCarthy (ed.), *Limerick's fighting story*, pp 214–20; Michael Hopkinson, *The Irish War of Independence* (Dublin, 2002), p. 94.
73 Augusteijn (ed.), *John M. Regan*, p. 135; Seán Clifford (UCDA, O'Malley notebooks, P17b/130, pp 4–5); Dave Hennessy (UCDA, O'Malley notebooks, P17b/129, pp 66–8).
74 *Times*, 4 Feb. 1920.
75 Patrick J. Twohig, *Blood on the flag: autobiography of a freedom fighter* (translated from *B'fhiú an braon fola* by Seamus Malone) (Cork, 1996), pp 127, 131.
76 Thomas Moynihan (BMH WS 1,452, p. 8).
77 Military court of inquiry on Dromkeen (TNA, WO 35/149A); Twohig, *Blood on the flag*, pp 130–1; Daily summaries, 5 Feb. 1921 (TNA, CO 904/144).
78 *LC*, 21 Dec. 1920; Harnett, *Victory and woe*, pp 161–8; Patrick Whelan (BMH WS 1,420, p. 15); Maloney, 'Mid Limerick activities', p. 164; Michael Hartney (BMH WS 1,415, p. 10); Richard O'Connell (BMH WS 656, p. 25).
79 'History of the 6th Division', p. 43 (IWM, Strickland papers).
80 Brennan, *The war in Clare*, pp 54–6; Hopkinson, *War of Independence*, p. 53; Tomás Malone (WS 845, pp 48–9); Jack MacCarthy (WS 883, p. 55); Richard O'Connell (BMH

WS 656, pp 11–12); Morgan Portley (BMH WS 1,559, pp 13–15); Uinseann MacEoin, *Survivors* (Dublin, 1980), p. 88; *LL*, 9 Aug. 1920.

81 Jack MacCarthy (WS 883, Appendix G); Tomás Malone (UCDA, O'Malley notebooks, P17b/106, p. 96).

82 Jack MacCarthy (WS 883, Appendix H); Liam Forde (BMH WS 1,710, p. 16).

83 MacEoin, *Survivors*, p. 93; Garret McAuliffe (UCDA, O'Malley notebooks, P17b/124, pp 47, 50, 52); James Collins (BMH WS 1,272, p. 19); Daniel O'Shaughnessy (BMH WS 1,435, pp 71, 84–6); Garret McAuliffe (UCDA, O'Malley notebooks, P17b/124, pp 47, 50, 52).

84 O'Callaghan, *Revolutionary Limerick*, p. 144.

85 Ned Tobin (BMH WS 1,451, pp 91–2); Bill Carty (UCDA, O'Malley notebooks, P17b/129, p. 10).

86 Green Howards Regimental History (Green Howards Regimental Museum); Ernie O'Malley, 2nd Southern Division, to GHQ, 1 July 1921 (UCDA, Mulcahy papers, P7A/21). On the ambushes at Sharharla and Lackelly, see also *LL*, 4 May 1921; 'History of the 6th Division', p. 102 (IWM, Strickland papers); Campbell, *Emergency law*, p. 98; Diary of Brigadier General Barron (UCDA, O'Malley papers, P17a/9); Daniel O'Shaughnessy (BMH WS 1,435, pp 87–93, Appendix B, pp 1–9); Michael Hennessy (BMH WS 1,412, pp 14–15); Liam Forde to GHQ (UCDA, Mulcahy papers, P7A/21); Richard Mulcahy to 2nd Southern Division, 16 June 1921 (UCDA, Mulcahy papers, P7A/38); Justin McCarthy (BMH WS 659, p. 3); Seán Clifford (BMH WS 1,279, pp 8–10); Dave Hennessy (UCDA, O'Malley notebooks, P17b/129, p. 61); Liam Forde (BMH WS 1,710, pp 17–22); Seán Carroll (UCDA, O'Malley notebooks, P17b/130, p. 13); Maurice Meade (BMH WS 891, pp 28–30); Séamus Malone (UCDA, O'Malley notebooks, P17b/103, pp 104–6).

87 Patrick Meehan (BMH WS 1,544, p. 12).

88 Forde to Mulcahy, 7 Feb. 1921 (UCDA, Mulcahy papers, P7A/116); Liam Forde (BMH WS 1,710, p. 16).

89 Mid Limerick Brigade report for Feb. 1921 to GHQ, 12 Mar. 1921; Mid Limerick Brigade report for Mar. 1921 to GHQ (UCDA, Mulcahy papers, P7A/38).

90 East Limerick Brigade training report, June 1921 (UCDA, Moloney papers, P9/248–14).

91 Eoin O'Duffy to GHQ, 'Report on Mid Limerick Brigade' (UCDA, Mulcahy papers, P7A/28).

92 O'Malley, *On another man's wound*, p. 351; Jack MacCarthy (BMH WS 883, p. 64).

93 Mid Limerick Brigade to GHQ, 21, 29 Apr. 1921; GHQ to Mid Limerick Brigade, 4 May 1921 (UCDA, Mulcahy papers, P7A/38).

94 Augusteijn (ed.), *John M. Regan*, p. 169.

95 Compensation claim of Ryan family (IMA, MSPC, 1D106).

96 West Limerick Brigade to 1st Southern Division, 2 Aug. 1921 (UCDA, Mulcahy papers, P7A/23); (UCDA, Moloney papers, P9/248–8).

97 Augusteijn (ed.), *John M. Regan*, p. 169.

98 East Limerick Brigade record of courts-martial, June 1921 (UCDA, Moloney papers, P9/248–12); Compensation claim of Morgan O'Brien (TNA, CO 762/19/13).

99 Ernie O'Malley report on East Limerick Brigade, June 1921 (UCDA, Moloney papers, P9/248–15).

100 O'Malley, *On another man's wound*, pp 350–1; Ernie O'Malley's Field Message Notebook, 'Army Book 153', May–June 1921 (NLI, O'Malley papers, MS 10,973/1); Ernie O'Malley, *The singing flame* (Dublin, 1992 [1978]), pp 37–9; Patrick Whelan (BMH WS 1,420, p. 17).

101 Jack MacCarthy (BMH WS 883, Appendix C2); British army report, 'Intelligence and contre-espionage: the IRA intelligence system' (IWM, Strickland papers).

102 O'Malley, *On another man's wound*, pp 350–1.

103 Mid Limerick Brigade to GHQ, 3 Mar. 1921; Richard Mulcahy to Mid Limerick Brigade, 9 Mar. 1921 (UCDA, Mulcahy papers, P7A/17).
104 Mid Limerick Brigade Intelligence Report to GHQ for July 1921, 25 July 1921 (UCDA, Mulcahy papers, P7a/8).
105 See, for instance, Military court of inquiry on David Tobin (TNA, WO 35/160); History of the 6th Division, pp 96–7 (IWM, Strickland papers).
106 'Blacklist No. 2, County of Limerick' (IWM, Lieutenant Colonel John Basil Jarvis papers, 98/11/1).
107 Jarvis's notebook (The Soldiers of Oxfordshire Museum, 3/7/A/1).
108 IRA GHQ General Order No. 24 (New Series), 9 June 1921 (UCDA, Mulcahy papers, P7/A/45); Quirke, 'My life and times', p. 34; Patrick Meehan (BMH WS 1,544, pp 4–5); Pension claim of Denis O'Leary (IMA, MSPC, MSP34REF12636); Military court of inquiry on William Sullivan (TNA, WO 35/159b); James Maloney (BMH WS 1,525, p. 28); Séamus Malone (UCDA, O'Malley notebooks, P17b/103, p. 97); Daniel O'Shaughnessy (BMH WS 1,435, pp 56–7); Twohig, *Blood on the flag*, p. 125; Daily summaries, 27 Nov. 1920 (TNA, CO 904/143); *LL*, 30 May, 16 Dec. 1921.
109 O'Callaghan, 'Munster', pp 553–4.
110 One unidentified man whose body was reportedly discovered in west Limerick in early January 1921 with the word 'Spy' printed on a piece of cardboard around his neck and a bullet wound in his chest was referred to in *LL*, 3 Jan. 1921. There is also anecdotal reference to a man being executed by the Castleconnell Battalion, Toomey, *The War of Independence*, pp 291–2. So, it is quite possible that there are two unmarked graves in Limerick containing the remains of victims of the intelligence war.
111 O'Callaghan, *Revolutionary Limerick*, pp 177–8; Pension claim of Patrick Ahern (IMA, MSPC, MSP34REF652).
112 Pádraig Ó Ruairc, *Truce: murder, myth and the last days of the Irish War of Independence* (Cork, 2016); Eunan O'Halpin, 'Problematic killing during the Irish War of Independence and its aftermath: civilian spies and informers' in James Kelly & Mary Ann Lyons (eds), *Death and dying in Ireland, Britain, and Europe: historical perspectives* (Dublin, 2013).
113 *LL*, 16 Feb., 17, 31 May 1920; *LC*, 27 May 1920; Séamus Malone (UCDA, O'Malley notebooks, P17b/103, p. 91); John J. Quilty (BMH WS 516, p 14–5, 17); Dave Hennessy (UCDA, O'Malley notebooks, P17b/129, p. 62); Kevin O'Shiel (BMH WS 1,770, Section 5, p. 746); Report of Dáil inquiry into Dalton (NAI, DÉ 2/121); Adjutant General Gearóid O'Sullivan to Rory O'Connor, 31 May 1920 (NLI, Count Plunkett papers, MS 11,406/2/4); John Dalton to Arthur Griffith, 23 June 1920 (NAI, DÉ 2/121); Michael Colivet to Michael Collins, 13 Aug. 1920 (NAI, DÉ 2/121); Frank Thornton (BMH WS 615, pp 12–3); Compensation claim of Annie Dalton (IMA, MSPC, ID467); James Dore (BMH WS 515, p. 4).
114 CI Limerick, June 1921 (TNA, CO 904/115).
115 *LL*, 29 Mar., 9, 30 Apr., 3 May 1920; *LC*, 27, 30 Mar., 1 Apr. 1920; Weekly summaries, 11 Apr. 1920 (TNA, CO 904/148); Harnett, *Victory and woe*, pp 47–50; Michael Sheehy (BMH WS 1,095, pp 3–5); James Collins (BMH WS 1,272, pp 4–5); Jimmy Roche (BMH WS 1,225, pp 12–3); William McCarthy (BMH WS 1,453, p. 6); Garret McAuliffe (UCDA, O'Malley notebooks, P17b/124, pp 56–7); *LL*, 30 Nov. 1935; Tomás Malone (UCDA, O'Malley notebooks, P17b/106, p. 90); Tom Wallace (UCDA, O'Malley notebooks, P17b/124, p. 59).
116 O'Callaghan, *Revolutionary Limerick*, pp 178–9.
117 *LL*, 8 July 1921; O'Malley's Field Message Notebook, 'Army Book 153', May–June 1921 (NLI, O'Malley papers, MS 10,973/1); Toomey, *The War of Independence*, p. 290; James Maloney (BMH WS 1,525, p.39); Séamus Malone (UCDA, O'Malley notebooks,

P17b/103, p. 110); Twohig, *Blood on the flag*, p. 125; Military court of inquiry on John Moloney (TNA, WO 35/155B); East Limerick Brigade Intelligence Report to GHQ for July 1921, 29 July 1921 (UCDA, Mulcahy papers, P7a/8).

118 Michael Geary and Richard Smith (BMH WS 754, pp 25–7).

119 Jane Leonard, 'Getting them at last: the IRA and ex-servicemen' in David Fitzpatrick (ed.), *Revolution? Ireland, 1917–23* (Dublin, 1990), p. 129; Peter Hart, *The IRA and its enemies: violence and community in Cork, 1916–23* (Oxford, 1998), p. 308; Borgonovo, *Spies, informers and the 'Anti-Sinn Féin Society'*, p. 91.

120 *LL*, 4 Nov. 1929; Garret McAuliffe (UCDA, O'Malley notebooks, P17b/124, p. 58); Army report, 24 June 1921 (TNA, WO 35/88); Jeremiah Kiely (BMH WS 851, p. 14); Patrick Mulcahy (BMH WS 815, p. 6); Ned Cregan (UCDA, O'Malley notebooks, P17b/124, p. 66); West Limerick Brigade to GHQ, 5 July 1921 (UCDA, Mulcahy papers, P7A/20); West Limerick Brigade Intelligence Report to GHQ for July 1921, 6 Aug. 1921 (UCDA, Mulcahy papers, P7a/7); *LL*, 27 June 1921.

121 IG, Jan. 1920 (TNA, CO 904/111); *LL*, 19, 23 Jan., 11 Feb. 1920; *LC*, 12 Feb. 1920; Seán, 'When the IRA held Newcastle West town', in *Limerick's fighting story*, pp 61–2.

122 Pension claim of Garret McAuliffe (IMA, MSPC, 34REF3694).

123 *LL*, 16 Feb. 1920.　　　124 Ibid., 30 Apr. 1920.

125 Ibid., 6 Sept. 1920.

126 A captured report on Gorman's court-martial is among Strickland's papers (IWM, Strickland papers).

127 Compensation claim of Crawford family (IMA, MSPC, 1D276).

128 Daniel O'Shaughnessy (BMH WS 1,435, pp 83–4); Michael Hennessy (BMH WS 1,412, pp 11–12); Ned Tobin (BMH WS 1,451, p. 92); Séamus Malone (UCDA, O'Malley notebooks, P17b/103, pp 97–8); Twohig, *Blood on the flag*, pp 122–4; Military court of inquiry on Ned Crawford (TNA, WO 35/148); Liam O'Dwyer & Michael O'Dwyer, *The parish of Emly: its history and heritage* (Emly, 1987), p. 153; *LL*, 30 Mar. 1921; *II*, 21 Oct. 1921.

129 Compensation claim of Michael Connery (TNA, CO 762/98/12).

130 IRA GHQ General Order No. 13 (New Series), 1 Nov. 1920 (UCDA, Mulcahy papers, P7/A/45).

131 James Maloney (BMH WS 1,525, p. 27).

132 Augusteijn (ed.), *John M. Regan*, pp 151–2.

133 *LL*, 1 Nov. 1920; Clarke, *Revolutionary woman*, p. 183; Madge Daly memoir, p. 257 (ULGLSC, Daly papers, Box 3, Folder 77).

134 'History of the 6th Division', p. 34 (IWM, Strickland papers).

135 *Irish Bulletin*, 19 May 1921.

136 CI Limerick and IG, July 1921 (TNA, CO 904/116); Daily summaries, 10 July 1921 (TNA, CO 904/146); West Limerick Brigade to 1st Southern Division, 2 Aug. 1921 (UCDA, Mulcahy papers, P7A/23); O'Callaghan, *Revolutionary Limerick*, p. 154.

CHAPTER SEVEN *'The people of Limerick want food, wages and work – not war': Civil War, 1922–3*

1 *LL*, 13, 15 July 1921.

2 Minutes, 31 Dec. 1921 (LA, Limerick Corporation minute book).

3 Liam Manahan (UCDA, O'Malley notebooks, P17b/117, p. 35).

4 *LL*, 2 Jan. 1922.

5 Field Message Notebook, 'No. 1 A.C.', of Ernie O'Malley, June–July 1921 (NLI, O'Malley papers, MS 10,973/2). A typescript copy of this Message Book is available in (BMH CD 53/2).

6 'Breaches of the truce' (TNA, CO 904/154); reported breaches of the truce (UCDA, Mulcahy papers, P7A/23).
7 CI Limerick and IG, Aug. 1921 (TNA, CO 904/116).
8 Limerick report (UCDA, O'Malley papers, P17a/9).
9 Mulcahy to 1st Southern Division, 6 Oct. 1921 (UCDA, Mulcahy papers, P7/A/26).
10 GHQ to 2nd Southern Division (UCDA, Moloney papers, P9/196); Daily summaries, 19, 23 Nov. 1921 (TNA, CO 904/147).
11 CI Limerick and IG, Sept. 1921 (TNA, CO 904/116); *FJ*, 27 Sept. 1921; *CE*, 27, 29 Sept. 1921.
12 Report on Mid Limerick Brigade, *circa* Aug. 1921 (UCDA, Moloney papers, P9/271).
13 Report on Mid Limerick Brigade, 23 Nov. 1921 (UCDA, O'Malley papers, P17a/111).
14 Report on Mid Limerick Brigade (UCDA, Mulcahy papers, P7A/28).
15 Report to GHQ, 24 Nov. 1921 (UCDA, O'Malley papers, P17A/105).
16 *CE*, 29 Sept. 1921; *II*, 26 Sept. 1921; *LL*, 23 Sept. 1921; *FJ*, 23 Sept. 1921.
17 *LL*, 10 Oct. 1921.
18 Mid Limerick Brigade intelligence report to GHQ for Aug. 1921, 18 Sept. 1921 (UCDA, Mulcahy papers, P7a/8).
19 RIC to Barry (IMA, Truce liaison and evacuation papers (1921–2), LE/B/4/12); 'Breaches of the truce' (TNA, CO 904/154); Augusteijn (ed.), *John M. Regan*, pp 176–8.
20 Strickland, HQ 6th Division, Cork, to Army GHQ Ireland, 22 Aug. 1921 (IWM, Strickland papers).
21 Augusteijn (ed.), *John M. Regan*, pp 148–50; Peter Hart (ed.), *British intelligence in Ireland: the final reports* (Cork, 2002), p. 49.
22 Séamus Malone (UCDA, O'Malley notebooks, P17b/103, pp 96–7, 99); Twohig, *Blood on the flag*, pp 114–16.
23 Extract from captured Crown document, *circa* Aug. 1921 (UCDA, O'Malley papers, P17a/9).
24 Rathkeale Workhouse correspondence (IMA, 'Specific breaches of the truce' in Truce liaison and evacuation papers (1921–22), LE/B/7); *IT*, 26 Nov. 1921.
25 *LC*, 6 Dec. 1921.
26 O'Malley, *The singing flame*, pp 41–2.
27 *Dáil Éireann debates*, 20 Dec. 1921, vol. T, no. 7, cols. 59–60; 4 Jan. 1922, vol. T, no. 11, cols. 241–2.
28 *LC*, 3, 7 Jan. 1921.
29 *LL*, 16 Dec. 1921; *CE*, 23 Dec. 1921, 5 Jan. 1922.
30 Maurice Meade (BMH WS 891, pp 43–4).
31 *Sunday Independent*, 12 Feb. 1922.
32 *CE*, 20 Feb. 1922.   33 *LC*, 21, 25 Feb. 1922.
34 NA – British GHQ correspondence (IMA, Truce liaison and evacuation papers (1921–2), LE/B/4/12).
35 J.R. Minshimpstead to Strickland, 4 Mar. 1922 (IWM, Strickland papers).
36 NA – British GHQ correspondence (IMA, Truce liaison and evacuation papers (1921–2), LE/B/4/12).
37 Keane, 'Class, religion and society', p. 32.   38 Logan, *Frugal comfort*, pp 573, 577.
39 *LC*, 16 Mar. 1922; *LL*, 17 Mar. 1922.   40 *LL*, 7 Apr. 1922.
41 *LC*, 17 Oct. 1922.   42 Logan, *Frugal comfort*, pp 573–4.
43 *LC*, 9, 19 Dec. 1922, 10 Jan. 1923; *LL*, 20 Dec. 1922; Keane, 'Class, religion and society', p. 38.
44 *LL*, 20 Feb. 1922.
45 *Dáil Éireann debates*, 26 Apr. 1922, vol. S2, no. 4, col. 255.

46 *CE*, 4 Mar. 1922.
47 Pádraig Ó Ruairc, *The battle for Limerick city* (Cork, 2010), p. 45.
48 Michael Brennan to assistant chief of staff, no date (NLI, Michael Collins papers, MS 22,127 (iii)).
49 Interview between O'Mara and Griffith, 9 Mar. 1922 (UCDA, Mulcahy papers, P7/B/191).
50 Seán Hurley to GHQ, 12 Mar. 1922 (NLI, Collins papers, MS 22,127 (iii)); O'Malley, *The singing flame*, p. 61.
51 Michael Hopkinson, *Green against green: the Irish Civil War* (Dublin, 2004 [1988]), p. 65.
52 Ó Ruairc, *Battle for Limerick city*, pp 50–1.
53 *CE*, 4, 17 Apr., 13 May 1922; *LC*, 6 Apr. 1922; Ó Ruairc, *Battle for Limerick city*, pp 50–1.
54 *Dáil Éireann debates*, 2 Mar. 1922, vol. S2, no. 3, cols. 197–201.
55 Collins to Quartermaster General, 17 Aug. 1922 (UCDA, Mulcahy papers, P7B/39).
56 *CE*, 17 July 1922.
57 General Dermot McManus to NA GHQ, 6 July 1922 (UCDA, Mulcahy papers, P7/B/60–61).
58 Seán Moylan to Liam Deasy, 6 July 1922 (IMA, Civil War captured documents collection, Lot 3, A/0991/2).
59 Compensation claim of Thomas O'Brien's family (IMA, MSPC, W2D122).
60 *II*, 20, 29 July 1922.   61 *IT*, 23 July 1922.
62 MacEoin, *Survivors*, pp 244–6.
63 *II*, 18, 22 July 1922; *IE*, 21 July 1922; *Sunday Independent*, 23 July 1922; *FJ*, 20, 24 July 1922; Ó Ruairc, *Battle for Limerick city*, pp 139–42.
64 *CE*, 25 Sept. 1922.   65 *LL*, 7 Nov. 1923.
66 South Western Command report, 29 Aug. 1922 (IMA, South Western Command papers, CW/OPS/09/01).
67 South Western Command report, 4 Aug. 1922 (UCDA, Mulcahy papers, P7/B/68).
68 Liam Deasy, *Brother against brother* (Cork, 1998 [1982]), p. 66.
69 General weekly survey for week ending 30 June 1923 (IMA, Limerick Command, 17 Mar. 1923–17 Oct. 1923, CW/OPS/09/12); Comment of General Seamás Hogan, Command Adjutant, South Western Command, 29 Dec. 1922 (IMA, Limerick Command papers, CW/OPS/09/04).
70 John O'Callaghan, *The battle for Kilmallock* (Cork, 2011), pp 82–4.
71 *II*, 31 July 1922.
72 Compensation claim of William O'Brien's family (IMA, MSPC, 3D221).
73 *CE*, 28 Aug. 1922; Compensation claim of Harry's Brazier's family (IMA, MSPC, WDP448); Compensation claim of Michael Danford's family (IMA, MSPC, DP60).
74 Adjutant Subdivisional Area to Adjutant 1st Southern Division, 17 Oct. 1922 (UCDA, O'Malley papers, P17a/88).   75 *LL*, 17 Aug. 1923.
76 Limerick Command reports, Mar. 1923 (IMA, Limerick Command papers, CW/OPS/09/12).
77 *FJ*, 3 Sept. 1923; *CE*, 3 Sept. 1923; *Nenagh News*, 8 Sept. 1923.
78 Limerick Command reports, May 1923 (IMA, Limerick Command papers, CW/OPS/09/12).
79 *Fermanagh Herald*, 27 Jan. 1923.
80 Ó Ruairc, *Battle for Limerick city*, pp 136–7.   81 *FJ*, 9 Feb. 1923.
82 Limerick Command reports, Oct. 1923 (IMA, Limerick Command papers, CW/OPS/09/16).
83 Limerick Command reports, Mar. 1923 (IMA, Limerick Command papers, CW/OPS/09/12).

84 Ibid., Oct. 1923 (ibid., CW/OPS/09/16).   85 Ibid.
86 *Kerryman*, 8 Mar. 1924; *EH*, 9 Apr. 1924; *FJ*, 8, 10 Apr. 1924; *LL*, 11 Apr. 1924.
87 *CE*, 28 Dec. 1923; *Southern Star*, 29 Dec. 1923; *FJ*, 2 Apr. 1924.
88 Prisoner lists (IMA, Civil War internment collection, CW/P/02/02/19).
89 *FJ*, 27 Dec. 1922, 17 Sept. 1923; *LC*, 28 Dec. 1922; Compensation claim of Kathleen Hehir's family (TNA, CO 762/50/8).
90 Compensation claim of Joseph Hanrahan's family (IMA, MSPC, 2D200).
91 McCarthy, *Waterford*, p. 121.
92 Gemma Clark, *Everyday violence in the Irish Civil War* (Cambridge, 2014), p. 93.

CHAPTER EIGHT *'We were obliged to leave our beautiful home': social strife, 1922–3*

1 *CE*, 21 Jan. 1898.
2 James Halpin (BMH WS 811, pp 4–5); David Moloney and Ned Enright (BMH WS 823, pp 3, 5); *LL*, 19 Apr. 1920; *LC*, 20 Apr. 1920; West Limerick Old IRA Memorial pamphlet (DLPC); CI Limerick, July 1920 (TNA, CO 904/112); Daily summaries, 29 Sept. 1920 (TNA, CO 904/142); Toomey, *War of Independence*.
3 *CE*, 11, 16, 17 Jan. 1922; *LC*, 12, 17 Jan. 1922; *Nenagh News*, 14 Jan. 1922; *FJ*, 17 Jan. 1922; *Anglo-Celt*, 21 Jan. 1922.
4 James Halpin (BMH WS 811, pp 4–5).
5 Augusteijn (ed.), *John M. Regan*, p. 181.
6 John Reynolds, *46 dead men: the Royal Irish Constabulary in County Tipperary, 1919–22* (Cork, 2016).
7 *IT*, 13 Apr., 2 May 1922.
8 Compensation claim of Maurice Reidy (TNA, CO 762/144/11).
9 Compensation claim of Patrick Sullivan (TNA, CO 762/169/3).
10 Compensation claim of Isaac Langrill (TNA, CO 762/11/5).
11 Compensation claim of Margaret Murphy (TNA, CO 762/49/6).
12 Compensation claim of Rachel Walker (TNA, CO 762/143/12).
13 Compensation claim of Michael O'Brien (TNA, CO 762/59/3).
14 Compensation claim of Maurice O'Brien (TNA, CO 762/59/2).
15 Compensation claim of John O'Brien (TNA, CO 762/141/13).
16 Compensation claim of Frances Ievers (TNA, CO 762/114/24, CO 762/185/6); Compensation claim of Frances Ievers (NAI, DF, 392/274).
17 Compensation claim of Denis Hickey (NAI, DF, 392/29, 31).
18 *LL*, 3 Mar. 1922.   19 Ibid., 28 Apr. 1922.
20 Compensation claim of Edward Westropp (NAI, DF, 392/227).
21 Compensation claim of Colonel William Yielding (NAI, DF, 392/305).
22 Compensation claim of Colonel William Yielding (TNA, CO 762/915/9).
23 McCarthy, *Waterford*, pp 122–6.   24 *Revolution Papers*, 28 Nov. 2016.
25 Compensation claim of Digby Hussey de Burgh (TNA, CO 762/37/9–10).
26 *EH*, 6 Sept. 1924; *Sunday Independent*, 7 Sept. 1924; *CE*, 8, 9, 11, 15, 19 Sept. 1924; *FJ*, 8 Sept. 1924; *II*, 9, 24 Sept., 1 Nov. 1924; *LL*, 24 Sept. 1924.
27 Digby Hussey de Burgh, *Western thugs: or, Ireland and the English speaking world* (London, 1925), p. 117.
28 Compensation claim of Digby Hussey de Burgh (TNA, CO 762/37/9–10).
29 *FJ*, 6 Apr. 1920; *CE*, 1 June 1920.
30 Daily summaries, 24 June 1921 (TNA, CO 904/146).
31 Minutes, 5 Aug. 1920 (LA, Limerick Corporation minute book).
32 *LL*, 25 Aug. 1920; *CE*, 25 Aug. 1920.   33 *CE*, 30 Mar. 1922.

34 *LC*, 28 Mar., 1 Apr. 1922.
35 Limerick Protestant Young Men's Association papers (ULGLSC); Compensation claims of William Benjamin Furlong and Archdeacon John Thomas Waller (TNA, CO 762/155/5; 762/98/9); *LC*, 30 Mar. 1922; *LL*, 31 Mar. 1922; *CE*, 31 Mar. 1922; *II*, 31 Mar. 1922; *EH*, 30 Mar. 1922.
36 *LC*, 4 Apr. 1922; *II*, 5 Apr. 1922; *CE*, 5 Apr. 1922; *LL*, 7 Apr. 1922.
37 *CE*, 24 Oct. 1922; *FJ*, 23 Oct. 1922.   38 Murphy, *Winnie Barrington*, p. xiii.
39 *CE*, 29 Nov. 1922; *FJ*, 26 Jan. 1923.   40 *CE*, 21, 23 Apr. 1923.
41 *II*, 6 Apr. 1922; *CE*, 28 Apr. 1922.   42 *LC*, 20 Apr. 1922.
43 *LC*, 4 May 1922.   44 Ibid., 9 May 1922.   45 Ibid., 6 May 1922.
46 *LL*, 10 May 1922   47 Limerick City Police Force archive (LA, IE LA L/PC).
48 Compensation claim of Canon Charles Atkinson (TNA, CO 762/184/3); Compensation claim of Canon Charles Atkinson (NAI, DF, 392/260).
49 Compensation claim of Reverend James Johnson, Arthur Bridge and Arthur Switzer (NAI, DF, 392/134).
50 Compensation claim of Edward and John Doupe (TNA, CO 762/195/18–19).
51 Compensation claim of Henry Gilliard (TNA, CO 762/195/13).
52 Compensation claim of Michael Ruttle (TNA, CO 762/195/21).
53 Compensation claim of Henry Ernest Shier (TNA, CO 762/195/20).
54 Compensation claim of John Sparling (TNA, CO 762/195/15).
55 Compensation claim of Sparling family (TNA, CO 762/195/16).
56 Compensation claim of John Clancy (TNA, CO 762/108/1).
57 *Church of Ireland Gazette*, 23 June, 6 Oct. 1922.
58 Compensation claim of Cleeve family (TNA, CO 762/189/6). Various members and combinations of the Cleeve family submitted a host of claims to the IGC (TNA, CO 762/189/6–16).
59 *EH*, 14 Apr. 1919.
60 *Voice of Labour*, 10 Nov. 1923; D.R. O'Connor Lysaght, 'The Munster Soviet Creameries', *Irish History Workshop*, 1 (1981), 43.
61 List of decisions at meeting of the Ministry of Economic Affairs, 2 Dec. 1921 (NAI, DÉ 2/5, Document No. 180).
62 *Munster News*, 21 Jan. 1922; Donal Ó Drisceoil, 'Losing a war it never fought: labour, socialism and the War of Independence' in Crowley et al. (eds), *Atlas of the Irish Revolution*, pp 490–3.
63 *LL*, 1, 15 Feb., 8 Mar. 1922.   64 *CE*, 15 Apr. 1922.
65 *LL*, 15, 17 May 1922.
66 Compensation claim of Cleeve family (TNA, CO 762/189/6).
67 V.S. Pritchett, *Midnight oil* (New York, 1973), p. 117.
68 *FJ*, 10 Mar. 1923.
69 South Western Command reports, Mar. 1923 (IMA, Limerick Command papers, CW/OPS/09/05).
70 Limerick Command reports, Oct. 1923 (IMA, Limerick Command papers, CW/OPS/09/16).
71 Compensation claim of Reverend Canon Sackville Taylor (TNA, CO 762/27/7).
72 Compensation claim of Cara Griffin (TNA, CO 762/116/19).
73 *Fermanagh Herald*, 9 July 1921.
74 *FJ*, 4 Nov. 1921; *CE*, 4 Nov. 1921.
75 *FJ*, 14, 23 June 1923.
76 Andy Bielenberg, 'Exodus: the emigration of southern Irish Protestants during the Irish War of Independence and the Civil War', *Past & Present*, 218:1 (2013), 202.
77 Ibid., p. 202 and Table 3, 205.   78 Ibid., Table 6, 223.

79 Statistical analyses are provided by Bielenberg, 'Exodus' and Enda Delaney, *Demography, state and society: Irish migration to Britain, 1921–71* (Liverpool, 2000).

80 Department of Industry and Commerce, *Saorstát Éireann: Census of Population 1926*. Vol. 3, Summary of Religion and Birthplaces, Table 9: Number of persons of each religion in each county and county borough in Saorstát Éireann at each census year from 1861, the first year for which figures are available (10 vols, Dublin, 1929). The original 1926 census returns will not be publicly available until 2026. Gemma Clark constructed a version of this table in her *Everyday violence*, p. 47.

81 Bielenberg, 'Exodus', p. 202 and Table 3, 205; Clark, *Everyday violence*, pp 38–51.

82 Department of Industry and Commerce, *Saorstát Éireann: Census of Population 1936*. Vol. 3, Religion and Birthplaces, Part 1, Religion, Table 9: Number of persons of each religion in each county and county borough in Saorstát Éireann at each census year from 1871 (8 vols, Dublin, 1939).

83 Keane, 'Class, religion and civil society', pp 107–35.

CHAPTER NINE *Limerick in 1923*

1 Department of Industry and Commerce, *Census of Population 1926*, Vol. 4, Housing (10 vols, Dublin, 1929).

2 Tomás Malone (UCDA, O'Malley notebooks, P17b/106, p. 122); Tomás Malone (BMH WS 845, p. 30); Daniel O'Shaughnessy (BMH WS 1,435, p. 23); Jack MacCarthy (BMH WS 883, pp 29–30); Maurice Meade (BMH WS 891, pp 33–4); Donnchadh O'Hannigan (BMH WS 600, pp 38–9); Seán Meade (BMH WS 737, p. 11).

3 Pension claim of Joseph Treacy (IMA, MSPC, MSP34REF12136; 1P120; 43SA2977).

4 David Leeson, *The Black and Tans: British police and Auxiliaries in the Irish War of Independence, 1920–21* (Oxford, 2012), p. 223.

5 Augusteijn (ed.), *John M. Regan*, p. 116.

6 O'Callaghan, *Revolutionary Limerick*.

7 Terence Dooley, *The plight of the Monaghan Protestants, 1912–26* (Dublin, 2000); Terence Dooley, *Monaghan: the Irish Revolution, 1912–23* (Dublin, 2017); Pádraig Deignan, *The Protestant community in Sligo, 1914–49* (Sligo, 2010); Michael Farry, *Sligo: the Irish Revolution, 1912–23* (Dublin, 2012).

8 Compensation claim of John Holmes (TNA, CO 762/177/4).

9 Limerick Command reports, Dec. 1923 (IMA, Limerick Command papers, CW/OPS/09/16).

Select bibliography

PRIMARY SOURCES

A. MANUSCRIPTS

Boston
John J. Burns Library, Boston College
Thomas J. Clarke and Kathleen Daly Clarke collection.

Dublin
Irish Military Archives
Bureau of Military History.
Civil War captured documents.
Civil War operations and intelligence reports collection.
Civil War internment collection.
Military Service Pensions Collection.
Truce liaison and evacuation papers (1921–2).

National Archives of Ireland
Chief Secretary's Office: Crime Branch Special papers.
Dáil Éireann Courts (Winding Up) Commission papers.
Dáil Éireann Department of Local Government papers.
Dáil Éireann Secretariat files, 1919–22.
Department of Finance, 392 compensation claims series.

National Library of Ireland
Michael Collins papers.
Lord Monteagle papers.
Maurice Moore papers.
Florence O'Donoghue papers.
Michael O'Dwyer papers.
Ernie O'Malley papers.
James O'Mara papers.
Stephen O'Mara papers.
Count Plunkett papers.
John Redmond papers.
Sinn Féin papers.
United Irish League, National Directory minute book.

National Museum of Ireland
Easter Week collection.

University College Dublin Archives
Con Moloney papers.
Richard Mulcahy papers.

Ernie O'Malley notebooks.
Ernie O'Malley papers.

Limerick
Limerick Archives
Limerick City Police Force archive.
Limerick Corporation minute books.
Limerick County Council minute books.
Medical Superintendent Officer of Health annual reports, 1912–38.

Limerick Museum
Michael Conway collection.
Diary of Captain Joseph Graham.
Limerick Corporation: miscellaneous files and correspondence.
Court diary of John Lynch.

Mary Immaculate College Library
Limerick Sinn Féin Comhairle Ceanntair minute book, 1917–19.

St Mary's Cathedral
Preachers' books 1906–16, 1916–26.

University of Limerick Glucksman Library Special Collections
Daly papers.
De Courcy papers.
Dunraven papers.
Knight of Glin papers.
Liam Manahan papers.
Limerick Young Men's Protestant Association papers.

London
Imperial War Museum
Lieutenant Colonel John Basil Jarvis papers.
Captain J.H.M. Staniforth papers.
General Sir Peter Strickland papers.

National Archives of the United Kingdom
Cabinet papers.
Colonial Office papers.
Home Office papers.
War Office papers.

Richmond
The Green Howards Museum
Green Howards regimental history.

Wiltshire
The Soldiers of Oxfordshire Museum
Lieutenant Colonel John Basil Jarvis notebook.

B. OFFICIAL RECORDS

Census of Ireland 1911: area, houses and population; also the ages, civil or conjugal condition, occupations, birthplaces, religion and education of the people. Province of Munster, county and city of Limerick. Table I: Area, houses and population of the city and county of Limerick in 1911, House of Commons, 1912–13 (Cd. 6050).

Dáil Éireann debates.

Department of Industry and Commerce, *Saorstát Éireann: Census of Population 1926* (10 vols, Dublin).

Department of Industry and Commerce, *Saorstát Éireann: Census of Population 1936* (8 vols, Dublin).

Report of the Royal Commission on the rebellion in Ireland. Minutes of evidence and appendix of documents, House of Commons, 1916 (Cd. 8311).

Report on recruiting in Ireland, House of Commons, 1914–16 (Cd. 8168).

Statement giving particulars of men of military age in Ireland. House of Commons, 1916 (Cd. 8390).

C. NEWSPAPERS AND PERIODICALS

Anglo-Celt
Bottom Dog
Church of Ireland Gazette
Cork Examiner
Evening Herald
Factionist
Fermanagh Herald
Freeman's Journal
Irish Bulletin
Irish Examiner
Irish Independent
Irish Times
Irish Volunteer
Kerryman
Limerick Chronicle
Limerick Leader
Limerick Post

Munster News
Nationality
Nenagh News
An tÓglach
Republic
Revolution Papers
Sgéal Chatha Luimnighe
Southern Democrat
Southern Star
Sunday Independent
Sunday Tribune
Times
Ulster Herald
Voice of Labour
Weekly Observer
Workers' Bulletin

D. PRINTED PRIMARY MATERIAL

Augeisteijn, Joost (ed.), *The memoirs of John M. Regan: a Catholic officer in the RIC and RUC, 1909–48* (Dublin, 2007).

Brennan, Michael, *The war in Clare, 1911–21* (Dublin, 1980).

Clarke, Kathleen, *Revolutionary woman*, ed. Helen Litton (Dublin, 1991).

Crozier, Frank Percy, *Ireland for ever* (London, 1932).

Deasy, Liam, *Brother against brother* (Cork, 1998 [1982]).

Gaughan, John Anthony (ed.), *Memoirs of Constable Jeremiah Mee* (Dublin, 1975).

Goldring, Douglas, *A stranger in Ireland* (Dublin, 1918).

Graves, Robert, *Good-bye to all that* (London, 1929).

Harnett, Mossie, *Victory and woe: the West Limerick Brigade in the War of Independence*, ed. James Joy (Dublin, 2002).

Hart, Peter (ed.), *British intelligence in Ireland: the final reports* (Cork, 2002).

Hussey de Burgh, Digby, *Western thugs: or, Ireland and the English speaking world* (London, 1925).

Long, J.J., *History of the Limerick medical mission* (London, 1911).

Mac Eoin, Uinseann, *Survivors* (Dublin, 1980).

Mac Giolla Choille, Breandán (ed.), *Intelligence notes, 1913–16* (Dublin, 1966).

Monteith, Robert, *Casement's last adventure* (Dublin, 1953).

O'Callaghan, Kate, *The Limerick curfew murders of March 7th 1921. The case of Michael O'Callaghan (councillor and ex-mayor). Presented by his widow* (Dublin, 1921).

O'Malley, Ernie, *On another man's wound* (Dublin, 2002 [1936]).

____, *The singing flame* (Dublin, 1992 [1978]).

Rashad, Ibrahim, *An Egyptian in Ireland* (private print, 1920).

Russell, Ruth, *What's the matter with Ireland?* (New York, 1920).

Wyndham-Quin, Windham Thomas, *Past times and pastimes* (London, 1922).

SELECT SECONDARY SOURCES

E. PUBLISHED WORKS

Limerick's fighting story, 1916–21 (Tralee, 1947).

aan de Wiel, Jérôme, 'From "castle" bishop to "moral leader"? Edward O'Dwyer and Irish nationalism, 1914–17', *History Studies*, 2 (2000), 55–68.

Bielenberg, Andy, 'Exodus: the emigration of southern Irish Protestants during the Irish War of Independence and the Civil War', *Past & Present*, 218:1 (2013), 199–233.

Borgonovo, John, *Spies, informers and the 'Anti-Sinn Féin Society': the intelligence war in Cork city, 1920–21* (Dublin, 2007).

Cahill, Liam, *Forgotten revolution. Limerick soviet 1919: a threat to British rule in Ireland* (Dublin, 1990).

Campbell, Colm, *Emergency law in Ireland, 1918–25* (Oxford, 1994).

Campbell, Fergus, *Land and revolution: nationalist politics in the west of Ireland, 1891–1921* (Oxford, 2005).

Cherry, Jonathan, 'Landlords, estates, demesnes and mansion houses in County Limerick *c*.1870–*c*.1920' in Liam Irwin, Gearóid Ó Tuathaigh & Matthew Potter (eds), *Limerick: history and society: interdisciplinary essays on the history of an Irish county* (Dublin, 2009), pp 533–56.

Clark, Gemma, *Everyday violence in the Irish Civil War* (Cambridge, 2014).

Coleman, Marie, *County Longford and the Irish Revolution, 1910–1923* (Dublin, 2003).

Costello, Francis, 'The republican courts and the decline of British rule in Ireland, 1919–21', *Éire–Ireland*, 25:2 (1990), 36–55.

Crean, Tom, 'Crowds and the labour movement in the southwest, 1914–23' in Peter Jupp & Eoin Magennis (eds), *Crowds in Ireland, c.1720–1920* (London, 2000), pp 249–68.

Daly, Mary, *The buffer state*: th*e historical roots of the Department of the Environment* (Dublin, 1997).

Deignan, Pádraig, *The Protestant community in Sligo, 1914–49* (Sligo, 2010).

Delaney, Enda, *Demography, state and society: Irish migration to Britain, 1921–71* (Liverpool, 2000).

Dooley, Terence, *The plight of the Monaghan Protestants, 1912–26* (Dublin, 2000).

_____, *Monaghan: the Irish Revolution, 1912–23* (Dublin, 2017).

Farry, Michael, *Sligo: the Irish Revolution, 1912–23* (Dublin, 2012).

Fitzpatrick, David, *Politics and Irish life, 1913–21: provincial experiences of war and revolution* (2nd ed., Cork, 1998 [1977]).

_____, 'The geography of Irish nationalism, 1910–21', *Past & Present*, 78 (1978), 113–44.

Foxton, David, *Revolutionary lawyers: Sinn Féin and Crown courts in Ireland and Britain, 1916–23* (Dublin, 2008).

Garvin, Tom, *1922: the birth of Irish democracy* (Dublin, 1996).

Guiry, Ruth, *Pigtown: a history of Limerick's bacon industry* (Limerick, 2016).

Hart, Peter, *The IRA at war, 1916–23* (Oxford, 2003).

_____, 'Definition: Defining the Irish Revolution' in Joost Augusteijn (ed.), *The Irish Revolution, 1913–23* (London, 2002), pp 17–33.

_____, 'The social structure of the Irish Republican Army, 1916–23', *The Historical Journal*, 42:1 (1999), 207–31.

_____, *The IRA and its enemies: violence and community in Cork, 1916–23* (Oxford, 1998).

Hay, Marnie, 'Moulding the future: Na Fianna Éireann and its members, 1909–23', *Studies*, 100:400 (2011), 441–54.

_____, 'The foundation and development of Na Fianna Éireann, 1909–16', *Irish Historical Studies*, 36:141 (2008), 53–71.

Hayes, Jacqui, Brian Hodkinson, William O'Neill & Matthew Potter, *They dreamed and are dead: Limerick 1916* (Limerick, 2016).

Hopkinson, Michael, *Green against green: the Irish Civil War* (Dublin, 2004 [1988]).

_____, *The Irish War of Independence* (Dublin, 2002).

Hughes, Brian, *Defying the IRA?: intimidation, coercion and communities during the Irish Revolution* (Liverpool, 2016).

Joyce, Mannix, 'The story of Limerick and Kerry in 1916', *Capuchin Annual* (1966), 327–70.

Kostick, Conor, *Revolution in Ireland: popular militancy, 1917–23* (London, 1996).

Laffan, Michael, *The resurrection of Ireland: the Sinn Féin party, 1916–23* (Cambridge, 1999).

Leeson, David, *The Black and Tans: British police and Auxiliaries in the Irish War of Independence, 1920–21* (Oxford, 2012).

Leonard, Jane, 'Getting them at last: the IRA and ex-servicemen' in David Fitzpatrick (ed.), *Revolution? Ireland, 1917–23* (Dublin, 1990), pp 118–29.

Logan, John, 'Frugal comfort: housing Limerick's labourers and artisans, 1841–1946' in Liam Irwin, Gearóid Ó Tuathaigh & Matthew Potter (eds), *Limerick: history and society: interdisciplinary essays on the history of an Irish county* (Dublin, 2009), pp 557–82.

Lovett, Phil, 'Quakers in Limerick', *Old Limerick Journal*, 37 (Summer 2001), 3–9.

Macardle, Dorothy, *The Irish Republic* (4th ed., Tralee, 1968 [1937]).

MacCarthy, Jack (ed.), *Limerick's fighting story from 1916 to the truce with Britain* (Tralee, 1965).

Maume, Patrick, *The long gestation: Irish nationalist life, 1891–1918* (Dublin, 1999).

McCarthy, Pat, *Waterford: the Irish Revolution, 1912–23* (Dublin, 2015).

McDowell, R.B., *Crisis and decline: the fate of the southern Unionists* (Dublin, 1997).

____, *The Irish Convention, 1917–18* (London, 1970).

McNamara, Patrick J., *The widow's penny: the memorial record of the Limerick men and women who gave their lives in the Great War* (Limerick, 2000).

Meghen, P.J., 'Social history' in Jeremiah Newman (ed.), *Limerick rural survey, 1958–64* (Tipperary, 1964), pp 53–157.

Mitchell, Arthur, 'Making the case for Irish independence' in John Crowley, Donal Ó Drisceoil, Mike Murphy & John Borgonovo (eds), *Atlas of the Irish Revolution* (Cork, 2017), pp 471–8.

Moloney, Tadhg, *The impact of World War One on Limerick* (Newcastle-on-Tyne, 2013).

Morrissey, Thomas J., *Bishop Edward Thomas O'Dwyer of Limerick, 1842–1917* (Dublin, 2003).

Murphy, Brian, *The life and tragic death of Winnie Barrington: the story of the Barrington family of Glenstal Castle, County Limerick, c.1800–1925* (Limerick, 2018).

Ó Broin, Leon, *The chief secretary: Augustine Birrell in Ireland* (London, 1969).

Ó Drisceoil, Donal, 'Losing a war it never fought: labour, socialism and the War of Independence' in John Crowley, William J. Smyth, Mike Murphy & John Borgonovo (eds), *Atlas of the Irish Revolution* (Cork, 2017), pp 490–3.

Ó Ruairc, Pádraig, *Truce: murder, myth and the last days of the Irish War of Independence* (Cork, 2016).

____, *The battle for Limerick city* (Cork, 2010).

O'Callaghan, John, 'Munster' in John Crowley, William J. Smyth, Mike Murphy & John Borgonovo (eds), *Atlas of the Irish Revolution* (Cork, 2017), pp 544–54.

____, *Con Colbert* (Dublin, 2015).

____, *The battle for Kilmallock* (Cork, 2011).

____, *Revolutionary Limerick: the republican campaign for independence in Limerick, 1913–21* (Dublin, 2010).

O'Connor Lysaght, D.R., *The story of the Limerick soviet: the 1919 strike against British militarism* (Limerick, 2003).

____, 'The Munster Soviet Creameries', *Irish History Workshop*, 1 (1981), 36–49.

O'Dwyer, Liam & Michael O'Dwyer, *The parish of Emly: its history and heritage* (Emly, 1987).

O'Halpin, Eunan, 'Problematic killing during the Irish War of Independence and its aftermath: civilian spies and informers' in James Kelly & Mary Ann Lyons (eds), *Death and dying in Ireland, Britain, and Europe: historical perspectives* (Dublin, 2013), pp 173–98.

O'Sullivan, Donal J., *The Irish constabularies, 1822–1922: a century of policing in Ireland* (Dingle, 1999).

Pritchett, V.S., *Midnight oil* (New York, 1973).

Reynolds, John, *46 dead men. The Royal Irish Constabulary in County Tipperary, 1919–22* (Cork, 2016).

Rumpf, Erhard, & Anthony C. Hepburn, *Nationalism and socialism in twentieth-century Ireland* (New York, 1977).

Ryan, Des, 'Women's suffrage associations in Limerick, 1912–14', *Old Limerick Journal* (Winter 1993), 41–6.

Michael V. Spillane, 'The fourth earl of Dunraven (1841–1926): local realities and "conciliation" politics' in Liam Irwin, Gearóid Ó Tuathaigh & Matthew Potter (eds), *Limerick: history and society: interdisciplinary essays on the history of an Irish county* (Dublin, 2009), pp 499–514.

Toomey, Tom, *The War of Independence in Limerick, 1912–21* (Limerick, 2010).

____, 'RIC consolidation in Limerick, 1919–21', *Old Limerick Journal*, 42 (Winter 2006), 33–5.

Townshend, Charles, *The British campaign in Ireland, 1919–21: the development of political and military policies* (Oxford, 1975).

____, *Political violence in Ireland: government and resistance since 1848* (Oxford, 1983).

Twohig, Patrick J., *Blood on the flag: autobiography of a freedom fighter* (translated from *B'fhiú an braon fola* by Séamus Malone) (Cork, 1996).

Vaughan, W.E. & A.J. Fitzpatrick (eds), *Irish historical statistics: population, 1821–1971* (Dublin, 1978).

F. THESES AND UNPUBLISHED WORK

Crean, Tom, 'The labour movement in Kerry and Limerick, 1914–21' (PhD, Trinity College, Dublin, 1996).

Jackson, Rev R.W., 'Notes on the history of St Michael's (Limerick) Company No. 653 of the Church Lads for use on the occasion of the laying up of the Company colour in St Michael's Church at Evening Service on Sunday, 28 June 1942' (courtesy of Johnny Conn).

Keane, Thomas, 'Class, religion and society in Limerick city, 1922–39' (PhD, Mary Immaculate College, 2015).

Maguire, Gloria, 'The political and military division in the Irish nationalist movement, January 1921–August 1923' (DPhil, Oxford University, 1986).

McCarthy, Deirdre, 'Cumann na mBan: the Limerick link' (MA, University of Limerick, 1992).

McCluskey, Fergal, 'The development of republican politics in East Tyrone, 1898–1918' (PhD, Queen's University Belfast, 2007).

Moloney, Tadhg, 'The impact of World War One on Limerick' (MA, Mary Immaculate College, Limerick, 2003).

Quirke, Mick, 'My life and times, 1896–1973' (Des Long private collection).

Toomey, Tom, 'The rise of militant nationalism in Limerick city, 1912–17' (MA, University of Limerick, 2006).

Index